Arthur Merton

The book of Israel

Arthur Merton

The book of Israel

ISBN/EAN: 9783744737531

Printed in Europe, USA, Canada, Australia, Japan

Cover: Foto ©ninafisch / pixelio.de

More available books at **www.hansebooks.com**

SEPHERVA

The Vision of Science penetrated many fields of physical knowledge before it could lift the veil of the Soul and survey the wonderful mechanism of the mind, from which arose the noble achievments that have built up civilization and glorified the race. Here alone it found the laws and the conditions of universal happiness.

Three great factors have been at work in the life of individuals and of nations. These factors are the Intellect, the Feelings, and the Will of man. They have produced Knowledge, Social life, and Industry.

Knowledge and Labor are the two hands with which the work of the world is done. They are the two instruments through which the Feelings must always be expressed. The office of Science, in its maturity, is not to suppress the emotions of the human heart. The highest work of science is to lift the veil of mystery from the mechanism of our inner life, and to furnish a clear and supreme guide in all the forms of personal conduct, and in the structure of civil society.

Design of this Book. We may consider the living framework of the human mind and body, as governed by twelve general laws. Each one of these laws has one chapter of the Book given to its elaborate exposition. The minor laws will be found included under these general ones. They form the constitution of man, as an individual and as a member of society.

All through the historic ages, and among all civilized nations, we may find fragments of the truths which are united under the light of these twelve laws into one clear System of Life. They have been elaborated by the work of many hands. But they were only fragments until the uniting laws were discovered.

This work has been done in our own time. First, by the physiologists who studied the mind in connection with the nervous mechanism and thus traced the location of the mental powers in the brain and body, and to some extent unfolded the law of the phases of life. Twenty-one years since, in the year of Israel 3445, the ten remaining laws of man's mental constitution were discovered. When this was done, it was at once seen that they included the forms and the methods of a great and perfect system of Social life, of Civil government and of Integral Education and Culture. They thus reach the most central interests of human life.

But these discoveries gave a still more surprising result. For they furnished the very first explanation of the great Doctrines of the Bible, and of the character, the mission, and the symbols of the ancient nation of Israel, and they show why its record stands as the central fact in the world's history.

The author occupied twelve years of close and careful labor in working out the details and demonstrations of these laws, and in comparing the immense mass of facts upon which they rest. Not only all human history and experience, but every branch of science and art, was laid under contribution in this extended examination.

The most direct proof of the truths stated in this book, is found in the fact that they precisely and clearly explain the phenomena of our inner and outer life. The detailed proof of these laws would fill many volumes. The most important laws in this book rest upon mathematical proof, and however condensed the demonstrations given, they are conclusive and final, and they cannot be refuted by logical forms of argument. Each one will stand the most rigorous tests of science.

The Conception of Law. In the childhood of the world, man looked upon nature everywhere as unstable, arbitrary and disorderly. It is only through science that we perceive the order and stability, the majesty and universality of her laws. Beneath all the changing and disconnected surfaces of objects and events, science reveals the play of eternal harmonies.

The man of science observes, classifies, and analyzes the objects of nature and their actions, in each domain he may seek to explore. He does more than this. He institutes experiments and evokes new phenomena. Through these methods he finds those regular forms of structure and those uniform methods of action which he terms the Laws of Nature.

He discovers that the atoms of spirit and of matter possess inherent forms and powers. Each one has its own modes of behavior, its intrinsic laws of form and action. Thus the laws of nature are within each object, and inseparable from it. They are not external rules or forces which the objects are compelled to obey. Hence these laws were never created, they are as eternal as matter and spirit.

The grouping of facts into the form of laws is the work of science. The lower steps of science are called Common Sense. In its higher stages of development, science always measures. It reveals to us exact relations of quantity. Thus, for example, common observation teaches us that water may be converted into steam by being heated. But science shows us the exact amount of heat required to produce this change.

All science is practical knowledge, for it is based upon an exact acquaintance with the objects of nature. It differs from other knowledge in possessing system, clearness, and certainty, in place of disorder, obscurity and uncertainty.

Criterion of Truth. As the lungs of all men are adapted to breathe the air, so the intellectual faculties of all men are adapted by nature to perceive and understand the laws which rule our own being, and those which relate us to the varied objects of the universe.

Every truth, every law, bears a fixed relation to the mental constitution of man. Therefore, when it is once fully understood, it must appear essentially the same to all minds.

Nature is not a system of jugglery. It was not contrived to mystify and perplex man. Every human being has an eternal right to understand the material and spiritual laws of nature. The methods of science apply to all of these with equal force and completeness.

The means of proof in science are open to all persons. But they must take the proper steps and institute the necessary conditions of proof. Thus it is a truth of science that in any circle every part of the circumference is equally distant from its centre. It is another truth that in a right angled triangle the squares erected on its two shorter sides are together equal to that erected on its longer side. And any person can convince himself of these truths by simply drawing the circle and the squares. And so of all truths in science. They never rest upon personal authority, or the testimony of witnesses, like truths received alone through inspiration. Thus science is the only standard of truth to which all men can agree, for it is the only one where the proof is always open to examination.

It is true that men differ in their capacity to investigate. The scientist makes allowance for this difference under the head of Personal Equation.

If we impose any doctrine or belief upon any person, then we violate a law of his reason. For through that faculty he has an eternal right to examine any and every idea presented to him, and to have its truth clearly demonstrated before he is obliged to accept it. When such demonstration is made, then he accepts it by a necessity of his intellectual nature. No persons actuated by the true spirit of science could ever persecute those who differed from themselves, or seek by physical force to make others adopt their ideas and practices.

Forms of Knowledge. In classifying the branches of knowledge for the purpose of study, two methods present themselves. By the older and now prevalent mode we should form three great branches, Art, Letters, and Science, and arrange the subdivisions of these as in the table "Analysis of Knowledge." The central branch is the storehouse of knowledge, while Science explains laws, and Art applies these in the practical work of life.

The difference between Science and Philosophy has been admirably stated as follows:

Science expresses in a single formula, a particular truth respecting a particular order of phenomena.

Philosophy expresses in a single formula a general truth respecting all phenomena.

Art consists of rules by which work is to be done. Skill is the mental and physical qualification required for the application of these rules.

CHAPTER FIRST.

PHYSICAL LIFE.

Within the human body three kinds of artizans carry on the unceasing work of life. Some are engaged in taking the elements of Air, Water and Food, and, after changing the form of these, they carry them to the various parts of the body, to sustain its action and to build up its wasted tissues. The organs which do this work, constitute the Nutritive System.

Another kind of organs consist of bundles of delicate tubules, which carry messages to and from all parts of the body, and center in the brain and other collections of nerve cells. These organs form the Nervous System with its three-fold functions of Thinking, Feeling and Volition.

All parts of the body are instruments for expressing the mind. They are united in relations of the closest sympathy. For this reason we must briefly consider the functions of the body as the basis of all mental phenomena.

If we do not understand the structure, the use and the care of these organs, then we will be very liable to do many things to injure them, and thus bring disease, pain and death upon ourselves. The science which teaches us this important knowledge is Physiology. When extended so as to include all living things, it is called Biology. A minute classification of the vital functions is given in the table at the close of this chapter.

Nutrition The work of digestion commences in the mouth, where the food is masticated by thirty-two teeth, and mixed with saliva from the parotid, the submaxillary and the sublingual glands. The food then passes along the pharnyx and down the esophagus to the stomach. The multitude of peptic glands then pour out the gastric juice, and this mixes with, or dissolves and digests, the albuminous parts of the food. As this process goes on, the mass of digested food passes through the pylorus and along the small intestine. Here it meets the juice of the pancreas and of the intestinal glands, and these complete the work of digestion by dissolving the fats, the starch and the sugar of the food.

The pulpy mass of the food is now called chyme, and it is forced slowly along over the mucous coat of the small intestine. From this coat a vast multitude of minute points, called villuses, project into the passing current of chyme. Within each one is the commencement of a little tube or lacteal.

The lacteals absorb the nutritious part of the food and carry it through the mesenteric glands to the chyle cyst. These glands modify the character of the current of chyle. They commence the work of organizing its materials into plastic cells. Reaching the chyle cyst, the milky liquid is carried up the thoracic duct, to the left side of the neck, where it is poured into the left subclavian vein. The chyle is thus mixed with the current of venous blood, and carried to the heart. Before tracing this farther, we must briefly consider the character of the chyle itself.

Our food contains three groups of elements:

First, the Proteid group, as gluten, albumen, fibrine and caseine. Each of these contain carbon, oxygen, hydrogen, and nitrogen, with lesser proportions of phosphorus, sulphur and mineral salts, as shown in the molecule of Bioplasm. The proteid group of food contains all the essential elements of nutrition. The tissues of the body have the same chemical composition, and they can all be formed from its materials.

Second, the Amyloid group includes starch, gum, sugar and the oils and fats. Each of these contains carbon, oxygen and hydrogen. They furnish elements to be used in forming the fats of the body, and for muscular action. In the process of digestion starch is changed to glucose before it can be assimilated.

Third, the Mineral group, including air, water and sodium chloride. Water contains oxygen and hydrogen, and air contains oxygen, nitrogen and traces of carbonic oxide.

A grain of wheat cut across, will show us how these elements are stored up in the food. The interior contains the starch cells, and the layer of gluten cells lies next to the bran. Here also are stored the iron and silica. In our food we require each day, 36,500 grains of water, 2,000 grains of proteids, 5,200 grains of amyloids, and 1,200 of the minerals.

We may now trace the distribution of these materials of life from the heart to all parts of the body. When once emptied into the veins, the current of chyle can not be distinguished from the blood. Both enter the right auricle of the heart. This contracts, and forces the blood into the right ventricle. The latter contracts in turn, driving the blood through the pulmonary arteries into the lungs. There it passes through the capillaries, over the clustered air cells, and is changed by the air which these 300,000 cells contain. The blood changes from a dark or bluish crimsom, to a bright scarlet color. The air imparts oxygen to the blood, and removes its carbonic oxide, watery vapor. and remains of wasted tissues. Seventeen times a minute the supply of air in the lungs is renewed by breathing.

The blood is returned to the heart by the pulmonary veins, and is poured into the left auricle. This chamber contracts, sending the blood into the left ventricle. The contraction of this ventricle forces the blood into the aorta, and through the branches of this artery the blood is carried to every part of the body, renewing the tissus of each organ, and supplying them with force for their activities.

The act of growth or nutrition takes place only when the blood reaches the capillaries, or minute arteries and veins which surround the cell tissues of all the organs. Nutrition involves *osmotic action*, or the passage of liquids and gases through basement membranes, covered with epithelial cells.

The blood is sent to all parts of the body by the arteries, and it is returned to the heart through the veins and lymphatics.

The veins from the intestines, stomach, spleen and kidneys, unite to form the portal vein. This enters the liver, branches around the hepatic cells, and these separate the bile and sugar from the passing current. The venous blood then goes to the heart.

The kidneys separate urea, water and salts, from arterial blood. The perspiratory glands of the skin also eliminate part of the waste products of the system.

In the corpuscles of the kidneys, the Renal artery is seen to end in a tuft, within the Glomerulus. The latter is formed of layers of cells, which separate the secretion of the kidneys. This is passed along the uriniferous tube of each minute lobule, and thence into the pelvis of the kidney, and along the ureter to the bladder, to be finally eliminated from the body.

Motive System. The four hundred and seventy muscles of the human body are disposed in layers. They consist of bundles of minute cells; as shown in Figure 1. They are attached to the bones as levers, and move them by contraction.

A current of nerve force is sent from the brain, or from other nerve centers, and this polarizes the muscle cells. One end of each cell is made negative, and the other end positive. When thus oppositely charged, the two ends approach each other, and thus the entire muscle is contracted or shortened about one-third. When the charge of nerve force is withdrawn, the cells return to their former position, and thus the whole muscle relaxes.

In the chart of the Nervous System, the large muscles of the upper arm are shown. The nerve is seen at BR, and the Biceps muscle is drawn with the cells immensely enlarged. This muscle, attached to the radius, at R, raises the forearm by its contraction.

THE SKIN presents an example of the nervous, nutritive and motive systems combined. Its protecting layers of the epidermis, and its elastic and contracting fibers, belong to the motive system. Its multitude of sensitive nerves are an important part of the nervous system. And its perspiratory, sebaceous and hair glands belong to the system of nutrition. The 5,000,000 of pores in the skin form an extensive system of drainage for the waste matters of the body, and justify the importance attached to bathing and cleanliness.

The Nervous System. The large figure in the chart of the nervous system, exhibits a side view of the brain and a back view of the body.

The Nervous System includes the Brain, the Nutro-nerves, and the Sensi-motor nerves.

On the left side of the body the muscles of the back have been removed. This displays the chain of nerve centers and fibres which form the great sympathetic or Nutro system of nerves. These lie back of the heart, lungs, stomach and other digestive organs, and are on each side of the body. They govern the action of all these organs. Each of these centers also sends a bundle of fibres to the spinal cord, and receives one in turn. The chief center of the nutro system, is the gasterus or solar plexus and ganglion, back of the Stomach, marked G. The Cardiacus is the center back of the heart, and the Pelvicus is the chief center of the pelvis.

Sensi-motors. The spinal cord consists of a vast multitude of fibres and cells. The motor fibres branch off to the muscles of the body, and the sensory fibres to the skin. Other bundles of sensory and motor fibres, like those in the face, branch directly from the brain.

In the eye, the nerves terminate in rods and cones 1–10,000th of an inch in diameter. See figure 7. These vibrate to the different waves of light, and carry into the brain the picture formed on the black pigment of the eye. This is the vital part of vision.

The nerves in the ear are distributed to the otoliths or ear stones; to the ends of the semi-circular canals; and to the vibrating fibres of Corti in the cochlea. These parts perceive the intensity, quality and pitch of sounds.

The nerves of Touch terminate in the microscopic papilla of the skin as seen in figure 6.

Centers. In all the centers of nervous action we find cells and fibres associated. The structure of these may be understood from figure 5 in the engraving of the Nervous System. This figure is magnified 350 diameters. Both the fibres and the cells, in the brain, have an average diameter of about the 1–1500th part of an inch. This would give at least 3,000,000,000, in each hemisphere of the brain.

The nerve cell has a nucleus, surrounded by layers of membranes and granules, and traversed

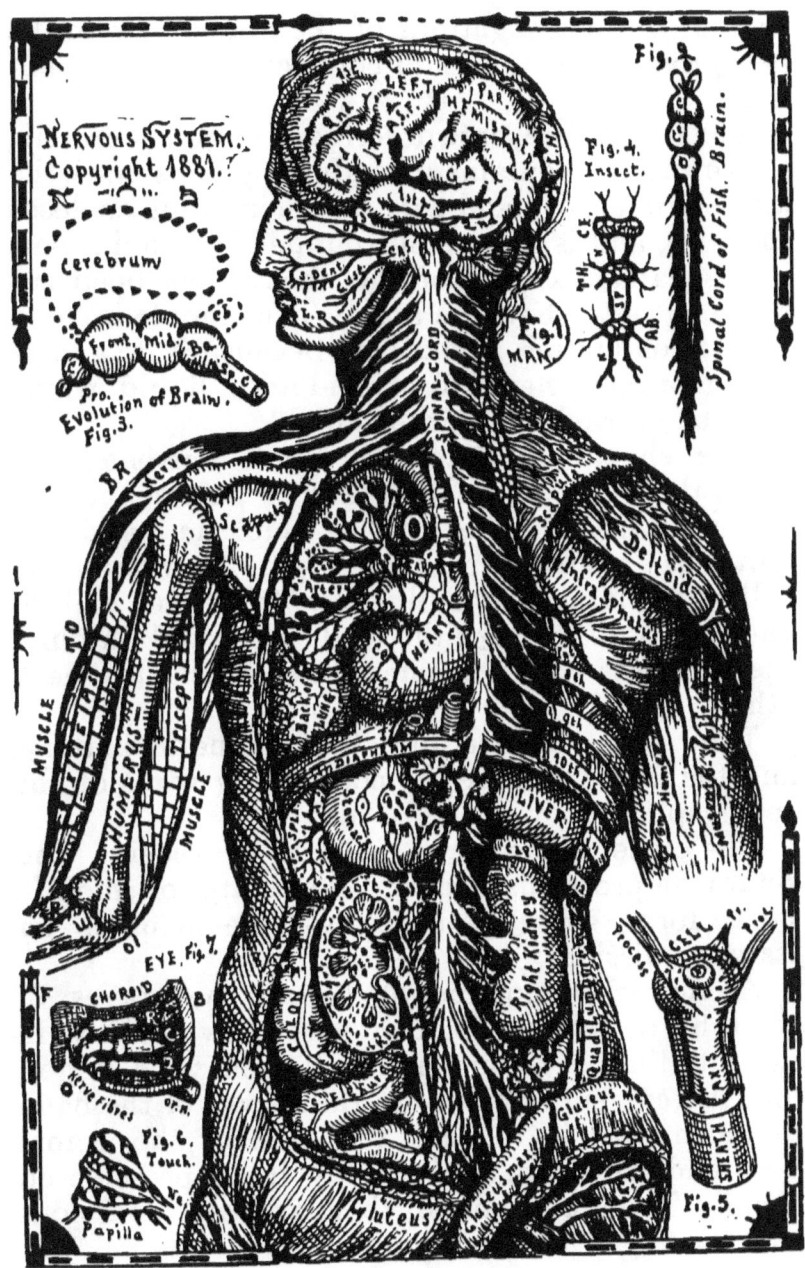

by delicate prolongations of the fibres. From the cell processes extend and connect it with adjacent cells.

The nerve fibre, or to describe it more accurately, nerve tubule, contains a conducting substance, the axis cylinder, or band axis. A membrane encloses this axis, and is in turn surrounded by an insulating sheath. A part of the sheath has been cut away so as to show the axis. The tubule is filled with a conducting substance, because it is a current motion or nerve force, and not a liquid which is to be carried along its channel.

The sheath insulates the nerve current as it flows along the cylinder so that no part of the current may escape to the tubules which lie beside it. But when a current reaches a center, where the cells are, it may readily flow from one cell to another, both through the cell walls and through the processes which connect the cells with each other.

The nerve cells are like the magnetic battery, and the fibres are like the conducting wires of the telegraph.

The office of the nerve cells is to receive and retain impressions, and to originate or modify nerve force, while the fibres are the channels for its transmission.

Along these conducting tubes the waves of thought, of feeling, and of will, flow swiftly in delicate lines of living light. Touch your finger, and the current will flow up the nerves of the hand and arm until it reaches the cells of the spinal cord and the brain, and makes its impression on them. Then, and not till then, you are conscious that the finger has been touched.

The office of the nerves is three fold, directive, sympathetic, and responsive. They are lines of communication between all parts of the animal body. Through these we are conscious of pleasure and pain. The doors of sensation open for the entrance of knowledge, and the motor nerves carry the directing impulses to the muscles. The conditions of each organ of the body are conveyed through the sensory nerves to the nerve centers, and become the source of responsive movements.

The Brain. The highest of all living structures is the human brain. Yet it was the last one in nature to yield its secrets of action to the questioning intellect of man.

When the brain is removed from its bony encasement, we observe a mass of folds or convolutions, as shown in the engraving of the Nervous System. The object of these folds seems to be to give a greater extent of surface, and consequently a greater number of cells to generate force, within a given space. The actual surface is said to be three hundred square inches in each hemisphere of the brain.

In some brains the convolutions are deep, and in others they are shallow. The amount of mental or nerve power increases in proportion to the surface here gained. In two brains of equal size, one might have deep convolutions and much mental power while the shallow convolutions of the other would give a much smaller thought-generating surface.

But the amount of mental power depends much more largely still, upon the good texture of the brain. One brain may be fine and powerful; another may be coarse and weak. One is like

PLAN OF THE BRAIN.

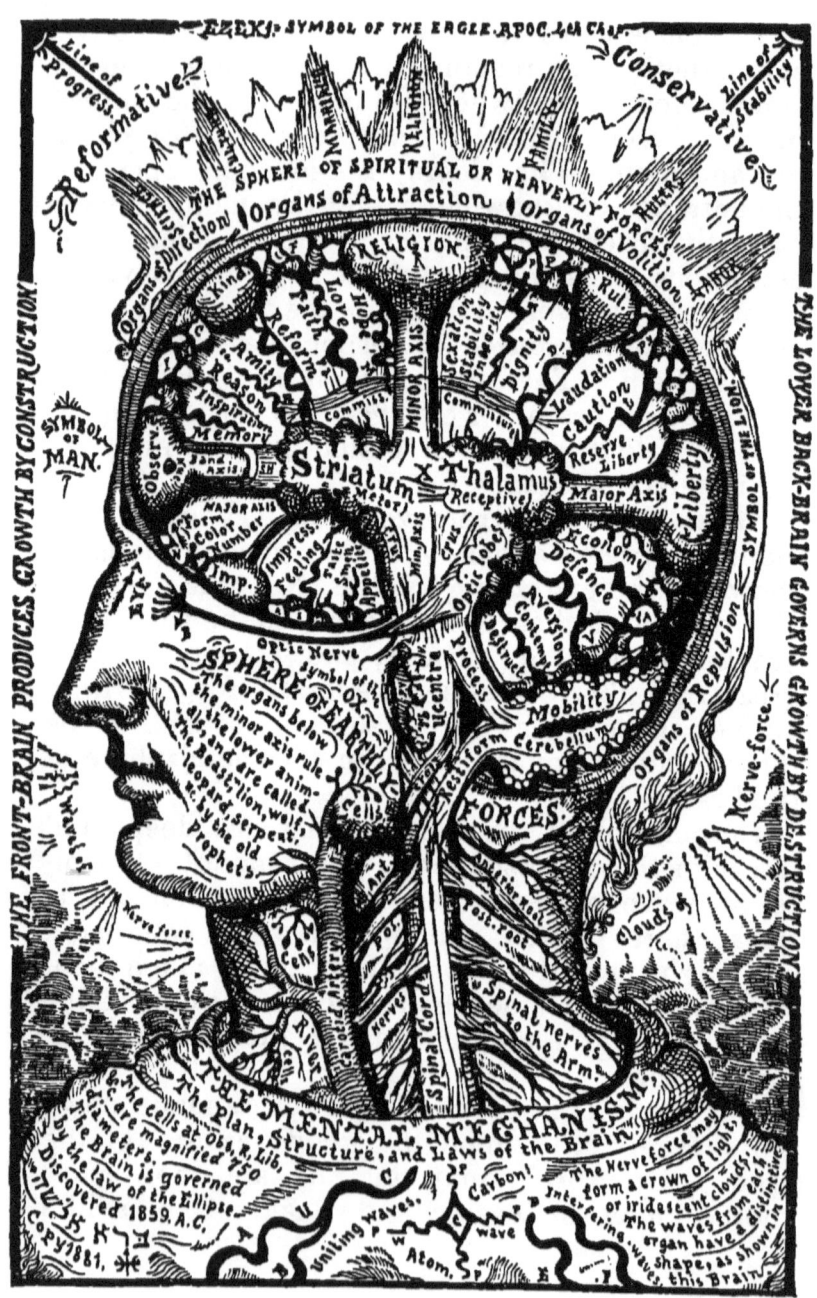

steel or the diamond; the other is like basswood or mud. The texture of the brain, in any given case, may be fairly judged by that of the organs of sense and of the body in general. Where these organs of sense, the eye, the ear, the nose, and the skin, are delicate and fine in texture, we may safely conclude that the brain has the same good texture and qualities.

The brain of man is about seven inches long, five inches high, and five in breadth. Its weight is about one-forty-fifth part of the entire body. It receives about one-sixth part of all the blood sent from the heart; an evidence that it produces the most concentrated form of vital force. This also shows why intense mental action is so much more exhausting than muscular labor. It consumes the blood more rapidly in proportion.

The brain has two sides or hemispheres, the right and the left. These are closely alike in form, size, and uses, like the right and left eye or hand.

The right and left hemispheres are united by transverse bands of fibres or commissures. The corpus callosum connects the upper parts, and smaller bands connect the centers. These bands are seen above VENT, in figure 2, and at CO, and CA, in the engraving of Polation. The hemispheres of the cerebellum are united by the pons varolii. The front and back of the hemispheres are united by the superior and inferior longitudinal commissures. These are shown on the engraved title page.

Brain Centers.—The Striatum, or front brain center is the chief focal point through which the organs of the brain send the impulses of motion to the muscles. It radiates force to all of the mental organs and receives from them. The Striatum, like the Thalamus, is a mass of nerve cells, with fibers passing to, through, and from it.

The Thalamus, or back brain centre is the chief point for receiving the incoming currents, containing the impressions which have been made on the organs of sense. All of the mental organs at their inner ends terminate in these two centers.

The Striatum and Thalamus thus stand between the mental organs on the one hand, and the outer world of sense and motion on the other. In passing through the centres the nerve force is usually modified, and more or less of all the impressions are stored in them.

Below the brain, are collections of cells which form a great center through which the brain acts on the body and the body acts on the brain. It is named the Ucenter.

The cerebellum has a center of its own, and it is connected in action with the larger brain by a process of fibres. It chiefly forms the organ of mobility, controlling the muscles of locomotion.

Vital Trinities. In studying the table of vital functions, we shall perceive that each divides into three parts. One of these three is always central, and each of its two side members supports its action in a characteristic way. The general relation of the three is formal, static, and dynamic. For example, the *state* of the body is maintained by Nutrition; the *form* of its movements is determined by Nervation; and its *dynamic* expression is through Motation.

In some of these trinities, the form element is less marked. For example, Respiration divides into Inspiration, or the taking of air into the lungs; Aeration or purifying the blood while in the air cells; and Expiration, or breathing out the air after it has done its work. Inspiration does not involve anything more than a temporary change in the form of the organs.

When carried to one thousand subdivisions, the analysis of vital functions still shows the law of the trinity governing them all with imperative exactness. One-third of these functions directly employ the organs of the brain and mind. And each one of the other two-thirds is connected by exact and constant laws of sympathetic action with some definite mental faculty. A rigid scientific analysis therefore proves that the great law of the Trinity governs no less absolutely in the true classification of the mental faculties as exhibited in the next chapter. Theological writers have speculated in vain about the trinity, for they had not the slightest idea that there is a fixed and well-defined relation between the three members of any trinity, and that the trinity is in each person, yea more, an essential part of the framework of the universe.

The vital organs show a trinal division in a no less conspicuous way. Thus the muscles divide according to their direction of movement into Flexors, Spincters, and Extensors; by their nervous relations they are Voluntary, Mixed, and Involuntary; and in their structure they are Striated, Non-striated, and Elastic tissue.

Units of Life. The microscope shows us that the tissues of the body, from delicate membranes to solid bones, are composed of minute cells. These are its units of structure.

TABULAR ANALYSIS OF LIFE.

MENTATION.

IDEATION.
    Thinking—Perception, Retention, Reflection.
    Mentocept—Percept, Recept, Concept.
    Theoration—Responding, Invention, Planning

FEELING.
    Sensation—Sentition, Gustation, Impression,
    Excitation—Pleasure, Consciousness, Pain.
    Loving—Association, Intercourse, Inchanging.

WILLING.
    Occupation—Profession, Employment, Trade.
    Reflexing—Impulse, Stimulation, Depulse.
    Practicing—Conducting, Co-operation, Execution.

VITATION.

REPRODUCTION.
    Ovulation—Menstruation, Blossoming, Ovoposition.
    Procreation—Copulation, Gestation, Engendering.
    Semination—Planting, Begetting, Sowing.

NUTRITION
    Ingestion—Mastication, Deglutition, Insalivation.
    Assimilation—Digestion, Cystation, Respiration.
    Excretion—Perspiration, Defecation, Urination,

CIRCULATION.
    Lymphation—Chylation, Absorption, Fibrination.
    Arteriation—Systolation, Pulsation, Diastolation.
    Veiniation—Osmosis, Capillation, Recursion.

MOTATION.

EXMENTATION.
    Speaking—Articulation, Utterance, Singing.
    Gesturing—Oration, Caressing, Directing.
    Playing—Gaming, Dancing, Sporting.

LOCOMOTION.
    Volation—Beating, Air-floating, Soaring.
    Pedestation—Walking, Running, Leaping.
    Natation—Paddling, Floating, Sailing.

WORKING.
    Handling—Fingering, Moulding, Tooling.
    Holding—Grasping, Clasping, Seizing.
    Moving—Pulling, Striking, Pushing.

TABULAR ANALYSIS OF LIFE.

MENTATION.

IDEATION.
    Thinking—Perception, Retention, Reflection.
    Mentocept—Precept, Recept, Concept.
    Theoration—Responding, Invention, Planning.

FEELING.
    Sensation—Sentition, Gustation, Impression.
    Excitation—Pleasure, Consciousness, Pain.
    Loving—Association, Intercourse, Interchanging.

WILLING.
    Occupation—Profession, Employment, Trade.
    Reflexing—Impulse, Stimulation, Depulse.
    Practicing—Conducting, Co-operation, Executing.

VITATION.

REPRODUCTION.
    Ovulation—Menstruation, Blossoming, Ovoposition.
    Procreation—Copulation, Gestation, Engendering.
    Semination—Planting, Begetting, Sowing.

NUTRITION.
    Ingestion—Mastication, Deglutition, Insalivation.
    Assimilation—Digestion, Cystation, Respiration.
    Excretion—Perspiration, Defecation, Urination.

CIRCULATION.
    Lymphation—Chylation, Absorption, Fibrination.
    Arteriation—Systolation, Pulsation, Diastolation.
    Veination—Osmosis, Capilliation, Recursion.

MOTATION.

EXMENTATION.
    Speaking—Articulation, Utterance, Singing.
    Gesturing—Orating, Caressing, Directing.
    Playing—Gaming, Dancing, Sporting.

LOCOMOTION.
    Volation—Beating, Air-floating, Soaring.
    Pedestation—Walking, Running, Leaping.
    Natation—Paddling, Floating, Sailing

WORKING.
    Handling—Fingering, Moulding, Tooling
    Holding—Grasping, Clasping, Seizing.
    Moving—Pulling, Striking, Pushing.

MAP OF THE ORGANS.

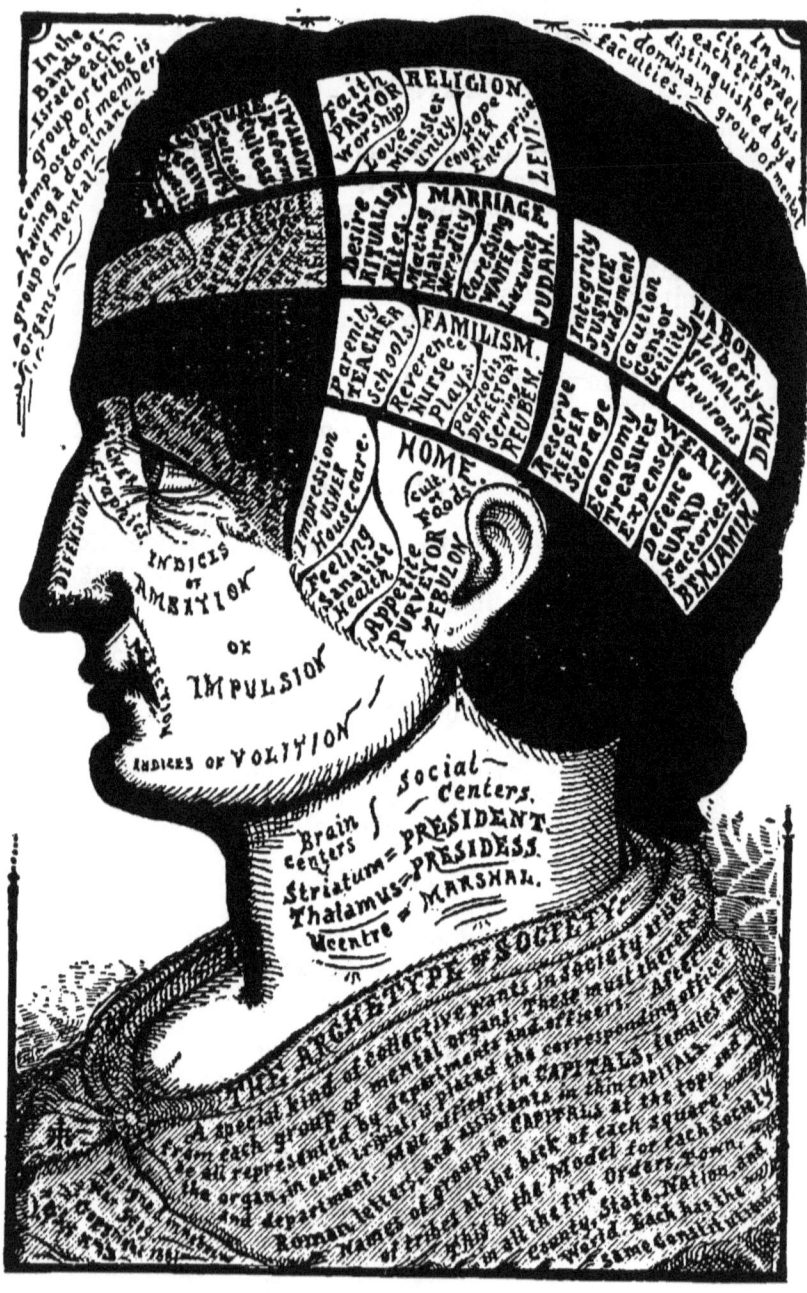

CHAPTER SECOND.

THE TRINITY.

From the motes that dance in the sunbeam to the central sun of our universe, each object has a three—fold nature. The far reaching analysis of modern science and profound search of historians, have proved that the intuitions of ancient thinkers in regard to sacred Numbers had a solid basis in the reality of things. The music of the spheres is not a mere figure of speech. The structure of the very atoms of matter makes them vibrate in rythmic pulses with the universal symphony.

The Laws of Numbers do more than simply gratify our sense of order and beauty. For they are practical guides in the works of art, the discoveries of science, and the conduct of life.

Modern chemistry rests upon the law of Definite Proportions. That law teaches that all the atoms of matter are grouped according to fixed numbers. Each kind of atom has a certain number of poles or points of attraction, and these limit the number and kind of other atoms with which it may unite. Thus in the molecule of Bioplasm the carbon atom in the center is shown with six poles, and at each one of these is found another kind of atom ; of oxygen, of nitrogen, of hydrogen, &c.

If we turn to any other branch of physical science we shall find the law of definite numbers ruling with absolute sway. No object is too minute and none too magnificent to be linked in its measured harmonies. The mechanical forces are of three kinds,—the Direct, the Lever, and the Inclined plane. The direct includes the pull, the blow, and the push. The lever in its simplest form has three elements, the fulcrum, weight and power.

The application of this law to the entire range of human knowledge, will be seen in the extended tables of Universal Synthesis.

Meaning of Numbers. Without entering into elaborate proofs, the meaning of the more important numbers is given here.

1. ONE is the number of unity, the beginning of every series, and the end of every synthesis.

2. Two is the number of duality. All the forces of nature are dual or polar. They are positive and receptive, masculine and feminine, active and passive, earthly and heavenly. By an inverse meaning, two is also the number of uncertainty or dubiety, as when we do not know which of two things to choose. By direct meaning, two stands

for certainty or assurance, as the mouth of two witnesses. The repetition of a number intensifies its meaning. 777 shows the fullest measure of meaning in seven.

3. THREE is the number of simple completeness, the Trinity. In every actual unit there is also a trinity. The two wings of a trinity are dual; three includes two. The two wings without a center would be easily divided, the center unites them, makes the three a unit.

In the indivisible atoms of matter there are three dimensions, length, breadth and thickness. The organic cell has three elements, cell-wall, nucleus, and circulating contents.

4. FOUR represents simple organization, or structure, the crossing of two lines of force at right angles. In the crystal, the poles A, B, C, D, are its lines of construction. In Segmentation, the organic cell is polarized by the sperm-cell, and divided into four parts, A, B, C, E. Four is the number of Life, and of the Family—a father and mother, a son and a daughter. It represents the heart with its four chambers; the river of life with its four heads.

12. TWELVE is produced when two axial lines, like the major and the minor axis in the brain, each terminates in a trinity. It includes a family of trinities, four threes. It is the high number of organized, spiritual perfection. It is the mathematical basis of construction in the human head, and in the human form, as will be shown in the next chapter. It is the number of Social Structure and of the New Jerusalem, the center of all earthly interests.

5 and 7. The number twelve divides into Five,

as its material or lower side; and Seven, as its higher or spiritual side. In the head, the brain is seven-twelfths of the circle, and the face and body, its servants, are five-twelfths. In the brain, the fibres of seven groups point upward and those of five groups point downward. Five is the number of the hand, the four fingers with the thumb as a pivot of action. Hence five is the number of the covenant and of material law. Seven includes two trinities with one as a pivot to unite them.

6. SIX has two trinities, but without a pivot. It stands for physical completeness, but lacks the spiritual bond of unity found in seven. 666 is the number of "the beast," of man under the reign of his lower faculties.

8. EIGHT contains twice four, the number of life. Hence it indicates the renewal of life, the resurrection, or a union of the physical and the spiritual life. The two fours which form eight are incomplete, or lack dynamic power, until the third four is added, and this makes twelve. It is a general law that the Even numbers form the Structural Series, while the Odd numbers form the Dynamic Series, or, that relating to the exertion of force. The trinity is an odd number, and in the structure of the mind, the trinity of Wisdom, Love, and Will is made even by duplicating it in the two hemispheres of the brain. Seven candle-sticks symbolize spiritual force, the dynamic work of light.

9. NINE is the number of Judgment, and of Labor. Its three trinities count a triangle, three sides of a square, the builder's measure of judgment. Labor is the ninth group, counting from the base of the brain. The date 1881 would read

"The double judgment of the earthly and the heavenly of the past, and the judgment by judgment of the present. This number reads the same backwards and forwards, it is the dividing line between the past and the future.

10. TEN is the complete number of material law, the duplicate of five.

11. ELEVEN indicates incompleteness, uncertainty, imperfection, or disorganization. Hence thirty-three, the years of Jesus, shows threefold uncertainty, and after three times six centuries, he is still without a kingdom.

13. THIRTEEN contains twelve, with one for a pivot. The twelve groups of mental faculties pivot upon the brain centers. The twelve masculine faculties have their pivot in the back center or Thalamus, and the twelve feminine ones on the front center or Striatum. The twelve assistant faculties pivot in the Ucenter. The twelve tribes in the New Jerusalem have their center in the great Temple. The twelve Princes of Israel had their pivot in the King, High Priest, or Judge. In every 13, the thirteenth number must be central or pivotal. For if they are all of equal rank, there can be no true balancing of parts, all will be discord. If we look at the twelve-rayed sun, we see that its points balance each other in every direction. But if we draw one with thirteen rays, no two of them will balance each other. We see from this and from the law of the trinity, that the doctrine of Pivotal Numbers assumes a high degree of importance. But it was quite unknown to the older writers on numbers.

26. TWENTY-SIX contains two twelves with a pivot for each. It represents the twenty-four

leading faculties and the two brain centers, a summary of the mental attributes of man. On these are based the twenty-four Rulers of the Kingdom, with the central King and Queen. Each group and each tribe has its material and its spiritual side, its masculine and its feminine rulers. Twenty-six is the number of the mystic and sacred Name, Yehovah. Among the Hebrews, every name and word had its number, and this number always shows its meaning. The attributes of Yehovah are therefore the same as those of man, for man was formed in the divine image. The Rabbis say that the full number of the sacred Name is seventy-two. This is the full number of thirty-six faculties, duplicated, as they are, in the two hemispheres of the encephalon. These faculties are again duplicated in the body, thus making one hundred and forty-four, the grand number of man and of the eternal City of Peace.

17. Seventeen is one number of the Chosen People Israel. 40 is another number of Israel, and signifies a renewal of the covenant, five times eight. The term 40 years occurs 12 times in the history of Israel.

31. Thirty-one is the number of AL, an ancient name of the Deity.

19. Nineteen signifies Judgment under the Law. The Nineteenth century of the Christian Era will witness the close of that Dispensation.

144. The meaning of this number is given above under twenty-six, and a proof is given in the third chapter.

The great events of human history, no less than the structure and laws of the individual man, have been arranged in harmony with the meaning of these numbers. These regular periods are best shown in the chronological tables.

THE TRINITY IN MIND.—The primary analysis of mental phenomena gives three divisions, Thought, Feeling, and Volition; or Wisdom, Love, and Will. These spring from the faculties of Intellect, Affection, and Expression. The intellect is directive, affection is attractive, and volition is impulsive.

Each of these classes is based upon three divisions of the bodily functions. The intellect acts in close sympathy with the entire nervous system; affection acts with the organs of nutrition; and volition governs the motive system.

The division of the classes into twelve groups and thirty-six faculties is given in the table. Each faculty again subdivides into three parts. This analysis is sufficiently minute for the purposes of art and science.

The groups of Sensation, Culture, and Impulsion are transitional in character, and this leaves a trinity of groups in each class.

The Intellect is *formal*, it determines the forms of knowlege, of feeling, and of action. The Affections are *static*, they maintain and perpetuate the race and unity of man. The Will is *dynamic*, it applies the powers of man in all his social and physical activities.

Brain and Body.—The brain is the great central organ of the mind, of Thought, Feeling and Will. We know this, FIRST, because the nerves of feeling and motion, from all parts of the body, all lead to and from the brain; SECOND, because in vivisection the removal of the brain destroys all mental manifestations, but not the bodily life of the animal; and THIRD, because the faculties can be excited by direct experiments on the brain, and observation shows a constant relation between the mental power and the degree and kind of brain developement, while the structure and plan of the brain corresponds to all the requirements of an instrument of mental action.

The front part of the brain is connected with the front part of the body and of the limbs, and the back of the brain with the back of these. From the map in this chapter, the student can readily trace these connections.

The arms partly repeat the signs of the body. The lower limbs relate us to the world of life below man, to the earth and its elements.

The upper and lower parts of the body repeat each other in action and sympathy. The anatomists have shown that the nose is thus connected with the anus; the upper lip with the perineum; the mouth with the genitals: the tongue with the penis and clitoris; the chin with the pubes; and the lungs with the allantois.

The size and texture of the signs in the form indicate the basic powers of the faculties, and their endurance; that is, the power of the brain to sustain long-continued action.

The body and the brain are usually developed in harmony with each other, but sometimes the organ of the brain is found to be either larger or smaller than the corresponding sign in the face and body. In that case, the activity and power of the faculty would be irregular, and not well sustained.

In the map it will be noticed that the intellect is not specialized in the body. The reason of this is found in the fact that the body is much more an instrument of feeling than it is of thought.

From the summit of mental to the base of bodily life, we have a sympathetic and responsive scale of forces. Touch any mental string in this harp of life, and instantly some part of the body responds with its sympathetic vibration.

The vibrations of mental excitement are larger and more noticeable in the body than in the corresponding parts of the brain. The heart throbs high under the impulse of love; but beats with irregular and arrested action when fear penetrates the soul. The whole language of gesture illustrates mental and bodily sympathies. They justify the instinctive sense which leads men to speak of Affection as the "Heart." We may still use the word heart in this way, if we will remember that the brain, the face, and the body, each contain the same scale of powers, pitched upon higher and lower keys.

The organs of the brain gradually change in the character of their functions as we pass from any given point to an entirely antagonistic region. There are no sharp lines of demarcation between them, and the lines thus drawn in the map of the organs are for the convenience of study.

The Human Face.—If the mental faculties were not connected with definite parts of the face, then the face could possess neither expression nor beauty. A look which indicated love at one moment, might indicate hate the very next. But the face is no such bundle of contradictions.

The lines on the face in the map of the organs show its principal divisions. These also correspond with the physiological functions of the face.

The mouth is directly connected, physically, with nutrition, and hence the signs of affection are around the mouth; for affection is related to nutrition.

The lower jaw is directly under control of the Will, and hence the signs of Coaction give downward length to this part of the face.

The intellect is closely related in sympathy with the lungs, and its facial signs give length and breadth to the lower end of the nose, the facial organ of breathing. We call the reception of knowledge inspiration, a word proper to the action of the lungs.

No person with a very short nose could have a great intellect, or produce a profound impression on the world.

Observation, Inspiration, Reason, Synthesis, and Analysis give prominence and length to the septum of the nose at the points indicated by their initial letters.

Imagination gives breadth to the back part of the septum.

Amity and Reform elevate the eyebrow at the places marked.

Truth and kindness elevate the inner third of the eyebrow. They form the upright and vertical wrinkles there; and Truth also produces folds and wrinkles above and below the eye.

Hospitality gives upright wrinkles back of the mouth corner, and Mirth draws the mouth corners up and backward. Mirth also causes converging wrinkles from the corner of the eye outward. Simplicity or candor curves the mouth corners slightly upward. Friendship causes slightly converging wrinkles in the red part of the lips.

BRAIN AND BODY.

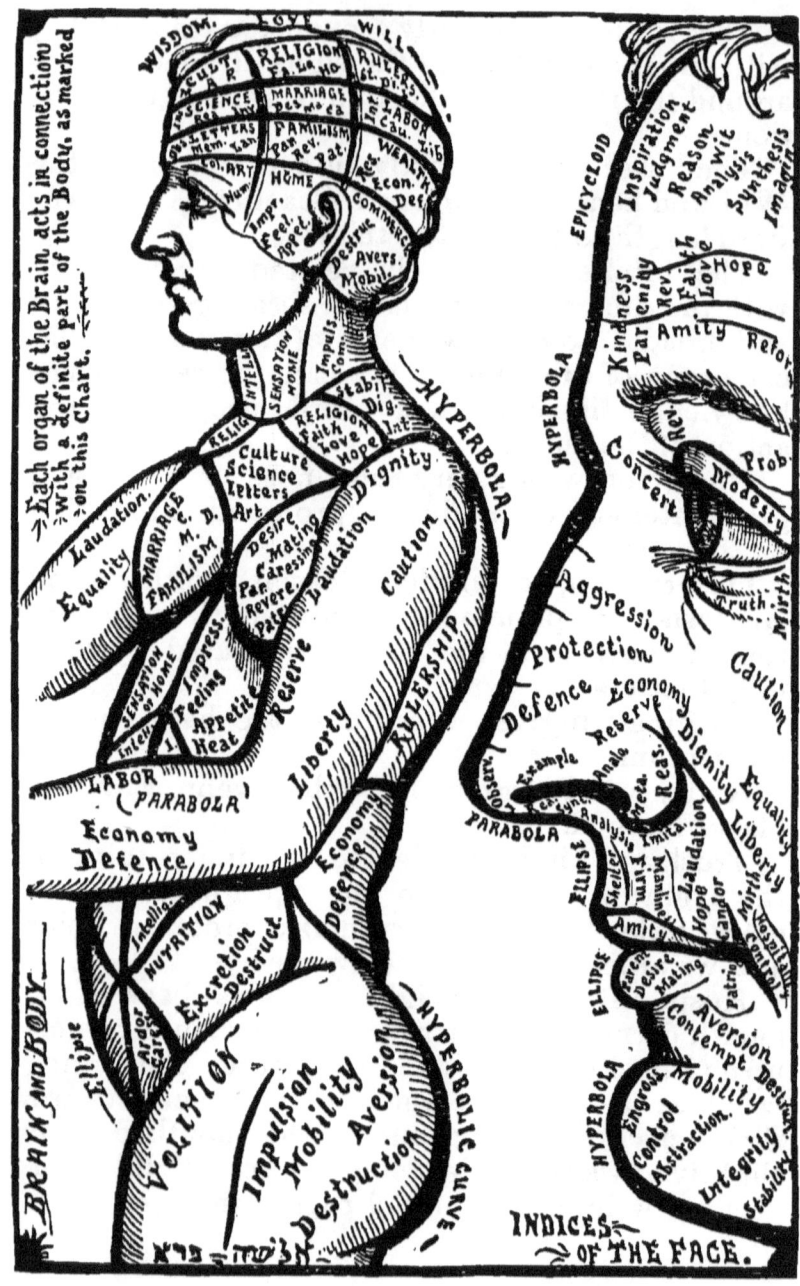

Signs of Affection.—Faith and Love elevate the middle of the eyebrow, above Amity and Reform. Farther outward, the elevation indicates Hope and Zeal. Hope also slightly raises the corners of the mouth. A noble brow is one where all of these are large.

The faculties of Sex love, such as Devotion, Fidelity, and Caressing, have their signs in the fullness and breadth of the red part of the lips. Persons with thin lips may, however, have large Fraternity and Kindness, and thus be kind and genial.

Parental and filial love elevate the inner end of the eyebrow, and are also connected with the lips near the center. Reverence turns the eye upward, and Modesty causes a drooping of the eyelids. Patriotism presses the lower lip against the upper, midway between the center and the corner.

The signs of the senses in the face are to be judged from their respective organs. Thus, development and fine structure of the mouth, especially of the tongue and lips, indicate the power and fineness of the sense of Taste. That of Touch has also its facial index in the lips, and its general index in the perfection of the skin. The development of the sense of Smell may be estimated by the perfection of structure of the nose; and that of hearing and vision by the same perfection in the ear and the eye.

The general quantity of attractive force in a person is indicated by the softness, fineness, and delicacy of the skin, and by the mobility and pliancy of the spine. Repulsive force is indicated by the length, strength, straitness, and stiffness of the spine. This quality is stronger in man, as attractiveness is in woman.

The downward length of the lower jaw indicates the faculties of Self-control, Integrity, Stability, and Caution. The breadth of the face at these points is thought to indicate the power of these faculties of the will to express affection. Mental control is indicated by an upright fulness back of the mouth.

Dignity and Laudation are connected with the muscles which elevate the upper lip and the wing of the nose. Laudation lifts the upper lip, as in the smile of approval. Dignity produces a muscular fulness at the place marked, and liberty below this.

Aggression, Protection, and Self-defense project the ridge of the nose at the upper, the middle, and the lower parts. These are small in the nose of the child; full in the Greek nose, and large in the Aquiline and Roman. Economy and Reserve give breadth to the nose at the place marked.

The intellect of a child is active, but like its nose, is not yet developed. The Greek nose has well developed signs of intellect, and the end of the nose is finely chiseled. It indicates refinement, taste, and a love of art. The Roman nose belongs to an executive, powerful, and power-loving character. It was common among the old Romans, and hence the name. The aquiline or Jewish nose indicates the commercial spirit, shrewdness, and combative energy and perseverance.

Destruction gives a fulness below the back of the mouth, and Aversion near its center. Contempt protrudes the lower lip.

Indications of the Eye.—Large eyes indicate

lively emotions, and activity of mind and body. Prominent eyes are quickly impressed, but deep-seated eyes have more accurate and deeper impressions.

The Hands.—As a rule, the general form of the hand corresponds with that of the head, in each case. A symmetrical hand indicates a symmetrical head and character. The long, bony hand is the hand of action and power. The short, fleshy hand indicates vivacity and versatility. The small, slender hand is an index of delicacy and artistic taste.

The different characters which exist among men have their types among the lower animals. The same traits of character which distinguish the lion among beasts, may be found strongly marked among men. Mary Stuart had a leonine face. Fenelon resembled a sheep; yet no one would think of applying the word beastly to their faces. The lower animals have only a fragmentary development of the faculties; man alone possesses them all in symmetry and completeness.

The Hebrew prophets represented the lower back faculties of man, by the lion, leopard, wolf, bear and serpent. The higher faculties were symbolized by the lamb, the kid, the dove, the eagle, and the horse. In the Messianic age, the lower faculties, the beast in man, were to be subject to the higher powers.

38 A   INTELLECT OR WISDOM

PERCEPTION—ART
  Form—Shape, outline, individuality.
  Color—Idea of color, size, location.
  Number—Trinity, unity, and plurality.
RETENTION—LETTERS.
  Memory—Retention of facts: time and system.
  Observation—Attention, mental focus, vision.
  Language—Mastery of words, sounds, music.
REFLECTION—SCIENCE.
  Reason—Analysis, synthesis, judgment.
  Inspiration—Foresight, intuition, spirituality.
  Construction—Skill, invention, imagination.
RECEPTION—CULTURE.
  Amity—Friendship, kindness, hospitality.
  Reform—Culture, progress, improvement.
  Communion—Candor, imitation, mirth.

AFFECTION OR LOVE.

RELIGION—RELIGION.
  Faith—Belief, love of Deity, worship.
  Love—Philanthropy, good-will, trust.
  Hope—Aspiration, zeal, immortality.
SEXATION—MARRIAGE.
  Devotion—Desire, sex-worship, romance.
  Fidelity—Mating, sex-fealty, ardency.
  Caressing—Fondness, sexuality, petting.
PARENTION—FAMILY.
  Parenity—Parental love, familism, providence.
  Reverence—Filial love, respect, modesty.
  Patriotism—Love of home, kin and country.
SENSATION—HOME.
  Appetite—Sense of hunger, taste and smell.
  Feeling—Sense of touch, heat and gravity.
  Impression—Of character, spheres, and aromas.

EXPRESSION OR WILL.

AMBITION—RULERSHIP.
  Dignity—Pride, self-esteem, authority.
  Laudation—Praise, emulation, display.
  Stability—Firmness, energy, perseverance.
COACTION—LABOR.
  Integrity—Justice, honor, balance.
  Caution—Vigilance, prudence, self-control.
  Liberty—Freedom, equality, independence.
DEFENSION—WEALTH..
  Defence—Self-defense, protection, aggression.
  Economy—Property, ownership, selfishness.
  Reserve—Secrecy, shrinking, fear.
IMPPULSION—COMMERCE.
  Mobility—Locomotion, travel, commerce.
  Aversion—Dislike, contempt, repugnance.
  Destruction—Vengeance, rigor, baseness.

MEASURE OF MAN.

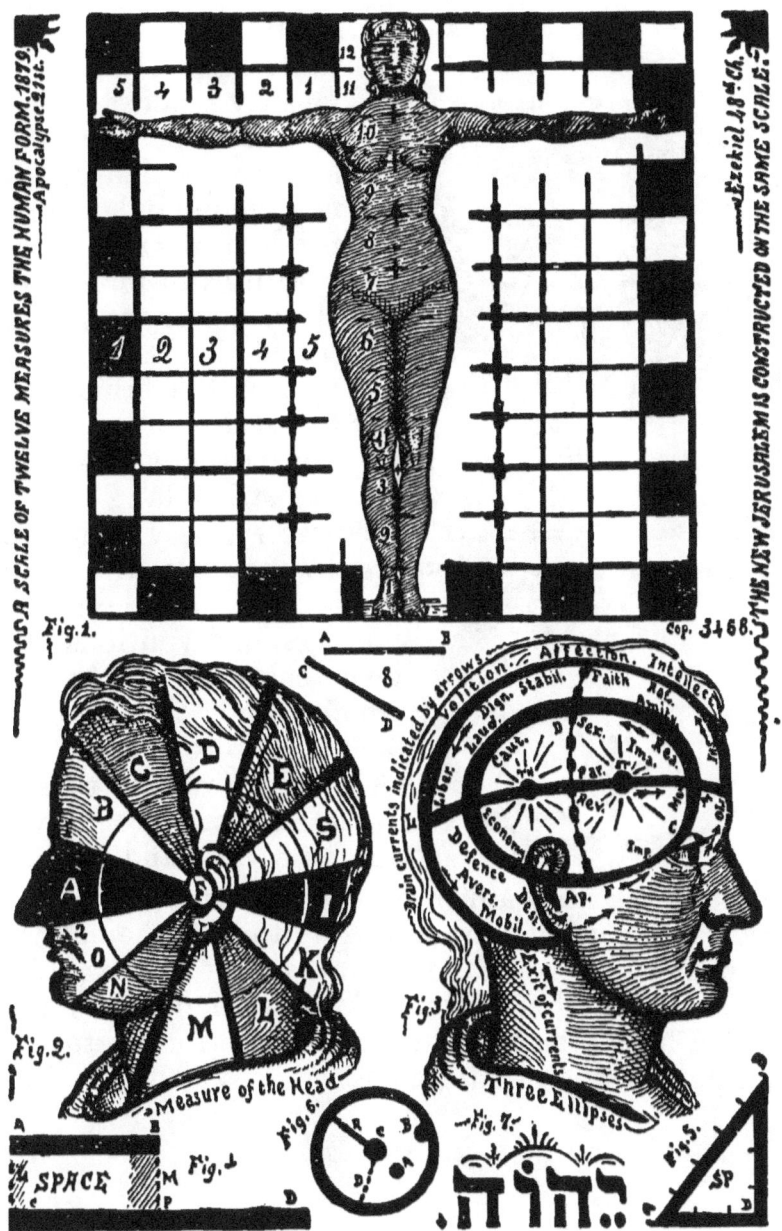

CHAPTER THIRD.

MENTAL MECHANISM.

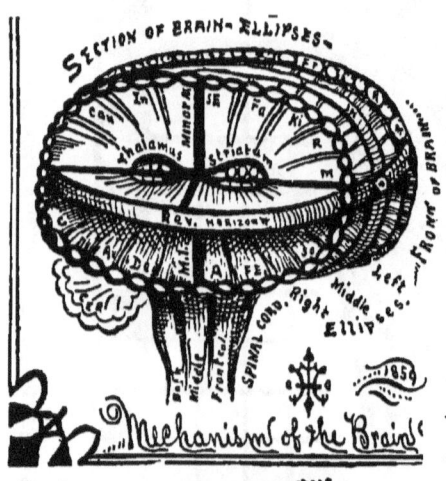

Beauty reaches deeper than the outward surface of things. It is a true index and product of their interior life and forces. In this chapter we are to learn that the structure of the brain and the action of its faculties, are governed by the strict laws of geometry. By these we are to measure the very shape of our thoughts, feelings, and volitions. In the celestial mechanics which bind the mental faculties into unison of movement, we are to see repeated those great laws which pervade and sustain the sublime mechanism of the heavens. The human brain is constructed on the mathematical plan of an Ellipse. At ST and TH are the two focal points of this curve. From each point is radiated both attractive and repulsive forces to all points of the circumference.

At the ends of the minor axis, A, B, the forces of the two centers are equal. This axis is the balancing line of unity. At all other points the forces vary. Thus at O the attractive force of TH is greater than that of ST. At L, the attraction of ST is the greater, and it reaches its maximum at C. Passing from C to R, B, S, the attraction of ST reaches its minimum point at D. Exactly the opposite has occurred with the repulsive forces of the two focuses. The repulsive forces have increased at each step as the attractive forces have lessened, or, have diminished as the attractive forces have increased. At every point, both attractive and repulsive forces are acting at the same instant.

The points at equal distances on either side of the minor axis, as O and L, balance each other and pivot on the axis, as at A. In a less conspicuous way, the upper and lower sides balance upon the major axis. All these balances are of extreme importance in understanding the action of the mental faculties.

A section of the brain shows that it contains four great elliptical planes, three of them vertical and one of them horizontal. Those in the right and in the left hemisphere are of course alike in function, so that we really have but to consider the relations of three ellipses. The united action of the two hemispheres takes place on the double middle ellipse, marked from OBS, to Mobility, in the engraved Measure of man.

Minor Axis.—The minor axis of the external ellipse extends from Appetite upward to Sexlove: Ap. to Sex. These faculties are the material pivots of all human life on the earth. For the physical existence of every individual depends upon the reception of food and drink, through appetite. From these materials of food every organ of the body is continually formed, and its action is maintained. The solid bones and the thinking brain are alike built up from these food materials. So much for the existence of the individual. But the existencs of the race or species depends upon the union of the sexes through Sexlove. Through this love, the child receives the materials for the original formation of every part of its physical organism. Thus Sexlove becomes the high material pivot of our existence, as the faculty of Appetite is the lower one. No other faculties can affect our mental and physical happiness so directly and so profoundly as these. From no others can we receive such exquisite and all-pervading pleasure as these give when they act in harmony, or such misery as these bring when in discord. In the eighth chapter, we shall find that Sexlove determines the classification of all offices and labors.

In the middle ellipse, the upper end of its minor axis is formed by the faculties of Faith, Love, and Hope. At its lower end are those of Feeling, Heat and Impression. These faculties are the channels through which we receive universal *forces*, even as we receive *materials* through the first ellipse.

The sense of Touch or Feeling, at the lower end of this axis, is the common standard for comparing all the other senses. Through this sense we perceive mathematical relations, which are the basis of all science. Through Faith and Love, at the upper end of this axis, we are related to the life of the Deity and to the collective life of Humanity, to the spiritual forces of the universe.

In a sectional view, the vertical and horizontal ellipse is formed by the organ of Reverence, of the two hemispheres. This organ points to each side, and relates equally to the past and present, the high and the low.

Eccentricity.—The Striatum and Thalamus are now regarded by all physiologists as the two great centers of brain action. The nerve fibres radiate from these centers to all parts of the circumference. In any ellipse, the farther its focal points are, the longer it will be in proportion to its breadth. The Striatum and Thalamus are a little too near together to be in the true mathematical focuses of the brain ellipses. The cause is this. The Intellect, and Volition at the front and the back, have more repulsive force in proportion than exists in Affection, which is along the middle of the ellipse. This excess of repulsive force in the Intellect and Volition pushes the brain out more at the front and back than at the sides, and this makes it relatively longer than it would otherwise be with the Striatum and Thalamus so near each other.

In any case, the mathematical analysis of a vital cnrve will give us the general law and relations of the organs which enter into its formation.

We know that the brain is an ellipse by simply dissecting it and studying its structure. The forces which produce its growth and form proceed from its centers, from within, and not from the outside. It is not cast in a mould. These forces are both mental and vital. That they are mental forces is clearly proved by the well known fact that the very thoughts and feelings of the parents during the embryonic life of a child determine the shape of its features and of its brain. And we know that either temporary or permanent changes of feeling or of character will change the curves of the head, the face, and the body.. It is mental forces then, which cause the brain to be an ellipse, and consequently the mental faculties must obey the mathematical law of this curve.

Sex in the Ellipse.—The forces of the two sexes in love act in strict harmony with the elliptical law of variation. The Striatum is dominantly masculine and the Thalamus feminine.

In their highest expression—that of originating a new being—the masculine and feminine forces are equal. From that moment forward, during the whole period of the child's prenatal development, the feminine forces increase in quantity and intensity, and the masculine diminish. After the direct parental functions are accomplished, the feminine forces slowly return to their equipoise with the masculine.

The affectional forces of the two sexes pass through elliptical variations of slighter extent when not engaged in parental relations. This law gives to sexlove—within its duality—a wide variety of emotion, the infinite charm of perpetual renewal.

THREE GREAT CURRENTS of nerve force sweep around the brain ellipses. They flow from cell to cell, and taking in their path all the principal organs, they awaken or excite these faculties in a definite order.

A large part of all the impressions received through the senses are conveyed along the fibres to the Thalamus and Striatum. On figure 3 of the measure of man, we may trace the course and effects of these currents around the brain. The arrows show the direction of the currents.

From the Sensitive group in front of the ear, the current sets forward toward the Perceptives at C. It then curves upward, and crossing the horizontal current at M, it flows over backward and downward.

The currents of the horizontal ellipse, starting forward from Reverence, at REV, meet the upward-moving current of the vertical ellipse, at M. The currents cross each other here, and a part of all the impressions composing the currents are here stored and retained. This crossing point is the organ of Memory. At no other place could Memory be so located as to store all impressions.

Moving still onward, the horizontal current crosses that of the middle vertical ellipse, at Obs. This is the organ of Observation, and the crossing here makes this the focal point of the whole intellect, the center of intellectual consciousness. The current goes on from right to left around the entire head.

The direction of this current determines an interesting fact,—it makes us right-handed instead of left-handed. The impulse, following the direction of the brain-current, flows out on the right hand and back on the left. Hence, the right hand takes the lead in most kinds of work, and the left hand is the recipient.

At points in the back of the head, corresponding to M and Obs. in front, there is a crossing of currents. These points are the organs of Equality and Liberty. This latter faculty makes us demand room for expansion ; it is a point for the *dispersion* of force in all directions. At the front brain,

Observation *concentrates* force from all directions. At Mobility a part of the currents pass to the body and thence make their exit from the system.

All of the principal organs of the brain are located on the line of these ellipses. So that wherever an impression may be made on the brain, or an action may be started, it will be carried in these currents to Memory, Observation, Reason, and Inspiration. We are thus made conscious of every mental action, and can reason about its relations.

This law of the ellipse would alone determine that the faculties are correctly located.

The course of these currents determines that in mental action, there is first Sensation, and this is followed, in orderly succession, by Perception, Memory, Reflection, Desire, and practical Action. Experience proves to us that this is just the order in which these mental processes normally succeed each other. But in cases of insanity the currents flow in irregular or reversed directions, and the ideas and actions are illogical and disorderly.

Radius Vector. A current of nerve force starting from Observation and flowing around the central ellipse, in the direction of Inspiration, Amity, Faith, Stability, Dignity and Liberty, would become slower and slower as it receded from Observation, its point nearest to its focus in the Thalamus. After the current reached Liberty, its speed would gradually increase toward Appetite and Feeling, until it reached its starting point. This variation corresponds to the law of radius vector of the planets. The shorter the fibres of any organ, the less will be the time required to perform the circuit.

Minor Currents. There are many minor currents in the brain, for they start at any organ which is the point of excitement, and spread more or less in all directions. Every organ, when in action, must therefore excite its neighbors, these waves establishing a universal sympathy among the organs, strong in proportion to their nearness. Hence, faculties which are similar to each other have adjacent locations. If Friendship and Aversion were side by side, then the more our Friendship were excited in loving a friend, the more would Aversion be aroused to repel him.

Other Curves.—The ellipse is the great curve upon which the brain is constructed. But it is not by any means the only curve which we find in the human form. The organs and signs of Sex-love in the brain, the face, and the body, form elliptical; those of Parental, filial and some of the intellectual, form parabolic; the Ambitious form hyperbolic; and the Reasoning, and Religious form epicycloidal curves. We shall only notice these briefly.

The Epicycloid forms a prominent part of our mental structure. This is the curve upon which all of the planets and suns move through space. In the brain a vertical range of organs, including Inspiration, Kindness, Faith, Love, Hope, Stability, and Dignity, are located upon this curve. These give us the widest possible range of relations so far as our feelings or affection is concerned. They unite us with universal life. Another range of organs, forming an epicycloid, includes Inspiration Reason, Imagination, and Construction. These faculties enable us to comprehend, and to harmonize ourselves with, universal law. These are the only two ranges which form this curve, and they are the only ones which establish universal relations.

In the map of the body, hyperbolic curves are formed by the ambitious faculties at the shoulder and the same curve is repeated by the analogous group of impulsion in the thigh. This curve is formed by the faculties of Will on the chin, and lower maxilla.

The straight line is a monotone. It does not possess that variation in the direction of line which is essential to beauty of curvation. It can occur but once in a beautiful form, and that is in the ridge of the nose. The circle, too, is a monotone, and only occurs in the iris of the eye.

Beauty of the Form. The curves of the head, face, and body seldom terminate abruptly, but gracefully blend with each other, like the organs of the brain. The number and perfect arrangement of these curves gives to the human form its wonderful beauty, so far surpassing that of all other physical objects that we cannot conceive of anything more beautiful; and our highest inspirations attribute the same form to beings in realms of existence more exhalted than our own.

The most beautiful face and figure is one in which all of the faculties are the most fully and symmetrically developed. If any organs or signs of a curve are deficient in size, this will destroy the regularity, and consequently the beauty of the curve. The most beautiful living object is one having the fullest and freest manifestation of life. For Life is a principle of unity, and the more complete the relation and harmony of its parts, the more perfect is the manifestation of life, in any living being. Living creatures appear ugly and deformed when the free play of life seems obstructed in them.

A homely face may have many of the higher faculties well developed, and express the goodness which comes from these, but it cannot belong to a complete and well-rounded character.

The angular character is really much better adapted to a discordant and defective civilization than a more symmetrical character would be. It sometimes happens that beautiful persons become perverted; and many persons have been called handsome who were really lacking in the higher indications and elements of beauty.

In the lowest of the animals, the simplest and fewest of the geometric curves prevail. The curves become more numerous and complex as we ascend the scale of life until we reach man. The divine beauty of the human form is expressed through one hundred and forty-four of these curves, and these are duplicated in its bi-lateral symmetry. Thirty-six of these curves belong to the head and face.

The more beautiful curves—the ellipse and its modification, the parabola—are repeated many times. The bosom of woman—the ivory throne of love, set with carnation, garnet, or amethyst—derives its exquisite beauty of form from both the ellipse and the parabola.

Proportions. The curves which make up the human form not only bear fixed relations to each other as regards their position, but also in regard to their proportional size. The upper figure in the Measure of Man will illustrate these proportions.

If we draw twelve squares, in each direction,

these squares will accurately divide off the proportion of the various parts of the human form. This divine measure of a man was rediscovered in modern times by the artist Page, from whom our drawing is copied.

The extended arms reach as far as the person is tall: the heighth and breadth are equal, as was said of the Celestial city.

These divisions of the form are not simply external, they belong to the bones, the muscles, and the viscera. They are exemplified in every well proportioned adult person, and in the great works of ancient and modern statuary.

The lowest square includes the foot and ancle; the second is the lower leg; the third its calf; the fourth is the knee; the fifth the upper leg; the sixth is the thigh; the seventh is the pelvis; the eighth is the abdomen; ninth, the stomach and liver; the tenth is the breast; the eleventh is the neck; and the twelfth is the brain. Its width also forms a twelfth. The arm is five-twelfths, the hand is one.

When we measure the head alone, we still find that a scale of twelve is the only one that will accurately fit its various parts. In the second figure, of the measure of man this scale is illustrated. A point, F, at the opening of the ear lies against the great physiological center of the nervous system as described in the second chapter. Drawing one line from this point to the top, and another to the lower end of the nose, these two lines, 1 and 2, include an angle of thirty degrees, or one-twelfth of a circle. Extending these same sized angles all the way around the head, there will be three in front, three above, three behind, and three below.

One includes from the nose to the chin, and one the forehead. If we divide the circle into any other number of angles, they will not fit any of the features of the head and face.

Here is the same division and arrangement into four sides, with three parts on each side, that we shall find in the plan of the city of the New Jerusalem, as described in the ninth chapter. The measure of the city is the measure of a man.

In the higher harmonies, the number twelve consists of two parts; five as the lower, and seven as the upper part. So in this measurement of the head, the brain occupies seven-twelvths of the great circle, or the angles B, C, D, E, S, I, and K. The face and the body, the servants of the mind and brain, include the five lower angles. The brain itself is divided into seven groups which point upward, and five which point downward.

In his vision of the New Palestine, the prophet Ezekiel, saw the gathered tribes of Israel all redistributed, so that seven were placed above or north, and five below the city. And, as we shall see iu the ninth chapter, the seven upper tribes had the upper groups of faculties dominant, while the five other tribes had the lower groups ruling in their traits of character.

We have thus proved, by the unanswerable facts of mathematics, that the number twelve is the basis of construction in thr human form, and that both our mental and bodily life express themselves through the numbers three and twelve. It is the faculties of the mind itself that give form to the brain and body, and we could not ask for any clearer proof that these faculties are classified by nature into three divisions and twelve groups.

CHAPTER FOURTH.

CROWN OF LIFE.

The theory of Wave movement is now generally accepted, as a well established truth, among scientific men.

We may safely assume that in Matter there are five, and in Spirit seven kinds or forms of Atoms. The atoms of matter differ from those of spirit in their forms, their size, and in their polarity.

The circular polarity of Spirit-atoms produces the rounded forms of organic cells and objects.

In the atom of spirit on the engraving of the mental mechanism the arrows show the direction of these circular currents of polarity. The rays show its straight polar lines.

The reason why spirit has no weight or gravity is because its atoms are smaller than the length of the waves of gravity, and therefore these waves cannot set the atoms of spirit into vibration, and consequently the attraction of gravitation has no effect on them. Suppose, for example, that the waves of gravity, in our engraving, were the 50,000th part of an inch in length, while the atoms of spirit were only the 70,000th of an inch. It is evident that one of these long waves could not vibrate within the smaller atom of spirit.

But the waves of spirit atoms may unite with each other, and according to the law of intensity, they may produce waves large enough to affect and set in vibration the atoms of matter. Thus in figure 2, the waves A and B unite at c, and the resulting wave is twice as large as when they were separate.

Every atom has its own inherent vibrations. These are a part of its essential properties. It may have different forms of waves at its different poles, and thus each pole possesses its special kind of attraction, and may exert its force over a special kind of matter. In the molecule of bioplasm the atom of carbon, in the center, attracts the atom of hydrogen at one, and that of nitrogen at another pole.

The atoms of spirit possess forms quite as distinct and persistent as those of matter. This has nothing to do with the question of their possessing weight, as was explained above. If spirit atoms have *form* they must of necessity have *space*. For we cannot conceive a form, a circle or triangle for instance, without there being space between its two sides. It does not follow that the ultimate atoms can be divided because they have parts, though some thinkers have tried to suppose it did.

Waves of Nerve Force.—The radiant waves from each organ of the brain and from each part of the body, have their own distinctive character. They differ in form, in length, and in altitude.

The engravings of the Mental Mechanism show the rounded form of the waves of Memory; the constructive waves of Reason; the articulated waves of Amity or Friendship; the smooth waves of Religion; the looped waves of Sexlove; the angulo-curves of Dignity; the sharp angles from Integrity and Liberty; the acute angles of Defense, and the hooked waves of Aversion.

These examples show that the form of the waves corresponds precisely with the character of the faculties from which they are radiated. The smooth, attractive waves of Affection are in broad and appropriate contrast to the harsh, repulsive waves of the Defensive faculties. Our very thoughts and feelings have their distinctive shapes and impress them upon the outflowing waves. The prickling sensations under the excitement of anger are very different from the soft thrills of affection. An instinctive preception of these truths has determined the figures of speech used in all languages. Men never speak of love as rough, or of anger as being smooth.

The nerve-force usually travels along its special

conductors, the nerve fibres, while it is within the brain and body. But, like magnetism it can readily flow outside of its conductors when it reaches their terminal ends. The sheaths of the fibres insulate the current while it is passing along the fibre, but when the current reaches either the cells or the free end of the fibre, then it may be freely radiated into space. Its rate of movement along the nerves is thought to be about two hundred feet per second, a rate which is very slow in comparison with that of magnetism or electricity.

Nerve–Spheres. The nerve-force constantly radiates from each organ, and it thus passes from us in all directions through space. Each person is thus constantly surrounded by a nerve-sphere which corresponds to his own character. Through these spheres we either attract or repel those who are around us. We mentally impress others and are impressed by them.

These pulsating brain-waves, these swift lines of thought and feeling, sometimes reach a few feet, and sometimes many miles. But whether extending a great or a less distance, there, around every person, is this vital sphere of silent power, reflecting and transmitting every mood and impulse that sweeps through the soul.

When two friends approach each other, there is a beautiful play of colors as the nerve currents from them meet and blend, one after another; and when the two friends become fixed in position, the waves returning to each give a new series of luminous harmonies. Sometimes the currents from some organs will blend, and that from others will not. In that case, the two friends can only partly sympathize in feeling or thought. When the blending is complete, we may read the very thoughts of our associates.

These exchanges are constantly taking place and all persons feel their influence, whether such persons are called sensitive or not. The highest effort of clairvoyance is but the exaltation of this nerve-sense, which all persons exercise in a greater or less degree.

Mesmerism. Mesmer and his followers have shown that the voluntary exertion of nerve-force in one person has enabled him for a time to control the muscular movements and apparently the whole thoughts of another. The operator makes passes over his subject, who must remain in a receptive condition, until his nerve-force has sufficiently penetrated the latter. Then whatever the operator may think or wish, the same thing is thought and wished by the subject. These experiments are abnormal uses of the nerve-force, but they serve to vividly illustrate its transfer between persons.

Mental Telegraph.—The nerve-force may extend between those who are great distances apart, and convey expressions of thought and emotion even more exact than by words. In these cases of mental telegraphing, the nerve-force may be passed through the air, or be conducted along solid objects, as along a road where a person has traveled. Many obstacles interfere with this method of communication. Every advance in culture and refinement will make its use more frequent and certain.

The nerve-force from large and active organs extends farther than that from small and inactive ones. So does that from the front and upper organs when compared with that from those of the lower and backhead. From Kindness, for example, it reaches farther than from Defence. The latter points to the earth and so must soon stop. Anger, hate, and all the evil passions die out sooner than love and the higher emotions. The reign of evil is limited by this law of brain-structure. The passion for military glory will be outgrown, while the beneficient triumphs of the intellect survive through all generations.

It is through these vital currents that the whole human race is to be united in one vast composite life. The high sensitiveness which would belong to such a universal sympathy, implies the entire dominance of the nobler faculties of man's nature. The invention of the magnetic telegraph was an external index that the development of man had reached nearly to a point where it would be possible to unite all the nations in bonds of amity. The telegraph was the physical nervous system of the nations.

The radiant nerve-force obeys the general laws of radiant forces. It has been carefully studied by competent observers, and the results are presented here without any attempt to state the multitude of separate facts upon which they rest.

All forces are convertible, transferrible, or counteractive, in measured proportions. A definite quantity of one always produces, or else counteracts, a definite quantity of another. In the steam engine, heat is converted into mechanical motion. When a body falls and strikes the earth. heat is developed—gravity has been converted into heat.

In no part of nature is there any such thing as

absolute rest. Matter, Spirit and Force are eternal. Either may assume a thousand complex forms in succession, but neither can ever be destroyed. To-day we behold the stately tree of the forest; a few centuries hence it will have fallen to decay, and its tissues be converted into gases or into the soil. Nay, before our very eyes the wonderful transformation is constantly taking place, but not an atom has been destroyed, not any force has been wasted. They have disappeared in one, to re-appear in another form. The entire quantity of matter and of motion remains always the same in the universe. We cannot take any atom of matter and by any possibility divest it of motion. For example, no atom of matter was ever found that did not possess gravity, or the power of movement toward other atoms.

Control of the Will.—The will appears to have a certain amount of control over these out-going currents. By thinking and steadily exerting the will on a particular person, the nerve currents may be directed towards him more definitely and effectively. Within the brain itself the will displays the same power in directing the currents of force. We can, by an effort of the will, call one faculty or another into activity, just as we choose. In the brain, however, the mechanism is so regular that this object is accomplished without difficulty and without our notice.

Modification of Currents.—A current flowing from an organ in any direction over other organs. mixes with the force peculiar to each, and is correspondingly modified. For instance, take a current starting from Excitement, the lower part of Caution, toward Stability. The harsh, angular character possessed by the waves when they start from Excitement is slightly modified by mingling with the force from Caution. At Patriotism, its forces make them much more quiet and smooth. Still further on, the blending nerve-force of Integrity imparts to them a more steady and even strength, and that of Perseverance gives them greater uniformity. At the end of their course, Stability or Firmness imparts its gentle and firm influence. The force of each organ tends to make the passing current resemble itself in character. If the intermediate organs are small and inactive, the current would pass around them, and over larger and more active ones.

Interference of Brain Waves.—A current of nerve-force from one organ may meet and neutralize that from another by interference. This is according to a general law of all the forces, that the crests of the waves in one correspond to those of the other, they are increased in their intensity; but when the crests of one fall into the depression of the other, they neutralize each other.

The new resulting force in the brain may be readily estimated by considering what the two organs were, and over what organ the currents met. A current from Parenity and one from Laudation might meet and neutralize each other over a large organ of Caution. The new force would be appropriated by Caution, and would probably impart to the organ a pleasing feeling of tender care.

Opposing currents are constantly meeting and being converted where no interference occurs. The organs of Imagination, Im, are located at the junction of the Reflective, the Receptive, Sexal and Parental groups. It follows that a multitude of minor currents must meet and be converted over this organ. Out of these conversions would naturally spring the whole system of metaphors and figures of speech which form so large a part of all languages. For if the nerve force of two organs may be converted into each other, then the forms of speech appropriate to each may be exchanged, as in the case of all metaphors.

Adhesion of Impressions.—When a new impression is made on the mind, it sets up its own peculiar vibration of the fibres and cells. Now if the mind already contains an impression which was in part similar to this new one, then some of the fibres have already vibrated in the same manner as the new impression would make them. According to a general law of all action, they could repeat their old vibrations more easily than they were produced at first. Hence new ideas tend to set in action those fibres and cells which have already responded to similar ideas, and thus similar ideas and feelings are stored up in the same parts of the brain. This fact is the basis of the important law of Association in memory and thinking.

If each new fact and new impression, as it comes in to the mind, is compared with those which are already there, and the mind decides which of the old ones it resembles most; then the new impresiion will be made on the cells which are adjacent to those which contain that old impression which is most like it.

As any excitement of one cluster of nerve cells will extend to and excite adjacent ones, it is clear that if the impressions of similar facts be made upon adjacent cells, when the excitement of recollecting one will awaken and recall the other.

Association of ideas also arises from analogous faculties, those which are polar in the second degree. Thus the color of an orange may recall its form and its flavor. The organs of form and of flavor are polar, but not adjacent to color.

These laws show us the vast importance of true classifications in teaching all branches of knowledge. If our facts and our ideas are all in disorder in our mind, it will be as difficult to find and recall them, as it would be to find anything you want in a disorderly house.

In childhood and youth the brain is more susceptible to impressions than at later periods of life, and they are retained with greater tenacity. The early part of life is the time to lay up a store of knowledge, to be worked out in the practical duties of mature years.

The actions of nature are full of measured repetitions. To these as a whole, we give the name of Time. The organ of Observation relates to the present moment. When time recedes into the past, it is cognized by the organ of Memory. When the facts become far enough past to be organized into periods, they come under the cognizance of the organ of Time, situated still further outward from the middle of the forehead. And when the periods assume definite relations to each other, they impress the organ of System.

Failure of Memory.—In the growth and nutrition of the brain—as each old and worn out nerve-cell is replaced by a new one—the impressions which were upon the old are transferred to the new, so that the mind is able to retain its images.

But there is a little force expended in making the transfer; consequently, it is never complete, and the mental impressions gradually lose their distinctness and intensity. Probably, many times the new impressions received by the mind are superimposed upon others, and this would impair their distinctness.

The organ of Memory is a general storehouse, but each mental faculty also retains or remembers its own kind of impressions. Thus the organ of Form remembers images, and that of Amity retains the impressions of friendship.

Nerve and Muscular Force. The nerve-force may be converted into either of the other forces. Whenever a muscle contracts, nerve-force has been sent to it and expended. Let a person of studious and sedentary habits engage in vigorous muscular labor, and he will quickly realize that the brain is using up its nerve-force in the effort, for his brain will soon feel exhausted.

There is an exact relation between the amount of nerve-force expended and the amount of mechanical force displayed in the contraction of the muscle. This is clearly proved by the fact that we know just how much nerve-force to expend in order to make the muscles contract to any required extent. All mechanic arts depend upon this certainty. In the acts of cutting, sawing, painting, and ten thousand acts of our daily life, it is necessary that the muscles contract just so far and no farther.

Waves in Dreaming.—In the act of dreaming, the fragments of mental impressions and images float about, and touching each other, they blend and adhere to each other in a disorderly and patchwork manner. During sleep, the great currents flow around the ellipses with exceeding slowness, and the minor and cross currents are thus allowed to dominate. The regular order of thought is suspended. Sensation, perception, memory, reflection, desire and action, no longer succeed each other in the manner of our waking hours. But many times in sleep the mind is especially sensitive and passive, and then clear impressions of ideas or of facts, may be received from other minds, or even from our own surroundings.

If a large current attempts to travel over a nerve which is too small for it, then one of two things may happen. It may be converted into heat, and we all know that a strong nervous current may produce a glow of warmth all through the body. Or it may be converted into a galvanic current, and then the person will feel those thrills which all have experienced under excitement.

Colors of Nerve-Force. Each organ of the brain radiates a nerve-light of a distinctive color. Thus, from Ambition the light may be bright or dull, clear or impure in tone, but it will always be a crimson or reddish purple. These colors are shown in the full-page view of the nerve spheres. The author of this book was the first person who analyzed these colors and traced them to their source in the separate groups. This was done, and the proper diagrams painted, in the Hebrew year 3445.

From the following table these colors may be readily learned, and also from the colored map of the mental organs in the second chapter, and from the colored plan of the New Jerusalem.

RECEPTION, Emerald.	**RELIGION,** Lemon.	**AMBITION,** Crimson.
REFLECTION, Azure.	**SEXATION,** Orange.	**COACTION,** Scarlet.
RETENTION, Blue.	**PARENTION,** Amber.	**DEFENSION,** Red.
PERCEPTION, Grey.	**SENSATION,** Salmon.	**IMPULSION,** Maroon.

These facts furnish a clear guide for the application of color in costume, architecture and landscape. Every color exerts a definite influence on that group of mental faculties which radiates a similar color. The world of color beauty, in nature and art, becomes full of living significance. Some of these applications are given in the twelfth chapter. The colors of the groups are shown in the plan of the New Jerusalem.

The nerve-force is finer than ordinary sunlight, and it is hence impossible to represent its extreme beauty and delicacy in a painting or an engraving.

The nerve-force bears closer analogies to light than to any other of the forces. It has often been seen by sensitives, under a slightly increased intensity of common vision. The rods and cones of the eye become more tense under some forms of mental excitement and consequently they vibrate to the fine waves of nerve force. It may then appear as a soft, diffused light around the head and form, or it may shoot out in broad glowing bands, like the aurora; or it may form iridescent clouds, at a greater or less distance from the person. The light from the seven upper groups often appears like a crown of spiritual brightness, decorated with flaming jewels.

Intensity of Colors.—When an organ is excited

and active, its nerve-force will be bright and intense, flashing up vividly. We express this condition by saying that our minds feel bright. A public speaker whose whole intellect is excited, is said to make a brilliant effort. Those who first used these terms regarded them as simply figures of speech, little dreaming that in the advance of science it would be proved that they were true in the most literal sense. When an organ is inactive, or when we are asleep, the light from it is dull and obscure. We can truly say that the mind is dull and the thought slow in this case.

The Crown of Life.—A well-cultivated and properly used organ gives forth a nerve-light that is pure ane clear in color. But from an organ in the opposite condition, it will be foul and impure in tone. We speak a literal truth, then, when we say that a good person is the light of a community, or that the bad dwell in darkness. When we enlighten the mind of a person, we actually increase the quantity and quality of the nerve-light radiated from his brain. To the eye of the sensitive, or the clairvoyant, the brain appears like a luminous sun, only its light is of infinite softness. Hence a sun with twelve rays is a true symbol of the human mind, and of a perfect man, a Sun of righteousness.

The seven-rayed crown of living nerve light may adorn the head of every good person in this life. It comes to them as the sure reward of intellectual culture and spiritual excellence. It is often seen in the form given at the head of this chapter.

Impressions..—Every object radiates forces which impress an image of itself upon surrounding objects. If we lay a key upon a smooth metal plate for a short time, and then remove it, the image of the key may be evoked by heating the plate. And this may be done years after the contact. Whether conscious or not, the objects of the universe are thus continually writing their history in these marvellous pictures.

The nerve cells of the brain and of the various nerve centers, are constituted on purpose to receive impressions. The extent of their impressibility is very great, and the results belong to a large part of our conscious life.

By coming in contact with an object, a sensitive person may perceive and describe the impression it has received and retained. For example, by holding a manuscript letter in gentle contact with the forehead or the hand, the whole character, personal appearance, and even the thoughts of the writer at the time of writing, may be faithfully described.

A fossil plant or animal, examined in this way, gives up a faithful picture of its ancient surroundings, in prehistoric ages. In the experiments made by Denton, this was done again and again.

It was through contact impressions, received through different parts of the brain, that the true location of the mental organs was finally discovered in the year 1841. These experiments, made by Buchanan, were numerous and decisive.

Here in a paragraph, is the statement of the method in the language of its discoverer: "CONCENTRATIVE EXCITEMENT.—This is the scientific demonstration of cerebral functions, the method which I discovered in 1841, of exciting the cerebral functions to compel them to manifest their functions. The application of heat and cold to the various parts of the body and head, of galvanic currents and of medical stimulants and sedatives, may concentrate the nervous excitement to any one spot, and diminish the activity of other parts so as to produce a decided predominance of the stimulated organ. By far the best method for such purposes, is to use the stimulus of the nervaura (nerve-force) by applying the hand. The finger or hand, applied to any portion of the head, excites the adjacent organs by an attractive influence, and in highly impressible persons will produce an immediate and striking effect. Thus anger, joy, avarice, mirth, pride, imagination, memory, fear, or any other faculty may be aroused by touching its locality for a few moments, and by a series of such experiments the functions of every organ may be demonstrated to the satisfaction of the experimenter and his subject. Since this discovery we no longer need to occupy ourselves in calculating the probable functions of the brain from a vast number of indefinite facts in cranilogy, as Gall and Spurtzheim did, for a simple and easy experiment places cerebral science upon as positive a foundation as chemistry, anatomy. or physiology. It must be remembered that all our experiments are made without any mesmeric preparation or somnambulism, and that both operator and subject are equally awake, intelligent, conscious, independent and self possessed."

The much later experiments of Hertzig, Ferrier and others, made by electricity upon the brains of lower animals, were undecisive and unreliable, These cannot report their sensations, and Ferrier made no allowance for the repetition of analogous functions, and the co-operation of back and front faculties. The pathological proofs of aphasia were more decisive, but they only located the faculty of Language where Buchanan's experiments had placed it, many years before.

Caressing. Those acts of contact which express the various forms of affection, prove the reality of these impressions beyond all possibility of doubt. All animals with a distinct nervous system, from the insignificant worm up to man, express their sexal, parental, filial or friendly affection by the contact of caressing. Taking man alone, here are twelve hundred millions of these facts occurring daily. And only one explanation is possible. There must be some actual force passing from one living being to another in these acts of caressing. This nerve-force is a vital part of us, and its reception in this way is just as real as the reception of force through the food which we eat. It does not depend upon imagination. We touch those parts of the face and body which are functionally connected with the actions which we wish to express. Thus parental, filial, fraternal, and sex-love are connected with the lips and with the bosom, and hence kissing or caressing these parts expresses these affections. A kiss on the back of the hand expresses protection and submission, for this part of the hand is connected with the defensive and ambitious faculties. A kiss on the forehead expresses fraternal and religious affection.

Spiritual Atmosphere. Through the radiated nerveforce we actually impart somewhat of our own being to everything we touch. And in turn we as constantly receive from the accumulated force left by others.

The presence of a large number of the wise.

and good in any locality fills the place with a nerve-sphere of light which may last for years. Such a luminous mental sphere is highly favorable to clearness of thought and social harmony. It is a part of human destiny to surround, in this way, the whole earth with the living glory of truth and love, its true and final spiritual atmosphere.

This law teaches us that we are responsible to our fellow beings for every thought and feeling which we entertain, as well as for every action which we perform. The silent waves of mental force vibrate from soul to soul. They unite us all by the inseparable links of a composite spiritual life.

CHAPTER FIFTH.

POLATION.

From the chemical union of atoms to the vast revolutions of the stars, all action is polar. It involves the concert of opposite forces or tendencies—the attractive and repulsive; receptive and positive; masculine and feminine. The phenomena of mental polarity play an important and conspicuous part in mental action.

The polar faculties, these all-sweeping levers of life, vibrate through the earthy and the heavenly spheres of our being. They sweep the past, the present, and the future. They move the progressive and the conservative phases of our existence. The rhythm of human life depends upon their equal development and concordant action.

Spheres of Contrast. The major axis of the brain extends from Memory to Liberty. The whole half of the brain below this points downward, and belongs to the earthly side of our natures. This lower side of the brain rules the life of the lower animals. Their chief attractions are earthly and material. This half relates to the lowest sphere of life, the lowest uses of all things.

Opposed to this inferior sphere is the upper half of the brain. Its organs of Inspiration, Integrity, Faith, Love, Hope, and Reform lead us to perceive the higher life; the spiritual, the better uses of all things, the heavenward phase of feeling and action. We should look up and not down, is the command of these faculties. They point upward and they fit us for an elevated life of purity, goodness, and harmony.

The perceptive faculties, around the eye, are concerned with the things of the present. Opposed to these are the conservative feelings of the ambitious organs, from D to L and Economy. They cling with tenacity to whatever the past has bequeathed to the present. When acting alone, they produce a clannish feeling, and desire to go with the oldest and strongest party, whether it be in the right or in the wrong.

The attractions to the past are opposed by the high front faculties of Inspiration, Reason, and Reform. These point forward to the future, and assure us that it is in the noonday of human history, and not in its gray dawn, that the sun of truth shines with the most life-giving beams. They command us to look forward, not backward. In the grand cycles of growth the old never fully returns. The new always has the first unfoldment of some truth or beauty.

The sensitive faculties, from Appetite to Impression, make us sensitive, yielding, and impressible. They are balanced by the vigorous organs from Stability to Caution. These organs render us firm, hardy, and tranquil.

The Defensive group, if acting alone, would make a person harsh, disagreeable, conservative,

PLAN OF THE BRAIN.

71

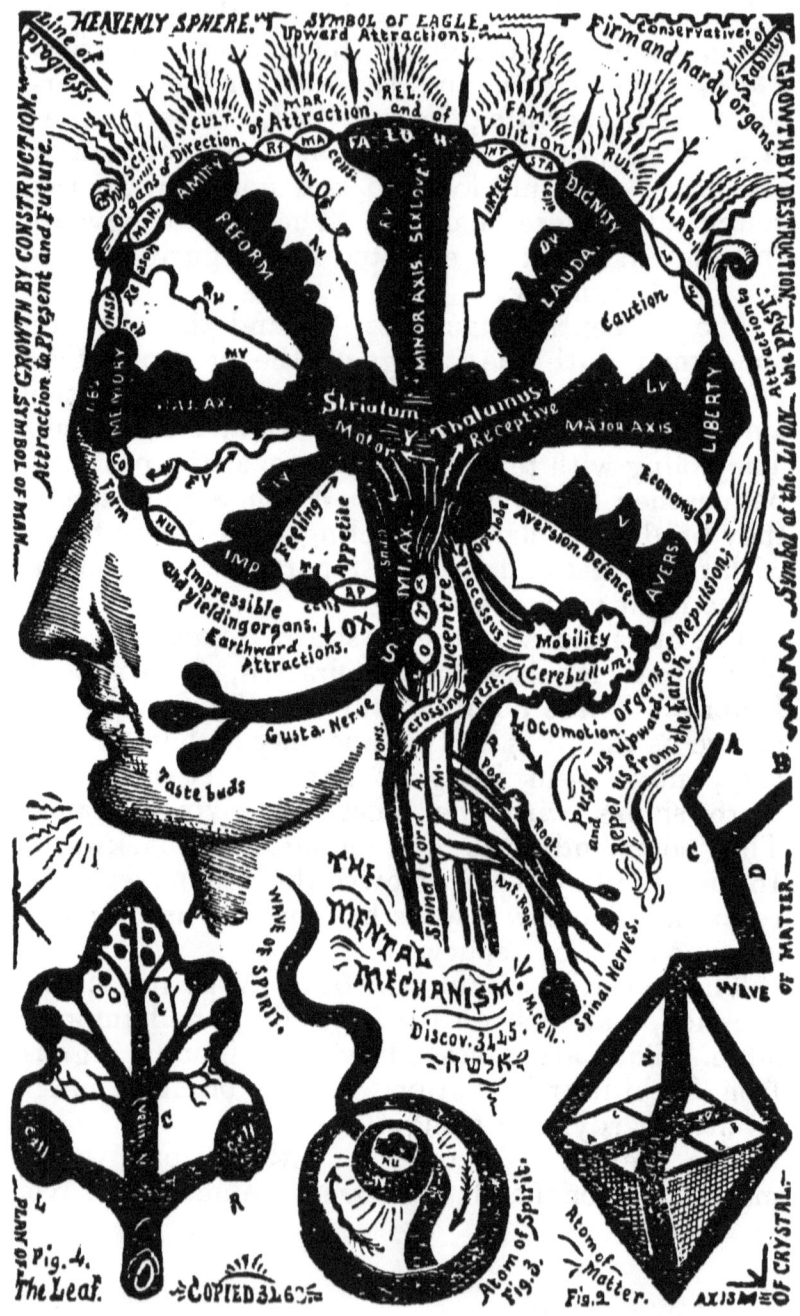

and selfish in manners and conduct, but when acting in conjunction with the opposite group of Amity, as they should do, than we have a careful regard for our own rights, but are careful to consider that our own rights are bound up in the interest and happiness of our fellow-beings.

The organs of repulsion, which point downward and backward, press against the earth, and thus push us upward and forward at every step. Their force thus acts in concert with that of the attractive organs in front.

In estimating the character of any person by the size of the organs, we must carefully take into account the opposite tendencies of these polar faculties. Thus a person may have very large Pride, and yet be modest and deferential through large Modesty and Reverence. When an organ and its polate are both small, the person will exhibit no decided tendencies in either direction. A person with small Kindness and small Economy would be neither a liberal nor a miser. His character would be negative in both respects. From the table of Mental Chords, the student can easily make these applications of the law.

Zones of Co-operation. It is a law that the organs all point toward their objects of relation. Thus the social organs point forward toward our associates and friends; the Perceptives point down toward the earth, which we are observing; and so of the rest. But the organs of the brain are, many of them, arranged so that different organs have the same, or almost the same, direction. As a consequence of this, they should have similar objects of relation; and such is the case. These organs occupy two parallel zones, and may be illustrated by the initial engraving. It represents an upright cross section of the brain, from right to left. We are looking at this view from behind. The fibres of Stability, at S, in the left hemisphere curve over toward the right. They take nearly the same direction as those of Control, C, in the right hemisphere. They must have similar objects of relation. The calmness and fortitude given by Stability are sustained by the co-operation of Control, which gives restraint and elevated caution. The two faculties are analogues.

In this engraving, the fibres of Integrity, at I, in one hemisphere, point in the same direction as those of this faculty in the other. At B, the fibres of Baseness are seen pointing exactly opposite to those of Integrity.

In the table of mental chords the most important of the co-operating organs, just described, will be found.

Where the hemispheres lie against and touch each other. is another zone. still more interior. Its faculties echo in a less definite way those of the outer zone.

Third Degree. This unites all of the faculties in pairs. In the table of mental faculties, the first and second one in each trinity form a pair.

The contrast between the two members of a pair is less strongly marked than in the other degrees. In some cases it required a most extended and careful analysis to discriminate them. The two are located near each other, and never act in antagonism.

The organ of Dignity is bold, positive, masculine, and impressive, tending to keep those upon whom it acts at a respectful distance, The organ of Laudation, its polate of the third degree, is receptive, attractive, and feminine, tending to win approval. It is strongest in the womanly character, while Dignity is stronger in man. Prevision is simply receptive, it is directly impressed by the forces which are to produce future events, and those which are now in action. But its polate, Reason, works externally, it combines and arranges impressions and produces new phenomena. Hence when compared with Prevision, it is the more positive.

But if we should compare Reason with Aggression, its polate of the first instead of the third degree, then Reason itself would appear receptive, while Aggression is positive. Defence and Economy, as a pair, are polar in the first degree to Amity and Reform. So long as the first pair predominate in human character, the influences of wealth are all enlisted on the side of conservatism.

Repetitions. It is a part of the law of evolution that all through life the higher organs and the higher animals repeat and elaborate functions which are found in the lower organs and types of life. In our mental structure and action this transfer and repetition of function is very important.

The organs of the sensitive group attract us to the objects of sense, and make us feel that " the earth is our mother." The higher group of parental love attracts us to our human parents. And highest of all, the religious group attracts us to the Deity, at once the infinite father and mother of our existence.

Among the lower animals, the attraction between the sexes originates in the organ of Impression. But in man, the higher group of Sexation takes the lead in this attraction, and surrounds sexlove with noble and refined sentiments.

The organs of reflection enable us to perceive laws and relations. This is a higher kind of perception than that of the Perceptive group, which only reveals objects.

As we shall discuss in the chapter on Social Unity. the lower organs everywhere in the brain supply materials for the use of those above them. Thus we cannot reason unless the lower group of memory supplies Reason with facts; nor can Memory retain facts themselves, until these are observed by the Perceptives which are still lower.

Mental Unity.—Whenever we allow the gratification of any back head or basenal organ to become the chief object of our existence, we are then failing to obey the laws of unity. The fullest power and most perfect pleasure of the senses can only be reached when they act in connection with the higher faculties. The organs of Appetite and Feeling lie at the base of all the social faculties, and they furnish the materials of force to all of the organs, as well as to themselves. Hence in their normal action they support and stimulate the noblest and most refined emotions of the mind.

The highest power of the Perceptives results from the culture and exercise of the Reflective faculties above them. The telescope and the microscope were the products of Reason and Construction, yet how immensely have they enlarged the scope and increased the accuracy of our perceptions.

The higher organs of the brain must rule in the

character of man. The larger part of the attractive organs and signs in the lower animals point downward toward the earth. Their chief attractions are earthly and sensual. But in man these attractive organs mostly point up and onward towards his fellow beings and the external universe. He alone, of all beings here, is released from a direct bondage to the earth, and united with his fellows in filling an exalted and immortal destiny.

Concert of Repulsions.—When the repulsive force of a person is directed against us, we are usually repelled from that person. But, for example, when Defense is not exerted with sufficient energy to terrify or conquer the person assailed, it usually rouses his defense in turn. In this case the Defense of the first person conflicts with the organs of Firmness and dignity in the second; and these organs being too strong to be overcome so easily, have roused up their assistant organs of the defensive group. The courageous man becomes firm or combative when attacked, when the person with little Firmness is frightened or paralyzed. But the repulsive force of two persons may act in concert instead of antagonism. In this way the courage of a leader arouses and inspires that of his followers. Where they are all pursuing the same object, each one imparts repulsive force to his associates, and they display the results of its accumulated strength

Mental Chords.—It is evident that if the higher and lower organs resemble each other in functions, then they may make an exchange of duties, and this is actually the case. Thus, Reason may exchange with Color. The latter gives the percep-

TABLE OF MENTAL CHORDS

These polar organs of the first degree, point in opposite directions, and display the most striking contrasts of action. Thus Amity attracts, but Defence repels. The repulsive organ is placed first in each contrast.

Energy	and	Feeling,	Secrecy and	Communion.
Control	"	Appetite	Aversion "	Sexation.
Courage	"	Fear.	Destruct'n "	Love
Mobility	"	Patriotism.	Defense "	Amity.
Control	"	Mobility.	Aggress'n "	Reform.
Economy	"	Kindness.	Liberty "	Serving.
Dignity	"	Modesty.	Integrity "	Destruction.

The organs compared in this table occupy zones of parallel direction in the two hemispheres. Thus firmness in one hemisphere, points in a direction parallel to that of control in the other. They are analogous, and they co-operate and exchange functions.

Form	and	Construct'n.	Love and	Reverence.
Observat'n	"	Impression.	Stability "	Control.
Inspiration	"	Imagination	Dignity "	Control.
Kindness	"	Hospitality.	Liberty "	Caution.
Reform	"	Devotion-	Aggress'n "	Economy.
Faith	"	Worship.	Mobility "	Excitement.

An organ may respond to, and exchange functions with, the third, fifth, or seventh one above or below it., and it also co-operates with those in front and back of itself. This action correponds to that of thirds, fifths and octaves in music.

THIRDS.

Form	and	Number.	Integrity and	Liberty.
Reason	"	Color.	Parenity "	Patriotism.
Memory	"	Imitation.	Fidelity "	Integrity.
Construct'n	"	Words.	Caution "	Defense.
Faith	"	Hope.	Defension "	Ambition.
Sensation	"	Sexation.	Parention "	Religion.

FIFTHS.

Color	and	Truth.
Form	"	Order.
Words	"	Imagination
Patriotism	"	Love.
Impression	"	Devotion.

OCTAVES.

Feeling	and	Zeal.
Serving	"	Victory.
Reverence	"	Faith.
Reason	"	Control.
Destruction	"	Integrity.

tion of light, and we say that we reason upon a subject to throw light upon it. Control may exchange with Stability; Defense with energy; Liberty with Dignity.

In general, an organ may exchange or co-operate with the third, the fifth, or the seventh one, either directly above, or directly in front of itself. This action corresponds with the chords in music. If musical notes which are thirds, fifths or octaves, are sounded together, they produce a sense of harmony, So, when these faculties respond to each other, it produces harmony of mental action, The princpal ones are given in the following table; and the intelligent reader, with the maps of the organs and signs before him, can easily work out the remainder for himself.

The harmonies of music are based upon purely mathematical relations. The sweet and graceful blending of voices in song, and the noble symphony of instruments, are each under the rule of strict physical laws of science. For in science we shall find graceful beauty and gentle sweetness no less than in the works of art.

The laws of music are exemplified in mental action, and these same laws of mental rythm must be the basis of social harmony, as will be shown in another place.

A train of thought or feeling may be carried on awhile by one faculty, and then its third, fifth or seventh complement will assume the train of thought and carry it forward, while the first rests or is engaged with other objects; or what is more usual, it may take on the proper functions of the first, thus effecting a direct exchange.

In the early ages of history, rulership depended

upon the impulsive group. The chief of a tribe must be its best hunter, warrior and runner. In time it came to depend more upon wealth and policy, functions of the higher group of defence. And in the future it will arise from the group of rulership itself, sustained by the eternal laws of justice, philanthropy and wisdom.

There are also frequent exchanges between organs of the third degree; that is, those which belong to the same pair. We may, for instance, make previsions through the organ of Reason; or, we may discover causes through the organ of Prevision or Inspiration.

Mental Order.—From the law of the ellipse it follows that impressions made on the sensitive group must flow forward through the cells, A, F, N, to the group of Perception. While in the sensitive group these impressions are more or less vague or indistinct, they are merely feelings. On reaching the Perceptives, they assume definite forms, and we recognize the size, location, form, color, and other properties of the objects which have made the impression. The current now passes up to Memory, where more or less of all impressions are stored or registered for the future use of all the faculties. From Memory the current flows up to the cells of the Reasoning organs. These faculties combine, arange and mould the impressions into the final form of mature ideas. They discover the relations among the objects which have produced the impressions, and the uses to which these laws of relation can be applied in practical life. The current then flows back over the Social organs, K, R, S, and these make us feel like using the knowledge in such actions as will gratify our own affections, and benefit our associates and the world. Passing on to the organs of Expression in the back head, the current stimulates these to activity, and they control the muscles to produce the bodily movements necessary to carry our ideas and plans into practical action.

The Sensitive group is the great portal of entrance for impressions, and the Impulsive group is the door of exit, through which they are finally ejected from the mental temple.

In the above brief description we have the order in which mental action must normally take place when the exciting cause is outside of ourselves. First there must be an Impression on the nerves. This part is physiological, not mental, action. Then in the first mental step we have a Sensation; next there is Perception; then Memory or Retention; next Reflection or Reason; then there are Social impulses and desires; and lastly there is Volition or Will, the practical execution of ideas and purposes. When a current starts within the brain, from the action of the mind upon its already accumulated materials, then it may commence in Observation, Memory, Reason, Amity or any other point.

A Mental Act. While currents of nerve-force are flowing through the cells around the ellipses, other currents are flowing over the fibres, to and from the centers. The combined action of these currents may be well illustratad by a single act, that of picking up a pencil.

The light from the pencil reaches the eye, and there makes its impression on the extremities of the optic nerve. The impression is carried in the

PLAN OF THE BRAIN.

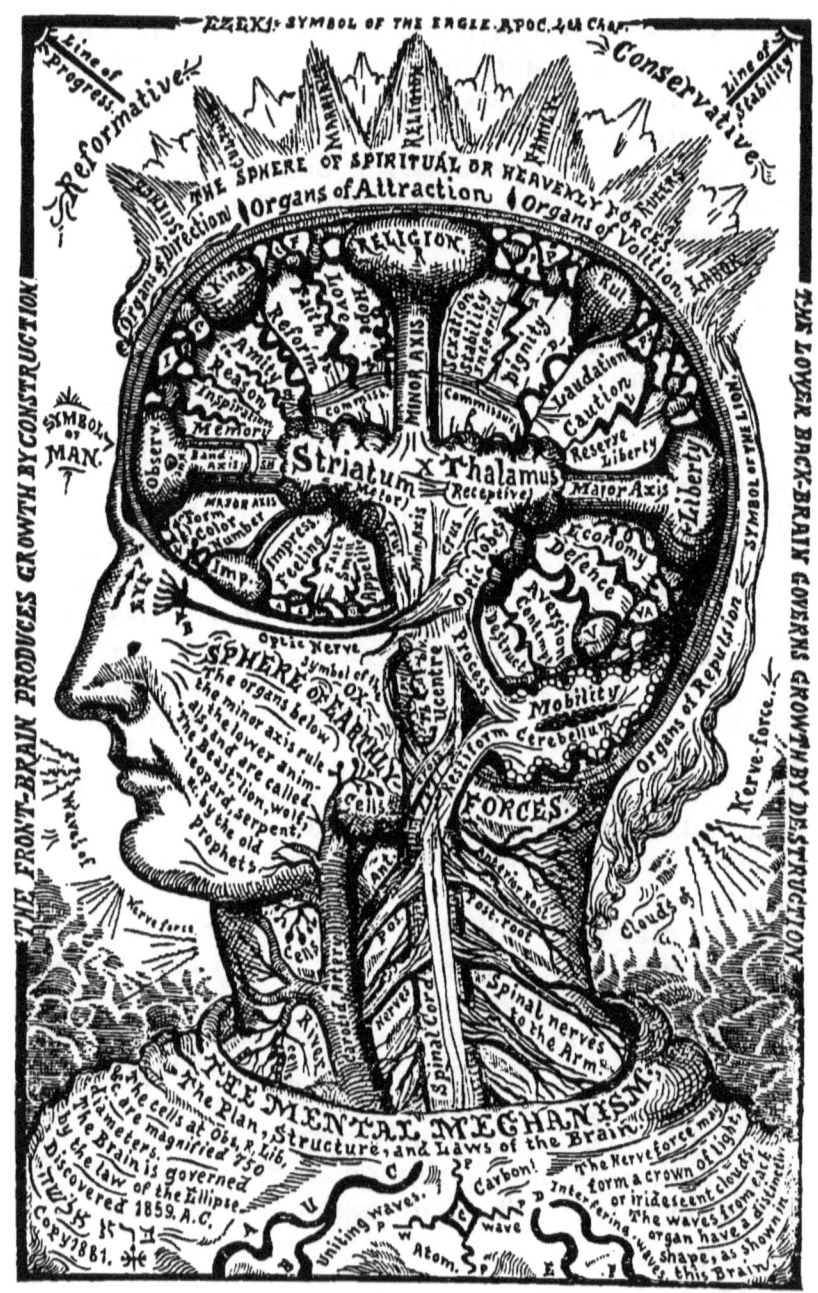

current of waves along the optic nerve, through the optic lobes, OP, to the thalamus and across the fibres, Y, to the striatum. From the striatum the current passes down the fibres of Form and Color, to their cells, at F, C. We then perceive the form, size, and locality of the pencil. A current now flows back to the striatum and then up the fibres of Reason. We then reason about the pencil and decide to pick it up. A current next flows from Reason down through the striatum and thalamus, and up to Integrity, Caution, and other organs which control the muscles of arm and hand. These organs now send down a current, which in the striatum meets and mixes with a directive current from the perceptives, and flowing down the spinal cord and the nerves, AN, it passes to the arm and hand, causing the muscular movements necessary in picking up a pencil. The law of the ellipse determines that Reason must thus respond to Perception, and the Will to Reason.

If an obstacle were presented to the action of the arm, then by the law of the ellipse the Defensive organs, below the major axis, would respond and assist in removing the obstacle.

The images formed in the eye are inverted. But in passing the circuit through the brain centers to the perceptive faculties, it of necessity returns to its erect position.

Responses. If we take the minor axis, from O to E, we shall find that any organ at a given distance directly back of this line must mathematically balance and co-operate with whatever organ is at the same distance in front. These organs are enabled to respond in action through bands of fibres which run directly from one to the other.

Language is full of expressions which illustrate these balances. Thus Truth and Fortitude respond, and we say "truthful and serene." Mirth and Playfulness balance, and are expressed in the phrase, " playful and witty." Memory and Economy balance, and hence we say that "language is the storehouse of thought."

As another example, take the faculties of Faith, Love, and Hope. At the front, the organ of Faith gives us strong confidence in human goodness and the possibility of improvement. The moment this faith is established, the organ of Hope responds and leads us to undertake great and beneficient enterprises for humanity, and thus satisfy Love or Philanthropy. The mental trinity of Intellect, Affection, and Expression occupies the front, the middle, and the back brain. Affection lies along the minor axis, and is, both mathematically and vitally, the central third of our mental life.

Thus when we desire anything, through Affection or feeling, the Intellect in front remembers, reasons, and decides about it, and then Expression in the back head moves the muscles to do what is necessary to gratify the desire.

The primary impulse to action comes from the central member or pivot of the mental trinities, and first the left wing responds and then the right.

The sense of hunger springs from Appetite, but it requires both Intellect and Expression to gratify its wants. We must see the food through the perceptives and the impulsive organs of the Will must move the muscles of the legs to go and get it.

Wisdom and Will are always the instruments to serve Love, from the low realm of sensation up to the exalted sphere of religion. Love without knowledge is blind. Without will and labor it is powerless. The richest fruits of Love must mature under the pure light of cultivated wisdom. The warm currents of affection sweep through all thoughts and volitions, giving them its own hues of life and beauty. It must transform the selfish impulses of the back brain into the noble forces of social life, and warm the cool blue rays of the intellect with its own golden light.

The organs above and below the major axis also respond to each other. Thus reason above responds to Perception below the line. So Ambition above responds to Defension below; and Sexation responds to Sensation.

The polar responses of the faculties reach the very highest degree of importance in adjusting the different departments and interests of society, as shown in the eight and ninth chapters. .

Physical Responses. The engraved Measure of a Man will illustrate a series of interesting and important responses between the different parts of the body. Each square of the body is numbered from the feet upward.

The first square responds in sympathy and action to the fourth; the 1st and the 7th respond; the 1st and 12th; the 4th and 7th; the 7th and 10th; the 10th and 12th; the 7th and 12th, and the 7th and 9th.

Uniting the arm and the body, and naming squares of the arm first each time, then the 5th and 7th respond; the 5th and 10th; the 5th and 12th.

These physical responses are the basis of physical culture, of caressing, of many sense-relations in the fine arts.

Mimetic Law.—In every animal tissue the direction of its fibres, if it have any, infallibly shows the direction in which its forces are and can be manifested. Thus the fibres of a muscle, running lengthwise, show that this is the line in which it can exert its force. This general law must of course apply fully to the brain. Its fibres have a definite direction, and this determines their lines of action with regard to each other in the brain, aud also the direction in which each one will cause the body to move when it acts upon that. The whole system of gestures, or natural language of the faculties, is a necessary product of this law. The location of the organs, and their direction being the same in all cases, the gestures which express any given passion or emotion must be the same in all ages, and all nations. And this is the fact. From the gestures alone we can prove that the organs of the brain are correctly located. Twelve hundred million human beings daily reproduce these decisive facts and no other interpretation can be put upon them. It would be extremely absurd to suppose that results so uniform and so universal could take place without the operation of such a natural law as the one here laid down.

Character in the Gestures.—Through the front organs we are attracted to what is before us and move forward. The organs of the back head repel us from what is behind us. The top head faculties elevate the features, the body, and the limbs, but the lower faculties depress all these. Many of these motions are matters of common observation. Everyone has noticed the lofty bearing of Dignity, the bowing of Submission, the erect attitude of Firmness and Integrity, and the reaching down and forward of Appetite.

In order to understand the subject of gestures clearly, we must remember that in the spinal cord the fibres from the right hemisphere of the brain go across and supply the left side of the body. This crossing is shown in the mental mechanism. Take, for example, the organ of Amity or Friendship. Its fibres in the brain point up, forward and outward. In expressing friendship by grasping the hand of a friend, we raise our *right* hand in the direction of our organ of Amity on the *left* side of the head. In embracing a friend in our arms, the same direction is observed. In reaching the hand down to take our food, the right hand follows the organ of Appetite on the left side, and *vice versa*. Gestures may be made either from or toward ourselves. In either case the line of the organ is followed. There are many compound gestures, produced by two or more organs, and taking a line of direction between them. By comparing the map of the mental organs with the drawings of the brain, the direction of all the gestures may be readily learned.

In the lower figure at the commencement of the fourth chapter, the organs of Caution and Economy on the *left side* draw the speaker's *right hand* toward himself to grasp his staff. His right organ of Caution moves his *left* hand outward to warn his hearers of impending danger. His finger points upward in the line of Stability to the source from which an everlasting kingdom shall proceed and be established.

Intellectual Motions.—The lines of the front brain point forward, and when a person is engaged in study or thought the head naturally inclines forward. It is seldom held high, and never is thrown back under intellectual excitement.

The Perceptive organs cause downward and forward motions of the head, as when we are picking up or closely examining objects. The larger number of the objects upon which the perceptives act lie beneath us or upon the surface of the earth.

The group of Memory is horizontal in its direction. Observation points the forefinger almost directly forward, and slightly upward when acting under the influence of reason, as when pursuing a close and direct train of thought. Observation relates to what is directly before us. Memory, Time and system are more external, and relate to events as they recede into the past and form fixed periods and systems of action.

Reason produces forward and upward gestures, as we see in a speaker who is reasoning and explaining logically. Prevision usually acts with Inspiration. and thus produces motions more lateral, and broader in their sweep. Reason produces similar ones when acting with Imagination. In planing and using a chisel, the movements are in the line of Construction. modified by Destruction and Aggression, as a part of the force comes from the latter organs.

Kindness throws the head forward and up, and raises the hands in the same direction when we are rendering assistance. The language of Friendship has already been mentioned.

Gestures of Affection.—Faith raises the hands above the head, slightly forward, and near each other, with the palms inward. This is the right atitude for expressing the true feelings of this lofty faculty. The act of bowing the knee comes from the organ of Serving, low down on the side head. It seemed appropriate enough in those ages when men regarded the Deity as a despotic monarch, only a little above themselves. The highest and purest religious fervor requires lofty, outspread gestures. And every artist gives these to the apostle and religious teacher, because they naturally express the superior sentiments. Hope, Belief, Zeal and Victory, all elevate the limbs and the features.

The organs of Sexation cause the upward and forward motions of caressing, the clasp, and the embrace. As we shall see hereafter, these organs are on the minor axis of the brain, and hence may use the gestures of all the other faculties to express themselves.

The natural motions of Parental love are seen in the act of nursing an infant, supporting and carrying it in the arms. Modesty and Reverence usually draw the hands close to the side of the body. When acting under the influence of the higher social faculties they may raise and clasp the hands. Reverence may greatly expand the feelings when we are gazing upon sublime scenery in nature, or when contemplating the grand achievements recorded in history.

Appetite, Feeling, and the other senses point to the earth. to their objects of relation and attraction on its surface.

The motions of Affection, as a whole, are of a gentle, refined, soothing, and quiet character, and they produce attractive and winning manners in social intercourse.

Gestures of Volition.—The vigorous organs give the upright walk, the firm, erect, and manly carriage of the head and person. Integrity raises the hand directly upward by and above the side of the head. Justice may also be expressed by extending both hands horizontally forward with the palms upward. The hands then take the line of the intellect and represent the idea of balancing, one of the functions of Justice. Caution and Economy, pointing out from the right side of the head, may bring the left hand in toward the body. They may also throw the hands outward, as when we reach out the hands to protect ourselves from danger at the side of us. Here we see that the same organ produces motions both *from* and *toward* the person. Both motions are in the same line of direction that of the mental fibres.

Dignity gives the erect attitude with the head and shoulders thrown slightly back, imparting an air of self-possession more marked and imposing than the simple attitude of Firmness. Laudation throws the head more to one side.

Defence moves the limbs back and to the sides, as seen in animals when kicking. The motion of striking with the fists is in the same line, but reversed by the signs of Defence in the back of the hand and arm. Economy draws the hands inward, as in the act of gathering materials.

Destruction, Baseness, and other impulsive organs cause motions still more downward than Defence, as we see in the acts of rending, tearing down, destroying, and stamping. When a carnivorous animal strikes its prey with the paws, the motions are in a line between Construction and

Destruction; it destroys the prey that it may construct its own body out of the materials. In walking, the motions of the feet against the earth are in the line of these organs.

Language and Gestures. From the foregoing descriptions the student will perceive that the language of gestures is in no way arbitrary, but strictly natural. Our spoken language is full of illustrations proving an instinctive perception of this mimetic law. We speak of actions which spring from the superior organs as being *high, lofty, noble, exalted*, and *heavenly*. While of those which result from the base of the brain we speak as being *low, debased, ignoble*, and *earthly*. We speak of the *summit* of power and of moral excellence; and of the *depth* of infamy and vice. We commonly think of these as mere figures of speech, but the mimetic law proves that the expressions are mathematically true. In a large number of cases, there is a direct, external. physical reason for the figures of speech. A parent is literally taller than the child, and therefore *superior*. But the mechanism of the brain must be exactly adapted to all these physical conditions, exactly fitted to produce the necessary actions in each case. Otherwise, the mind and body would work in a confusing and impractical antagonism.

Character in the Walk. With a knowledge of the various gestures we can easily read the general character of a person by the walk. For, in walking, the head, the arms, the body, and the legs are all making gestures. If a person in his walk habitually assumes and makes the gestures belonging to any group of faculties, we may be certain that those faculties are leading ones in his character

In the walk of a tall, healthy, well-balanced man, both Dignity and Firmness may be seen. Where these qualities are deficient in the character, the stooping posture and unsteady gait will be assumed. The mincing, affected walk of the dandy, and the heavy, ungainly tramp of the boor, each express corresponding mental characteristics.

Effect on Locomotion. The attractive organs are in the front, and the repulsive ones are in the back of the body. As a consequence of this arrangement, we are attracted to what is before us, and we move forward. At the same time the organs of the back head repel us from what is behind us, pushing us forward, and thus acting in concert with those in front. Attractions and repulsions are proportional to destinies, for they are the motor forces which carry us onward and upward. This is as true in the physical as it is in the mental sense.

The upward attractions center in Religion, and the forward ones center in Retention or the group of Letters.

According to the law for the composition of forces, their united action is on the diagonal line between them, and this takes the organs of Culture, the line of progress and reform. It is upward and forward.

The organs of the side head are alike on each side, and consequently we are equally attracted or repelled from each, so that these do not determine our course.

The Voice and Character. The vocal gestures or Inflections follow the mimetic law. Thus the organ of Reason, which asks questions, points somewhat upward. Hence, all questions have the rising inflection or slide of the voice either at the end of the sentence or upon a principal word. The returning answer must reach us through the same organ, and, of course, take a downward direction to do this. Therefore answers have the falling inflection.

The upper organs give rising and the lower organs falling inflections. Supplication, entreaty, sympathy, praise, ambition, hope, and affection illustrate the rising; while authority, aggression, aversion, contempt, and other manifestations of the lower organs illustrate the falling inflections. The monotone may express either the upper or the lower organs. The circumflex, or union of the up and the down slides, is properly used in irony, where we say one thing and mean another, or, in some cases, expressing surprise or a sudden turn of thought and feeling.

When the lower faculties predominate in a person, his voice will be coarse, harsh, and discordant, The indistinct, guttural voice of the savage expresses his low and undeveloped nature. The musical, flexible, rich, and sonorous voice of the civilized and cultured man speaks the language of the superior sentiments, of self-control, affection, and intelligence.

In the Messianic age, the law of gestures will be the basis of a true and natural system of ceremonies in religion and all the intercourse of social life.

CHAPTER SIXTH.

PHASES OF LIFE.

The mental faculties are subject to a law of evolution which embraces in its sweep the entire career of vertebrate life on our globe.

The human brain proceeds from the development and rule of the organs at the base and back to that of the top and front. This gives the three great phases of life, Preturity, Maturity, and Senility. These phases are separated by horizontal lines in the map of the mental organs.

From the first moment to the close of fœtal life, the brain presents a constant increase in its complexity of structure. At different parts of this period, the embyro resembles, in succession, the members of an ascending series of the lower animals; but the brains of these lower animals are arrested, some at a low and some at a higher point, that of man alone passes onward to completion.

In doing this, the fœtus but conforms to the general law ruling all organic bodies,—that the individual development of every organism, or the series of forms through which it passes from the germ to the complete form, repeats approximately the development of its race, or the series of forms through which its ancestral types have passed.

In the chart of the Nervous System, figure 3 shows the embryonic evolution of the brain. An enlargement of the end of the "Primitive Trace" becomes divided into three vesicles, front, middle and back. From the front one of these a little process, C, arises. This process enlarges, turns upward, and increases in size until finally it forms the cerebrum or the principal mass of the brain, as seen in the dotted outline. From the back vesicle, the cerebellum, CB, arises. The developing force in this growth is applied from behind, from the direction of the spinal cord SP C.

In the insect, figure 4, the nervous system is formed on a very simple plan. A collection of cells or nerve centre, is found in the head, CE, in the thorax, TH, and in the abdomen, AB. Bands of fibres connect these with each other. In the spinal cord of man, the centers are continuous with each other, and the fibres are outside of them. The first stage of growth in the human brain, is as complex in structure as the mature insect.

In the ameba, the whole animal is so extremely simple in structure that no nervous system is required to establish a sympathy of action between its different parts The few necessary sympathetic impulses are conveyed from cell to cell through its tissues, just as they are in the carnivorous plants.

Heredity.—An organic being resembles its parents with such variations as are induced by the temporary activity of special organs or functions in them during its pernatal existence, and also such as are caused by the external influences which bear upon it after birth.

All impressions made upon the mind and body of the mother during the prenatal phase are transmitted, in a greater or less degree, to those of the child. If the parents exercise their higher faculties during this period, the child will be superior in mental endowments. If they exercise the lower faculties chiefly, it will be inferior. The law of Heredity places within our voluntary control a powerful instrument for human exaltation. It is for the vital interests of society that all parents should have the favorable conditions which these laws demand. Both the parents and society are responsible for the organization of every child. They can make it good or bad as they choose.

The child, after it reaches maturity, is to be a member of society forty or fifty years, four times as long as it is directly dependent upon its parents; therefore society has a much greater right than the parents, to control the child's development and education.

Phases of Personal Life.—The brain is not perfect at birth. It must pass through phases of development each well marked at its central period, and at their points of union insensibly gliding into each other. We may consider life, after birth, in three phases. The ascending phase of Preturity, includes childhood and youth. The central phase of Maturity is the highest altitude of life. It is succeeded by the descending phase of old age or Senility. Each phase is marked by the dominant activity of certain faculties.

Childhood.—During the periods of Infancy and Childhood, from the first to the tenth year, the groups of Impulsion, Sensation and Perception rule the character. The child is restless, impul-

receives impressions in infancy; but these are indistinct, and soon replaced by others. In the latter part of childhood the impressions are the most permanent of any made during life. The child learns through Sensation and Perception almost wholly. It constantly asks questions, yet reasons very little. Although the organs of the top brain are often very large in Childhood, yet they are dormant, and not roused into activity until later.

Youth.—The range of organs which rule in this period, from the tenth to the twentieth year, includes the groups of Memory, Parention, and Defension. Through Observation, Memory, and Language, the youth acquires stores of knowledge; through Reverence, Parenity, and Patriotism, he learns some of his relations to his superiors, his equals, and his inferiors; and through Economy, Defense, and Reserve, he gets an idea of property and of personal rights.

Maturity.—In this period, from twenty to sixty, the high faculties of Integrity, Control, Energy, Sexual, Parental, Fraternal, and Religious Love, with Reason and Inspiration, come into prominence and rule the character. The crude ideas of Childhood and Youth are displaced by exact knowledge. The powers of mind and body attain their full solidity and vigor, and the character is rounded out into completeness and symmetry.

Senility.—At last old age or Senility comes creeping slowly on. The faculties gradually lose their vigor, and the senses become unretentive; the body demands rest and quiet, and its powers pass into decadence.

CHAPTER SEVENTH.

EVOLUTION OF SOCIETY.

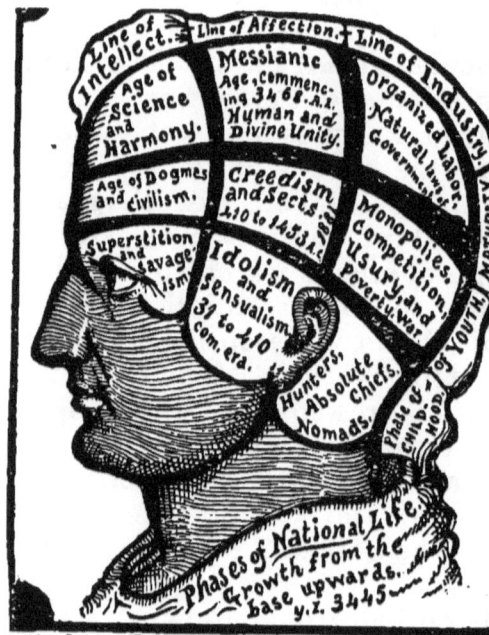

The voice of inspiration and the teachings of science unite in proclaiming the exalted social destiny of man.

The advancement of the human race in past ages has not been guided solely by the caprices of statesmen and kings, nor by the fluctuating impulses of men. The mighty drama of human history has been an impressive and majestic procession, moving forward under the dominion of eternal laws.

These laws of development are not only an inherent part of the nature of man, but they also control the physical world, and have their center in the Life of the Universe.

In the fossil-written record of this earth's history we may examine its many steps of preparation for the noble advent of man.

The facts of geology, as at present understood, teach us that the matter composing any star or planet, like our earth, was once attenuated and diffused in space, like that of some nebulæ which we may now see in the heavens, This matter was gradually collected around central points and solidified.

If the earth was at one time a vast globe of molten rock-material, then as the portions of its surface became solid by losing heat, they would sink into the interior. This process would go on until the sunk portions of the crust would build up from the bottom a sufficiently close-ribbed framework to allow fresh solidifications to remain on the surface, bridging across the now small areas of lava-pools or lakes of molten matter. Some of these still remain as the source of volcanoes and earthquakes.

After the general surface was formed, vast areas of the primitive rocks were thrown up, and the materials of these were afterward worn down and produced successive formations, through the agency of heat, water, and the atmosphere.

Were all the formations which compose the crust of the earth to be found in one place, they would appear as in the first diagram of this book, on the third page.

These formations are divided into seven ages, according to the dominant kinds of animal, or of plant life by which each is characterized.

From the age of molluscs up to that of man, the climate, the atmosphere, and the soil, were constantly becoming more perfect, and better adapted to sustain the higher types of life. And through all of these ages there was a steady and resistless march of organic life toward more perfect forms.

The first vertebrates were Fishes, the lowest animals of this division. Then came Reptiles, a little higher in structure; then Mammals, above these; and at last came Man, the crowning form of the organic series.

It is the marvellous brain of man that gives him the most exalted rank in the scale of earthly life. The development of the nervous system and the brain is therefore the most interesting of all the facts revealed by geologic science.

If we compare the nervous system of the lowest vertebrate, a fish, with that of man, who is the highest, we shall be at once struck by the great relative development of the brain in man. As shown in the initial engraving of this chapter, the brain of the fish is only about one third greater in diameter than his spinal cord. The balance of nerve power in the fish is only slightly in favor of the head. But the brain of man exceeds in diameter that of his spinal cord seven times. Its structure, too, is correspondingly complex and elaborate. In man alone the front limbs are entirely relieved from the duty of locomotion, and are so specialized in form as to be perfect servants of the head. He alone has a real hand.

Through all the many species of vertebrates, from the fish up to man, the spinal cord and lower parts of the nervous system have steadily diminished in size and importance, while the brain has quite as steadily increased in relative size and in perfection of structure.

This all-sweeping law must also embrace the brain itself when we compare its lower with its higher parts. It must determine the successive development of its organs from the base to the top, as was illustrated in the phases of personal life. The ultimate rule of the higher faculties of the brain, the nobler powers of the human mind, is secured by a law as extensive in its way as the existence of organic life itself. No hand of conservatism can turn back that upward march of humanity.

Whatever may be the functions of the top brain, this well proved law of science assures us that these functions must rule in the future of national life, in the political conduct of men, no less than in that of the individual members of society.

This law sums up the experience of the whole human race, and that of all life below man. If selfishness has thus far ruled in the affairs of nations, this law shows that it can not in the future.

National Phases. Nations are composed of persons, and hence the laws which govern the individual also determine the national life.

A nation, like a person, has its childhood, its youth, and its maturity.

Through these national and race phases we observe the same successive rule of organs from the base to the top, and from the back to the front, which mark the life career of a single person.

The first ages of the human race were sensual, debased, and ignorant. As a nation, or the race advances to maturity, the higher and nobler faculties come into activity and elevate the whole character of civil and domestic life.

But so far in history, no nation has completely developed its phase of maturity. Many nations have just entered this phase and then have been cut off prematurely, or have remained with a dwarfed growth for centuries.

This part of the law of evolution is regarded by all scientific men as established by the clearest of proof. We may safely build upon it, as an everlasting foundation. We shall first see what changes this law has produced in the past, and then show what it points out in regard to the future of national life.

On three great lines of movement we may trace the influence of higher and higher faculties, as nations pass through the phases of childhood, youth, and maturity. The lines of Intellect, of Affection, and of Industry are separated in the engraving by dark upright lines. Each one is subject to the same great law of development.

In the childhood of the race, the low faculties of Mobility, Destruction, and Aversion, lead to absolute forms of government. The most successful warrior and hunter becomes the chief of the tribe by his prowess. Labor is insulated, it is confined to hunting, fishing, and pastoral life, except in a few localities where a rude earth culture is very easy.

In the phase of national youth, the higher organs of the Defensive group lead to forms of government in which the power of its rulers is limited by fixed laws and customs. The war power and the money power are then regarded as the true indications of a nation's rank in greatness. Labor then assumes the form of competitism, a fierce strife of the few to accumulate wealth from the labor of the many. This phase produces war, monopolies, competition, usury and poverty.

When a nation, or the race, reaches maturity, the group of Rulership comes into full power in government, and it is under the guidance of the groups of Science and Culture, which have then become dominant in the front brain. Labor now takes the form of combinism, it secures the organized unity and specialization of all industrial interests.

The line of religious evolution begins low down in the Sensitive group. It is idolism and sensualism, a worship of the objects of sense. In national youth, under the influence of the faculties of Familism and Memory, Religion passes into the phase of Creedism, where the doctrines rest upon the real or the supposed authority of ancient inspirations. This was the condition of Christianity and of Judaism in the middle of the nineteenth century. Reason does not yet exert its influence, and hence religious doctrines are shrouded in mysteries, are separated from practical life, and are divided among hostile sects. Religion finally becomes a conscious union of the human with the divine life, and the organized unity of the human race, as exemplified in the Messianic reign of peace. It is based upon an intelligent obedience to the eternal laws of spiritual harmony.

The line of Intellectual growth gives us superstition and savageism as the product of the perceptive faculties. The succeeding age of dogmatism and civilism is produced by the group of Memory. Science and harmony complete the upward march on this line.

Each line of advancement is supported by the other two lines at every successive point. Thus the creeds of religion are sustained by dogmas of the intellect and by competitive labor. Idolism is sustained on one side by superstition and on the other by absolute forms of government. Messian-

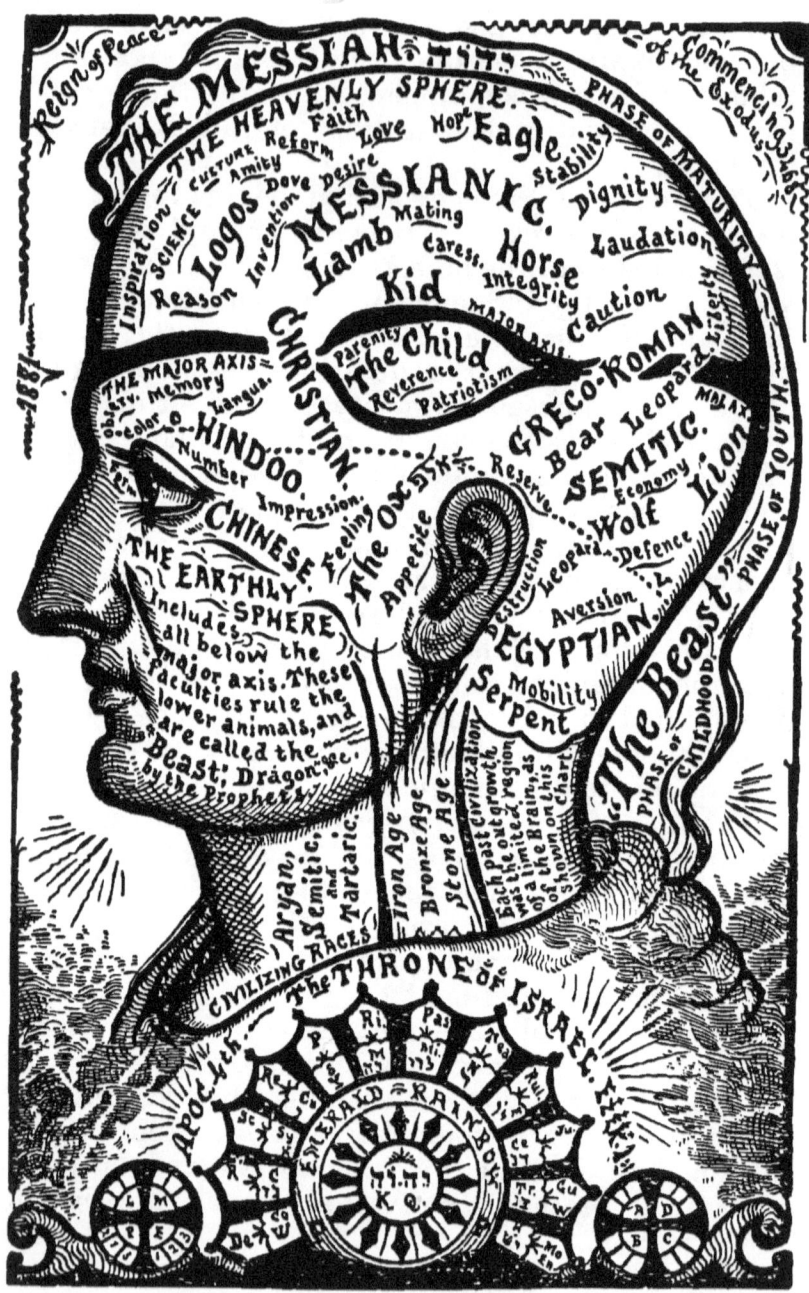

MESSIANISM.
WISDOMATE.
CULTURE.
  Receiver—Amity.
  Cultess—Reform.
SCIENCE,
  Scientist—Reason.
  Symbolist—Inspiration.
LETTERS.
  Recorder—Memory.
  Curator—Observation
ART,
  Designer—Form
  Costumist—Color.

SOCIALATE
RELIGION.
  Pastor—Faith.
  Minister—Love.
MARRIAGE.
  Ritualist—Desire.
  Matron—Mating.
FAMILY.
  Teacher.
  Nurse.
HOME.
  Purveyor—Appetite.
  Sanatist—Feeling.

LABORATE.
RULERSHIP.
  Ruler—Dignity.
  Elector—Laudation.
LABOR.
  Justice—Integrity.
  Censor—Caution.
WEALTH.
  Guard—Defense
  Treasurer—Economy.
COMMERCE.
  Engineer—Mobility.
  Herder—Aversion.

CIVILISM.

LEGISLATIVE.
Secretaries—Curators—Senators.
Representatives.

Schools—Teachers.
Libraries—Museums.

CHURCHES.
Clergy—Priests—Bishops,
Sunday Schools.

Agricultural Soc.—Hospitals.
Temperance—Insurance.

JUDICIAL & EXECUTIVE.
Judges—Courts.
President, Governors.

Cabinet—Ministers.
Marshals—Police.

ism will use scientific knowledge as its instrument on one side, and on the other, organized industry.

Seven Civilizations. There have been six great forms of civilization in past times; each was the outgrowth of a limited region of mental faculties, as shown in the engraving. Their characteristics are placed in a table, as are those of Greek life.

The civilized nations of the earth have already passed through the phases of childhood and youth on these different lines of growth. They have organized their institutions to correspond with these phases. We therefore have the supreme warrant of science in affirming that the nations will go on and organize the higher institutions which are required by the phase of Maturity. The ablest scientific men and the profoundest historians teach that such an organization of society, based upon science, is not only possible, but absolutely certain.

In Europe, America, India, China, and Japan, the average development of the brain is far above the line that separates the phase of youth from that of maturity. The people have outgrown their institutions and are prepared for higher social forms.

It is impossible to learn these new forms from past experience. For history does not furnish a single example of a nation with a perfect government, or a complete national life for us to imitate. All the statesmen of the present time (1880) confess that they do not know what a perfect form of government would be. We cannot discover the science of society by gathering and comparing statistics, as Spencer has attempted to do. No Science was ever developed in that way.

We must have a new method. In the railway, the steamboat, the telegraph, and numberless improvements of modern life, we see that the superior methods of modern science have supplanted those of mere experience. Not one of these great inventions was produced by imitating the past. Science puts exact knowledge in place of mere guesses and imitati

The time has now come to extend the sure and safe methods of science into the domain of politics. And science will quickly tell us why the old methods have been and must be failures. It will explain why, " after nearly two thousand years of Christian rule, we find the mass of the population struggling for a bare existence, like ravenous brutes for food. In the most favored of countries, men fight for individual advantage, everyone for himself, as if the golden rule had never been laid down, and men were governed by the cruel law that life is a fight in which the strongest conquer and the weakest go to the wall."

In regard to the true constitution of society, the argument of science is a direct statement of facts which cannot be denied or set aside. They are all self-evident, when once stated, and they also contain the most positive proof that the new methods will be entirely successful, as soon as they are applied.

The argument may be summed up in three self-evident propositions.

FIRST. The collective wants of society arise from each of the mental faculties, and we can know the number of these wants only by knowing the number of the faculties.

In the engraved archetype of society, after

each faculty is placed that want of society which arises directly from it. Each one of these may include a number of subdivisions. From the faculties of Memory arises the need for publishing houses, of libraries, museums, school, and of music associations. From the Defensive group arises the need of factories, stores, machinery, and trading. And thus around the entire circle, every faculty originates its own special kind of wants. There is no exception to the law. There must be as many kinds of wants in society as there is of faculties in the mind of man. If there are twelve groups of faculties, then there must be twelve groups of wants in society. Destroy any faculty, and you will also destroy the want. If men had no organ of memory, they would care nothing for facts; if they had no organs of Integrity they would have no desire for justice.

SECOND. The wants of society are represented and provided for by its departments and officers.

The Secretary represents the organs of Memory, and leads in supplying the wants which arise from this faculty. The Treasurer represents the organ of Economy; the Justice is intended to represent Integrity; and so of every officer.

This method of representing is perfecty natural. It is the only way in which the result can be reached. All action in nature takes place around central points or pivots. An officer is a pivot of social action.

The nature of these wants is such that single persons, working alone, can not get or use the means to satisfy them. Each requires combined action, through some fixed provision in the structure and offices of society.

Impelled by those wants, men have organized all their institutions, and elected all their officers. If men had possessed no organ of Economy, there would have been no Treasurers in any society. If the organ of Memory did not exist, man would not know that a society required a Secretary. As the organs of the brain correspond to those of the body, this analysis includes all of the bodily wants.

THIRD. A complete form of society must have as many departments and officers as there are groups and faculties of the brain. If there is a less number, then either some wants would be left unsupplied, or some officers must fill diverse and complex functions.

Taking both the past and the present institutions of the most highly civilized nations, a critical examination shows that only one half, that is, the six lower groups, are in any manner represented. These groups are all below the major axis in the brain. It is true that in the departments above this line are some terms already used in civilism. But they represented analogous functions far lower down in the brain. Thus the courts of Justice only represented the low organs of Destruction, Economy, and Reserve. Hence they destroyed the life, confiscated the property, or imprisoned the evil doer. But in the new plan, the Justice represents Integrity, and seeks to restore the criminal to a state of moral health and social integrity. the true function of this faculty.

The reason why the higher faculties have not been provided for, lies in the fact that they belong to the phase of maturity, and the nations have only passed through the phases of childhood and youth.

They have been dominated by the base of the brain. Fraud and Force are the two black parents from which most of the institutions of civilism have been born.

But the nations have now entered the phase of maturity. They are everywhere dissatisfied with the old, and are waiting for the new. The analysis of man's constitution in this Book of Israel proves mathematically the exact number of his faculties, and from this we know the exact number of his societary wants. Before this analysis was made, the statesman did not know that the wants of society spring from the faculties, and without this key of social science, they could never know how many departments and officers should be in the plan of society. Nor could they know how these should be arranged.

The new and final structure of society is fully shown in the Model of Society, in the eighth chapter. It reproduces all parts of the constitution of man, and consequently it represents all of his possible wants. Its plan is so complete that no committees are ever required, in any of the orders The duties of each officer are clearly defined and are different from those of all others. It is not like the House of Commons, or of Represenatives, where hundreds of members have exactly the same duties, making the whole an unwieldy mob, instead of an organism.

Although civilism represents the lower half of the faculties, it does not do this in a complete and methodical way. For example, in Great Britain and America the three departments of government are Legislative, Executive, and Judicial. But the great classes of wants in society are Intelluctal,

Social, and Industrial, for they arise from the great divisions of his nature, from Intellect, Affection, and Volition.

The table of Man and Society presents a fair and just comparison of the new with the old structure of society. In the first column are placed the titles of the Leaders in Israel, and after each of these is the faculty which that officer represents. On the right side of the page are the corresponding parts of civilized institutions. While civilism represents some of the single faculties by fifty differently named officers, it leaves fully, one-half without any representation at all, as we see in the blanks of the table.

When thus compared with the constitution of man, the structure of civilized society is fatally defective in the number and character of its parts. It cannot give man the highest conditions of life, it can not, and never did satisfy the aspirations of man.

Not only were the parts of civilized society so sadly deficient, but the natural relations and mutual dependence of its various parts were disregarded, or not established, as we shall now consider under the head of Specialization.

Specialization. For below man, and extending too, far up through all phases of his national life, is the great law known to scientific men as that of Specialization. It teaches us that in the career of every thing, whether it be the formation of a world, of an animal, or of a nation, the method by which its growth is effected consists in the division of labor or of action. That is, those functions and actions which in the early stages of evolution are performed in a rude and general way by a few organs or parts, or else by many parts of similar form, are gradually divided up among a greater and greater number of unlike parts, each assuming some special portion of the work.

While in the early stages of evolution there is scarcely any mutual dependence of parts, this becomes greater and greater with the increasing complexity, so that at last the full life and activity of each part is more possible only by that of the rest.

A few examples will show clearly the application of this important law to national life. Thus in some of the lower forms of animals, like the crinoid figured at the head of this chapter, the entire function of digestion is performed by a simple sac or stomach. As we pass upward in the scale of life, we find that in other animals there has been added to this sac various other organs, each doing a special part of the work of digestion. Thus we have a liver added to separate the bile; pancreas to help digest the fat in the food; intestinal and salivary glands to digest its starchy portions, and teeth to masticate. Of course where all of these exist the whole process of digestion is carried on much more perfectly.

Now this law of Specialization, this division of labor, governs the social progress of man no less than it does that of his body. For example, in national infancy each person performs every kind of labor pursued by any of the rest. Each man, in a rude way, is at once hunter, farmer, mechanic, and merchant. The savage chief hunts his own game, dresses and cooks it, gathers his own nuts and wild fruit, and makes his own rude clothing of skins, and his ruder hut of sticks and mud. In later periods, persons who show particular aptitudes for special kinds of labor begin to devote themselves to the kinds in which they excel, and thus the various trades and professions come into existence.

One man makes arrowheads, another blankets, another huts, and so on. Out of, and along with, this division of labor there grows a far greater degree of mutual dependence between the members of society, and this increases just in proportion to the advance in civilization and social unfolding. For the men of each trade must exchange their products with those of the other trades. But while it makes men more dependent, it also makes them more completely individualized. The most highly individualized man is the one who has depended upon the greatest number of his fellow-beings for the materials, the comforts, and the luxuries of life. The farmer is dependent upon the tradesman, the grocer, the carpenter, the shoemaker, and those of a hundred other trades. And conversely, each of these is dependent upon the farmer, and upon all the others. The greater the degree of individuality, the greater is the degree of mutual dependence, and of social unity of action and of feeling.

But while labor remains in the stage of competion, there is no formal recognition of these mutual dependencies. There is no provision to secure organized unity of action. Instead of this we only find a selfish antagonism of interests. Everyman's hand is against that of his neighbor. What is for the interest of one man in civilism, is against the interest of the rest. Such is the state of industry in all civilized nations in this year of

1880, common era. The agricultural society is not connected with the state government, the temperance society is severed from the schools, commerce is divorced from art, literature is separated from finance, the scientists do not mingle with the laborers, and culture is not made a test of fitness for official positions. No civilized statesman was wise enough to provide for the united action of these dependent interests. Science proves, and experience confirms, their constant and important interdependence. The statesmen have left their connection wholly to chance or accident. The result of this chance-work is that society is a vast aggregation of discordant and mutually destructive organizations. The social structure thus resembles the very low forms of animal life, instead of the higher. In the next chapter we shall see how these different parts of society are adjusted to each other and respond in action by laws which are a part of the very nature of man, and which will produce in the collective, political life of society a rythm of movement, which has its lesser counterpart and image only in the noblest of musical symphonies.

The division of labor in any organism, or in any series of animals, is not affected chiefly or simply by increasing the number of organs or parts. It is accomplished by changing their form and arrangement. For example, one of the crinoids had 300,000 muscles. But these were all alike in form and the only motions they permitted were reaching out its tentacles, grasping its food, and drawing this into its mouth. But in man, the small number of 232 muscles are constructed and arranged so differently from each other that they enable him to perform an exceedingly great variety of movements.

And so, in the true social organism we shall find a less number of officers than in the Christian and other civilizations. The whole structure of society, the duties of its officers, and the relations of its departments, are so clearly defined that a child can understand them. And the youth who learns this in the band where he lives will then have a clear and true idea of the mechanism and the workings of society through all its orders. The expense of conducting the affairs of society are reduced to a very small part of what was necessary in civilism. Ninetenths of all the labor in civilism was misdirected, wasted, or nugatory.

Final Test.—The final and supreme test of any form of government and society is to compare it with the constitution of man. This we have now done, and have shown that the very best of civilized institutions have failed and must fail to secure human happiness. No matter how high the personal character and attainments of its officers may be, the mechanism of civilized society does not admit of the higher functions. It is as if we should put the spirit or mind of man into the body of a horse and compel it to use that body as its instrument of work and manifestation. We can see at once that in that case the mind of man could not do any of the great deeds, produce any of the high works of art, or give form to the thoughts which place man so far above the brutes. So in civilized society, when men wish to unite in any noble and necessary work for their common welfare, there is no organized means suitable for their use. If they form an organization for the purpose, it is not connected with the rest of the social structure, and it is impractical and useless as a human arm and hand would be, if they were cut off from their connection with the body and the brain. There would be nothing to sustain and nothing to direct their movements.

There is only one course to be taken, and that is to reorganize the whole structure of society in harmony with the wants and nature of man. There is nothing difficult in this work of reconstruction. Men have already represented a part of the faculties by officers. There is nothing in the nature of the higher faculties that makes it either impossible or difficult to represent them by officers. For example, it is no more difficult to represent Reason than it has been to represent Memory.

Science proposes new methods here, just as it has done in other departments of life. And the new methods will be as successful here as they have been in other directions. The statesman who thinks that he can prevent this change, seeks to turn back the movements of the moral universe.

In the ninth chapter it will be proved that the plan of society thus wrought out through the positive methods of science, fulfils precisely the entire description of the great Messianic Age, which has so long inspired the hopes of mankind.

The next chapter presents a formal statement of the natural Constitution of Society, thus elaborated through the methods of science. The remaining chapters will sketch its most important applications to the branches of practical life.

CHAPTER EIGHT.

LIFE IN ISRAEL.

The whole evolution of society in past times has been an attempt of man to organize institutions which shall satisfy his various needs desires, and aspirations.

The wants of man arise from his faculties, and hence the first step in this work is to ascertain precisely how many groups and faculties exist in the mind. This shows the great importance of that positive mathematical analysis of mind which proves that the mind contains three classes, twelve groups, and thirty-six faculties. These, with the corresponding parts of the body, include the entire nature of man. By representing all of these, the work will be complete. The perfect plan of society is thus reached by a series of logical and natural steps, not one of which can be disputed or disproved.

Man is the Archetype of Society. This is not a mere analogy, but a direct statement of facts. For each part of society is a direct product of some mental faculty. These faculties include the Reasoning organs, and hence a complete structure of society is not simply an unconscious and merely spontaneous growth. Intelligence, science and well defined intentions, are an inseparable part of its producing causes.

A concise statement of the laws of society is given on one page, under the head of Bands of Israel. This is followed by a more elaborate statement through the rest of the chapter. The constitution of all human society may be thus written in a single page, or it may be minutely detailed through volumes, just as a work upon any other science may be either a synopsis or a lengthened exposition.

The engraved Archetype of Society exhibits the classes, departments and officers, with thirty-six subdepartments. In the groupate of Letters, the organ of Memory is represented by the Recorder, who leads in the subdepartment of Records.

The Curator represents Observation, and presides over the subdepartment of Publication. The assistant officer here is the Musician and she presides over music. The duties of all the officers can thus be readily learned from the engraving.

Orders of Society. The societies are placed in five orders or ranks. These are called the Town, County, State, Nation, and Israel.

A groupate, or tribe, when full, contains from twelve to thirty-six members, besides the children. Its two central officers are called the Rabbin and Rabbiness. The members are grouped according to their characters, tastes, and attractions, each groupate being composed of those who have the corresponding group of mental faculties dominant. Twelve groupates form a complete society or Band of Israel, which thus contains from one hundred and forty-four to four or five hundred members. The School is formed on the same plan as the parent society, and the Home School is presided over by the Home groupate.

Twelve Bands of the lowest rank are united in a Town. Thirty-six towns are united to form a County. This has the same number and kind of officers in its general government. The State contains one hundred and forty-four counties. Thirty-six or more States form a Nation.

The wants of a Town, of a State, or of a Nation are alike in kind, and they differ from each other only in the degree in which these wants descend to details. For example, a town may require roads which reach no farther than simply through it. Other roads may extend through the State, and others still, through the Nation. But in either case, it is the same kind of a need, and differs only in extent.

If the wants of all these orders are the same in number and kind, they must each have the same kind of officers, and be governed by the same constitution. From the lowest to the highest rank, the Model of Society gives the plan of government in each Order. The only titles changed are those of the two central officers. These changes are shown in engraving at the head of this chapter.

When all the nations of the world are united, the central nation is Israel, with its capital in Palestine Its officers are elected every twelve years.

BANDS OF ISRAEL.

THE MESSIANIC KINGDOM contains twelve departments, in each society or Band of Israel, namely—Art, Letters, Science, Culture, Religion, Marriage, Familism, Home, Rulership, Labor, Wealth, and Commerce. The plan, relations, and officers of these are shown in the engraved Archetype of Society. The Kingdom establishes and secures twelve things:—

1st. AUTHORITY. All the true laws of structure and action in Society, whether physical, spiritual, or political, are inherent in the nature of man, and must be proved by the methods of science before adoption. The office of legislation and rulership is to discover, adopt, and execute the natural laws of society, but not to invent or manufacture laws, except merely as temporary expedients.

2nd. ELECTIONS. All officers must be chosen, or deposed, by a free majority vote of the adult members which they are to lead.

3rd. EDUCATION. This must secure normal methods of teaching; the systematic, daily culture of all the mental faculties; and physical training.

4th. OWNERSHIP. There must be common ownership for all things used in common by two or more persons, such as Buildings, Lands, Highways and Machinery.

5th. EMPLOYMENT. All members must have constant employment, and the full results of their labor. Members must be grouped according to their characters, tastes and attractions.

6th. SEXALITY. There must be dual equality of man and woman in all the offices, employments, and labors of society.

7th. HEREDITY. Society must control and establish the conditions of heredity, and a providence over children.

8th. THE HOME. There must be unitary dwellings, systematic earth culture, and sanitary conditions for all societies.

9th. COMMERCE. There must be organized distribution of labor and art products, and established lines of transit, messages, and commerce.

10th. CONVENTIONS. Annual conventions of each nation, and semi-annual ones of each State, to secure unity of action.

11th. REPRESENTATION. The wants of the lower orders of Societies are represented in the corresponding parts of the higher orders.

12th. RELIGION. There must be a unity of all human interests in society. The good of each must be secured through the good of all. The unity of the Human with the Divine life must be established through an obedience to the intellectual, moral, and physical laws of the human constitution, for this is an image of the divine constitution.

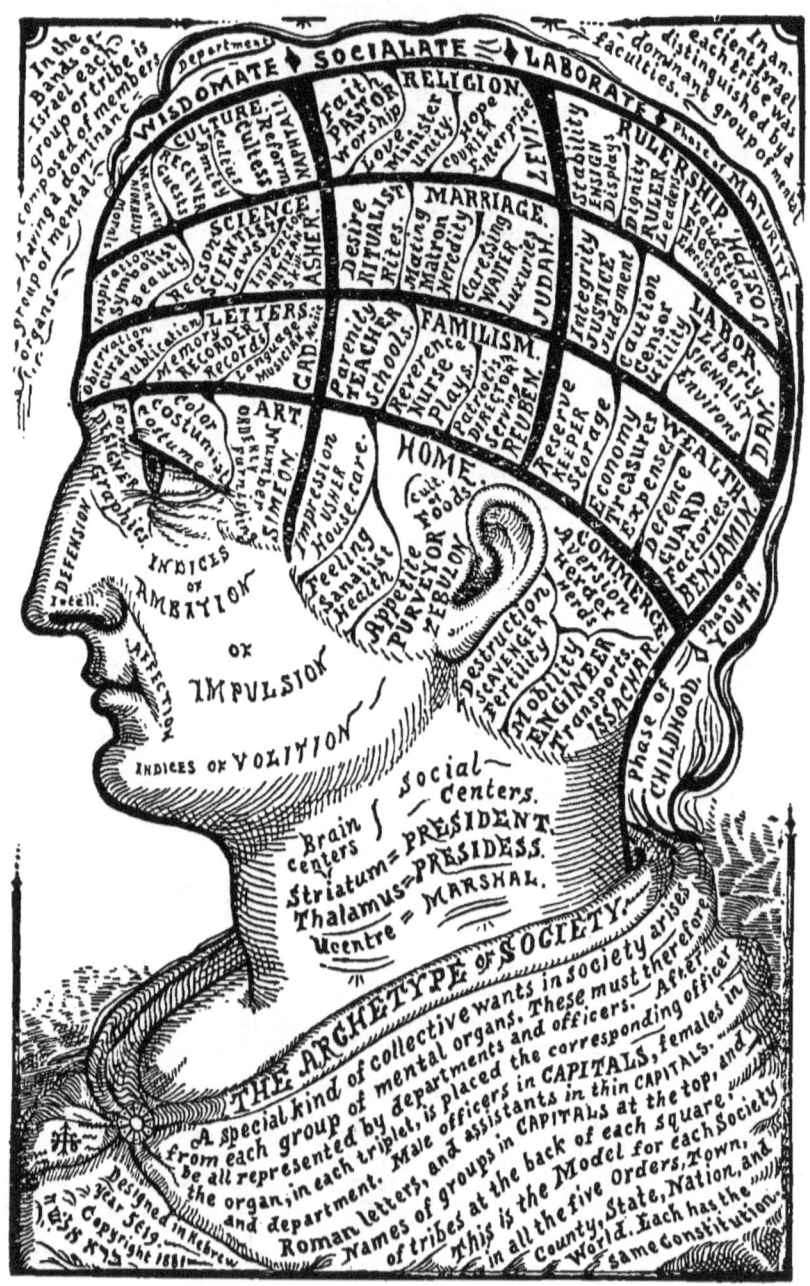

In serving as a pivot of international action and unity, this central government must have the consent of each nation involved in any project or proposed line of action, before it is put into practical execution. It can not force its measures on them without their consent. The legal title of the two highest central officers in Israel, is Prince and Princess, the word Prince meaning one who is first.

Authority. The laws of the human constitution include the only true laws of society. Therefore the office of legislation is to discover and express these natural laws. Or, when this cannot be at once done, it may devise temporary rules and expedients until the required natural law can be discovered.

The proof that each law of society does thus truly express a natural law, should be such as to satisfy all members who are to be affected by the law, so that no person shall be compelled to obey a law which he does not regard as true and based on justice.

Every permanent law of society must be referred back to the people for their acceptance or rejection, and it must be accepted by a three-fourths vote before it is practically adopted. Temporary expedients, in the case of emergencies, need not be subject to this rule.

The methods and tests of science legitimately apply to every sphere of knowledge. And scientific proof is of such a character that it can be understood in the same way by all persons. Therefore no doctrine or belief which is not susceptible of scientific demonstration must ever be made a part of the laws or constitution of society.

True freedom consists, first, in the presence of

the right conditions for the full and natural exercise of every faculty; second, in a normal internal state of the faculties; and third. in the absence of false external restraint.

It is not in any sense true that when men enter civil society they surrender certain rights or liberties, in exchange for other benefits conferred. On the contrary, it is only by uniting in organized society. that man can gain the conditions required for the free exercise of each and all of his faculties. If isolated from his fellows, he would lose the freedom to use all his social organs, and none of his other faculties could attain a full development.

Man is adapted by his nature to live in a social organism like the Kingdom, where all parts of his nature are represented. By fulfilling the duties of such a life, by acting in concert with others, by loving and being loved, by these alone can any person secure the full measure of freedom. The laws of such a society can not restrict any person's freedom, because they are true statements of those laws which are a part of the nature of each person. The acting forces are from within and not from without.

Every person has a natural right to the proper development, conditions, and use of each faculty. Rights cannot be created or transferred by men.

As all human beings, of either sex and of all races, have the same number and kind of faculties, therefore all have the same classes of rights, and are adapted to the same great forms of government and social life.

The quantity of a right may depend upon the degree to which its faculty is developed. A man with a small organ of Reason would have a right to exercise it in learning science, but not in leading the scientific pursuits of society.

In every natural law, the inseparable results of obedience are integrity and happiness, and those of disobedience are destruction and pain.

When the laws of society are transgressed, the Justice, Censor, and Scientist, must ascertain what are the natural penalties, and see that only these follow any transgression. The object of all penal measures should be, to restore the transgressor to a condition of normal action, of social health and power.

A member of society might become so vicious or discordant that the other members could not work with him, or he might possibly become dangerous to the peace or lives of others. But he is still susceptible to influences from the higher faculties of his fellows, and these influences must be brought to bear, so that they will make his own higher faculties rule in his conduct thereafter.

In the Messianic kingdom, the chief motives which impel men to crime in civilism will be removed. This is done through the system of integral education, of organized and attractive industry, and of universal wealth. The great criminal causes in civilism are ignorance, intemperance, and poverty.

In depending upon the higher forces to secure obedience, the structure of society is such that it secures the constant rule of the higher faculties in all of its activities. But it still retains as much compulsory power as in civilism, only it is not necessary to use this lower force.

Elections. The act of voting is the formal expression of a choice in regard to officers, laws, or social action. As all adult persons, of either sex and of all races, possess this choice or preference, therefore all have a natural right to vote, and may exercise this right after the sixteenth year of age.

All officers must be elected by a direct vote of the members which they are to lead and rule. Thus, the members of a Town Band elect its officers, those of all the Town Bands in a County elect the officers of that County, and so through all the orders up to the Nation. But in case of vacancies the Centers may appoint temporary officers until elections can be held.

The assistant officers are each elected by the groupate in which he is to act. The same rule applies to sub-leaders of the subdivisions of departments.

The Curator and Recorder take and record the votes in each society

Each officer must have the represented faculty large. Thus, the Scientist should have large Reason, and the Justice large Integrity. The Centers should have a full development of all the faculties.

Regular elections are held on the fifteenth day of March, officers entering upon their duties the twenty-first day. In the Nation, elections are held once in seven years ; in the State, once in six years ; in the County, once in five years ; and in the Town, every year. In elections to permanently fill vacancies, notice thereof must be given at least twelve days previous to the election.

The times of election may be changed by a two-thirds vote of the members in all the societies.

In case of official misconduct, any officer may be tried before the Justice and Censor of an adjacent society, and the evidence elicited be published

The members within the jurisdiction of that society shall then vote for or against his or her expulsion from office, and their decision shall be final in the case, because they had the original right of selection.

Education. The methods of integral education require the elaborate explanations of an entire chapter, the tenth of this work.

Rights of Wealth. The right to own property arises from the mental faculty of Economy, and hence this right exists in all persons. But man is normally a member of society, and he cannot acquire extensive wealth unless he combines his labor with that of his fellows. The rights of wealth thus become Common and Social, as well as Personal.

Three objects are gained through combined labors. *First*, Increased power of production. *Second*, Facilities for making exchanges of property. *Third*, Economy and Security in the use of wealth.

The grouping of members in the Kingdom secures to each one a free choice in employment. The industries are so organized that the mental and physical labor of each member is fully productive, and no part of it wasted. And each member receives back the full product of his labor, or else receives in exchange with some one else, that which has cost that person an equal amount of labor.

By the law of Conservation every person expends just as much force as he receives, and no more. Hence where the plan or society makes these forces wholly productive, the wants of each member may be safely made the basis for the distribution of the products of labor. There is no danger that any one will receive more than his just share. This law applies to all the produced necessities and comforts of life.

Those things which are used by one person alone, should be owned by that person. This includes clothing, private rooms, and many kinds of tools. In all these, each person has individual character, peculiarities, and tastes to gratify, and what is adapted to one person, is not adapted to another.

All those things which are used together by two or more persons, should be owned by them in common. One person alone could not occupy and use a house, and therefore should not own it. Each Band of Israel would own a unitary home, with common rooms used by all, and with private rooms which are used and owned by each member exclusively, and furnished in harmony with that member's character and tastes.

A railway is to be used by the whole public, and they should be its owners. A farm can only be well cultivated by a group or a society, and should be owned by them. Homes, temples, workshops, storerooms, machinery, lands, and highways of all kinds, are all used by a common public, and should therefore be owned in common.

The Town, the County, the State and Nation, each owns property. For example, the County owns the county roads; the State owns those which only pass through it, and the Nation owns those roads which are national in their extent.

The two Centers, with the Guard, Treasurer, Secretary, Curator, and Marshal, constitute a Board of Trustees in each of the five orders and they have the general care of the property in each society.

The whole growth of society is through the Specialization of Labor, the division of the different employments, among those who have the talent to excel in each special kind of work. Thus the whole community gets the benefit of each person's skill. The carpenter builds as good houses for others as he does for himself. The shoemaker does as skillful work for his neighbor's children as for his own. One talent alone, the ability to control men and make their labor productive, this talent alone in civilism is used wholly for selfish purposes. The financier uses his talent to accumulate wealth for himself out of the labor of others. But in the Kingdom, this talent must be specialized the same as all other kinds of skill. In demanding this, we are doing no more than we have already done for the rest. Financial talent is not any more godlike than the painter's skill, or the artizan's technical acquirements. It has no more right to be exempt from this great law which has lifted man from savageism to civilization.

Employment. When the youth, of either sex, graduates from school, the course of study has fitted that youth for a definite place in the productive work of society. And society must secure this place to every youth, and it must thereafter furnish constant occupation.

Civilism left its industry without organization, to be the prey of fierce and selfish competition. Its best possible results brought only wealth and comfort to the few, while poverty was the lot of the masses. Surely the political wisdom which produced nothing better than these conditions was not worth boasting about.

The national organization of Intellect, even in

the imperfect schools of civilism, secured to every member of society the benefits of a general education. The manifold benefits of wealth will in like manner be secured to all members of society through the national organization of Industry. If it is wise and practical to establish order in the work of imparting knowledge, then it is equally wise, practical and necessary to organize the application of knowledge in the methods of labor, in a complete system of production and distribution. This will displace competitive labor by combined industry, and establish equity in supreme dominion.

The system of combined industry in the Kingdom, opens a thousand new channels for the highest ambition, in the fields of science, labor, culture and religion. And, unlike the grovelling lust for wealth, these higher channels lead only to the welfare of humanity.

In every Band, through all the five Orders, there is a department of enterprises, of displays, and of awards, so that every person is sure to receive, not only assistance in his undertakings, but the fullest measure of reward and praise for whatever good and great thing he may achieve.

Every person has a natural right to associate with others who are attractive and congenial.

This right must be gratified by arranging the members of each society into twelve groupates, according to their characters.

Members in whose characters the reflective faculties are dominant would unite to form the groupate of Science; those who have the faculties of religion as leading elements of their characters would form the groupate of Religion; and those in whom the ambitious faculties were strongest would form the groupate of Government.

This process is followed in forming each one of the twelve groupates and the various sub-groups which each of these may require. Each member will then be associated with others of similar ideas, tastes, and capacities. A person who is fully and evenly developed in all his traits, may pass and repass, in succession, through all the groupates. Such persons would also be qualified for Centers.

In order to join any groupate, a person must be accepted by all its members, by vote or otherwise. If dissatisfied with any groupate or society, a member may, without censure, leave it for another. The Pastor and Minister lead and assist in this grouping of the members, and they must provide every facility for the satisfactory adjustment of these relations.

We may learn the character of persons by reading the indices of the face; by the development of the brain; by psychometry; or by an actual acquaintance with the facts of their lives. The Pastor, Minister, and Scientist must understand all these methods of reading character.

As each group of faculties gives a taste for its particular kinds of employment, this grouping of members places each person where his natural tastes and capacities can be most fully satisfied. Thus persons with the faculties of Defense or Wealth dominant, prefer those employments named in the square of Wealth in the Social Model. And so of all the other groups.

Spheres of the Sexes. Man and woman are mental and physical complements of each other. Each sex is more developed in some directions than in others, but neither can claim superiority as a whole. They possess equal quantities of power, but it differs in kind.

The physical differences of sex must produce mental differences, because the brain and body are definitely related in action and sympathy. So long as woman must fill the offices of maternity, so long must her nutritive organs predominate over the nervous and muscular. The effect on her brain would be that she would be ruled more by her affections and emotions, and less by ideas and material influences.

In the table of faculties, the first one given in each trinity dominates in the character of man,. and the second one in the character of woman. Man is positive, woman is receptive. In general, man is the more vigorous, muscular, hardy, bold, cool, and scientific. Woman is the more sensitive, yielding, gentle, loving, ardent, and intuitive.

In woman, the nerve-currents from the body to the brain first flow outward on the mental organs which are feminine. In man they first flow outward on the mental organs which are masculine. Thus in examining a truth, man looks at it first through his Reason; while woman gets her first idea of it through her Intuition.

These natural differences of the two sexes adapt them to different spheres of intellectual, social, and industrial activity. Their spheres, like their characters, are complements.

The offices and labors of society are all dual, as shown in the Model of Society. Each has its masculine and its feminine side. Thus the department and labors of Illustration are feminine complements to those of Building. So is that of

Inspiration to that of Law ; and that of exchanges to that of Machinery.

The office and employments of harmonic society are assigned to the two sexes on the basis of this difference. The first officer in each pair is a man and the second is a woman. The twelve Assistant officers may be arranged as masculine and feminine, as follows: Orderly and Musician ; Artisan and Moralist; Courier and Waiter; Director and Usher ; Signalist and Ensign ; Scavenger and Keeper.

The sexes are thus everywhere equal in rank, they go together in all the groupates, and to each is assigned duties and employments in harmony with its natural adaptations. While woman thus takes an equal part in the government and conduct of society, she does not become less womanly nor does man become less manly, in development and character. This is the societary or external side of marriage. It is the high material pivot of the entire social organism.

Marriage. The polarity of the sexes finds its most intense expression in the high and enduring attraction of Marriage. The mental force of sex-love has its focus of intensity in the group of Sexation, but it originates from and permeates every part of the mental and physical system.

All marriages must be based upon the existence and duration of mutual love and adaptation between the parties. Persons who do not love each other have no right to live together in this relation, for it derives its sancity from love only. No ceremony and no legislative act can justify that which is a violation of natural law. The bond of union is internal, not external. We can not compel any one to love another; but we can repress its expression. If persons make mistakes in choosing their mates, they should be allowed every opportunity to rectify their mistakes, and form true unions.

Two persons who are united through Sex-love should also have their other faculties developed in harmony with each other. There should exist between sex-mates a sympathy of ideas, tastes, and aspirations; and this sympathy may result from either similarities or complements of organization.

If a person have an organ somewhat deficient, he may make up or neutralize the deficiency by uniting with a mate who has the organ better developed. But persons of widely contrasted characters should not unite, for they would not see things in a similar light, and could not work together in that close sympathy demanded by this kind of love.

The same qualities which make a man and a woman adapted to love each other, also best adapt them to work together in the offices of society. Hence in a complete state of harmonism the two officers or workers of each pair are husband and wife.

The permanence of sex-love must be secured by carefully teaching youth, of either sex, the physical and mental laws of sex-harmony; by giving them opportunity to make an intelligent choice of mates; and by surrounding them after marriage with conditions which are favorable to its perpetuity and perfection. The Ritualist and Matron are the leaders in securing these conditions, in each society.

The group of sex-love, or Sexation, is surrounded by the faculties of Integrity, Self-control,

Imagination, Faith, Love, and Hope. The action of all these faculties is constantly required to develop, perfect, and sustain sex-love. These organs have the same location and sustain the same relations after marriage that they did before.

If we would make love perpetual, we must exercise it in connection with the full activity of these higher organs, and not allow it to be led by those at the base of the brain, by mere sensation and impulse.

In the most complete expression of love,—the physical union of the sexes,—the highest faculties of the mind must be called into dominant activity. If they are not, it will surely debase both parties, and the physical pleasure itself will lose the best of its sweetness and intensity. If impulse takes the place of self-control, if modesty and reverence cease between sex-mates, if they cease to refine and inspire each other, then their love will certainly be made impure and its beauty will be destroyed; its golden fruit will turn to dust and ashes.

Purity is in the right and normal use of any organ, not in its disuse, or suppression. It is a positive and active, not a negative quality. Purity of the stomach does not consist in its not digesting food. The lungs would not be pure if they did not work actively in changing the blood. We must not define sexual purity as the absence of all sex-relations. Nor must we imagine that an external ceremony is sufficient to secure purity here. That is not a pure sex-relation which brings forth children who are badly organized in mind and body. In our eating and drinking, purity is not less central, and its violations are not less corrupting, than in the relation of the sexes. It requires all the different kinds of purity to make a pure character.

Like all the other faculties, those of Sex-love have their harmonies of thirds, fifths, and octaves, as shown in the table of mental chords. Love is therefore an art no less definite than that of music. In the expression of love by conversation, by caressing, or in labors, these harmonies should be secured.

A gentle, or even close contact, greatly increases and intensifies the exchange of nerve-force. By placing our hands upon any part of another person we may receive the force peculiar to that part, or we may excite it to activity by communicating our own force. Thus caressing the bosom, which is connected with Sex-love, Parental, and Filial love, tends to excite these affections. The signs of these faculties and that of Friendship are also in the lips, and hence kissing is a natural expression of either or of all these kinds of love. This reception of pleasure and of force is as real as that through the food which we consume.

In caressing we should, therefore, touch the different parts of the body in such a way as to excite together, or in succession, such faculties as are thirds, fifths, octaves, or polates of the second degree. The touch may be made by the hand, or by corresponding parts of the body, or by parts which are polar to each other. A careful study of the mental chords in connection with the map of the body will place this art within our power.

For example, it will produce harmony if we caress in succession, the faculties or signs of Ambition Culture, and Religion ; of Impulsion, Rulership, and Culture; of Sex-love, Labor and Intellect; or of Intellect, Sensation and Ardor.

The faculties may also be excited in polar harmonies by the current of conversation, by material surroundings, and by our employments. Love may and should use all these as its instruments. All thoughts and actions, all desires, whatever thrills the human frame, find centers in love's aural fires and feed the raptures of its flame.

Before these laws of harmony were known, sex-love was subject to all the mistakes of instinctive impulses and erroneous notions. The few high harmonies it secured were reached more through accident than through wisdom.

The relation of two sex-mates is one of equality of rank. Therefore the exchanges of labor and employment between members of higher and those of lower groups do not involve a physical relation of sexes between the lower and higher members.

Among the lower animals, mere instinct is sufficient to rule the sex-relations. But the nature of man is so complex that sexlove stands at the center of a vast multitude of forces, and any one of these may disturb its harmony if wrongly exerted, or if properly united and controlled, each may contribute to its lofty symphony.

In the new life, the ceremonies of Sex-love are many, beautiful and interesting. And they are not confined to a single event once during a person's life; they are repeated every day. The groupate of Marriage includes the subdepartments of Luxuries, Rites, Waiters, Maternity, Heredity, and Florists. And each day these occupy one hour of the harmonic life. In the lower phases of life, Sexlove exhausts its forces in physical intercourse. In the new life it becomes the high and inspiring center of a thousand new relations of harmony.

Conditions of Heredity.—Society must give to all prospective parents the best conditions of heredity, so that the forming structure of the child shall be perfect, mentally and physically. Private effort can never secure and maintain these conditions. In every child, society has rights no less than the parents. But the two claims can never be in conflict. The child is to be under the direct influence of its parents for perhaps twenty years, but it is to be an active member of society more than three times as long. Whatever tends to develop the individual character into symmetry, that also tends, most directly, to qualify the person to fill his place in society with honor.

The laws of Biology teach us what are the conditions and influences which mould the character of children previous to birth.

It is comparatively an easy task to train children into virtuous men and women, if their original organization of brain and body has been made such as these good prenatal conditions will secure. Society has a right to protect itself by insisting that prospective parents shall avail themselves of these conditions.

Home Work.—The division of human labor into classes or separate trades and pursuits has lifted man from barbarism to civilization. But this division of labor affected the pursuits of the male sex chiefly. From the most primitive times woman remained merely a housekeeper, and her advance depended upon the incidental influence of her connection with man.

The isolated household made this restriction of woman's sphere a necessity, while it left man free to follow varied occupations. It was not until the analysis in this book was made, showing that every office and every labor is dual, having its masculine and its feminine side, that it became possible to give woman her true place in society, to specialize her labor as much as that of man, and to organize a unitary home which should equally secure the privacy and the sacredness of domestic life, and the widest range of social action and sympathy.

The domestic work of the home is divided into the branches of Purveying, Cooking, Table-serving, House care, Sanitary and Laundry. Separate groups of men and women labor in each of these branches. But woman also takes one half the labor, the feminine side, in all the employments of society. Her range of choice is as wide as that of man. Only one twelfth of the women in a society are engaged in household duties.

The whole society is interested in seeing that each of its members has its free choice of employments, and place gratified. In the home each person has at least three hundred others from which to choose the group with which he or she will work and be most intimately associated. And the whole community accepts this choice as right, proper, and according to the laws of harmony in adaptation. The employments of each society are so arranged that persons who are not adapted never come in contact. But in civilism, just the opposite constantly occurred. In the unitary dwelling the groups of members pass in regular directions through the building, in going to the central rooms, and to and from their employments. These directions correspond to that of the currents through the brain, from which the temple is modelled. They are thus in harmony with the laws of each person's mind. In grouping at the table, and in the kinds of food, the same free choice is regarded.

And third, within the unitary home is a circle of three hundred persons, or varied characters, and all of them chosen friends, seeking each other's welfare, and meeting often together. The facilities of social intercourse are carried to the highest possible point, but at the same time it provides for a privacy much more secure and complete than could be obtained in civilism.

A true social life cannot exist along with dominant selfishness. And neither can social happiness. The sooner all selfishness disappears from the earth, the better it will be for us all.

Commerce.— The thirty-six sub-departments given in the model of society, are found in all the orders from the band up to the nation. The six departments of Wealth and Commerce, in all these, constitute a vast and perfect mechanism for the distribution and exchange of wealth through every nation and throughout the world.

At the yearly and half-yearly conventions, the higher societies receive from those of lower rank exact reports of their various productions, and of their present and prospective needs; and these are made the basis of state and national distribution.

Society in harmonism is thus able to proportion its productions to its wants, to guard against the vicissitudes of climate, and in every way to protect its composite life.

The wealth of society is the product of its united industries. No person, by wholly isolated industry, could accumulate wealth. The right to superintend its distribution is therefore much more a society than it is a personal right.

The organ of Economy, the desire for property, has not as much right to dominate the life of society as any one of the higher faculties possesses In civilism, the love of wealth was a dominant power.

If a member were so selfish as to require more luxuries and comforts than his proportion of the labor would have produced, then that is simply a proof that the society has not educated him up to the proper idea of social justice.

In effecting the commercial exchanges between the various societies, the same law is followed. Each is supplied in proportion to its wants.

Conventions.—Each State society may hold a semi-annual convention, lasting seven days or more. As delegates and voting members of this convention, each town may send its Pastor and Minister. The temporary absence of these officers is supplied by their assistants.

Each Nation holds an annual convention, to which each of its States sends its Pastor and Minister as acting members.

In a state convention, the regular officers of that state preside; and in a national convention, the officers of that nation preside.

Each convention receives reports from its component societies, and devises plans for their concerted action, their social welfare, and their material prosperity.

Representation.—The wants of the lower orders

are answered by the higher, through like parts of each. Thus, if a want in regard to food arises in the Home groupate of some town and cannot be answered there, it would be represented in, and answered by the Home groupate of its ruling County. Or, if necessary, it would be carried up to the corresponding groupates in the still higher orders. These wants may be made known through any of the ordinary channels of communication, by messages or by special delegates. All the interests, employments, and professions of society are organized, secured and represented in the twelve groupates, with invariable certainty and equality.

Religion. The faculties of man are exactly adapted to the reception and practical realization of all religious truth. The group of religious organs forms the key-stone in the great mental arch. Their action is supported by that of all the rest, below and around them.

Under the Polar law of Responses in the fifth chapter, it was shown that the feelings can not act without using the intellect. We would not know a friend from an enemy if we had no intellectual faculties of Form and Memory. The religious faculties are completely subject to this law. If a truth is addressed to the religious faculties, the very constitution of our minds compels us to use Reason and other intellectual faculties in deciding what the truth means, and upon what proofs it rests. But Reason acts by the methods of science and therefore the methods and tests of science legitimately apply to all religious truth.

Religion aims at the symmetrical development of every person, at the intellectual, the social and industrial unity of the human race here on the earth, and the harmony of human life with that of all beings in the supernal spheres. As those beings are constituted on the same plan as ourselves, religion only requires a fulfilment of all the natural laws of man.

The Bible declares that man is in the image of Yehovah. He must therefore have the same mental constitution, and if he fulfils its laws he will be obeying the laws of the divine mind. The laws of Yehovah are not issued like the mandates of an autocrat. They are in the inner nature of man.

The modes of Angelic life very much resemble our own. Every evidence goes to show that the spirit must have organs or parts like all those of the body; and this would fit them for the same great methods of existence.

Our relations with the spirit world can only be adjusted by harmonizing our relations with each other here, and for this reason it is not necessary to dwell at length upon this part of our subject.

Our communion with the angelic world takes place through the nerve-spheres, and the laws which govern these have been stated in the fourth chapter.

When the institutions of society are all in harmony with the nature of man, then the religious faculties will have full and free scope for the exercise of their beneficent influence. Our faculties and their laws of action will remain the same in all spheres of being. Science decides what forms of life are best adapted to our natures here, and, consequently, it determines what the forms of life must be in a spiritual existence.

The faculties which compose the groups of Cultture, religion, sexation, and parention have a most important law of social action. In the true and natural action of these organs, their nerve force flows out from one person to another as its object, and is then answered by a returning current from the latter person. Thus, when I exercise my Friendship, the current flows from this organ to my friend, and from his organ of Friendship a returning current flows to me. On the other hand, only four organs, and these are all low ones, have self as the first object upon which their actions terminate. Our high and true life must flow through that of others. We can maintain it only by perpetual interchange. We must look out and not in. The members of a harmonic society must be as vitally related to each other as are the parts of our physical organism.

If we are selfish and seek to draw everything to ourselves, we must of necessity contract our minds and our pleasures. Selfishness defeats itself. Expansion of the mind means outward growth, and this law explains its method. To give is the way to live. Through the social law which we are discussing, all humanity is made one, and we receive the full benefit of its common growth and advancement.

We are by nature social beings, and a universal sympathy may through this law unite all nations and communities in one vast, composite life. To effect this sublime result and give full sway to this beneficent law, the institutions and government of society must be formed in harmony with the nature of man, as planned in the Model of Society.

Humanity must be regarded as a unit, made up of the past, the present, and the future. We all inherit the results of many centuries of human culture and improvement ; and we should violate the deepest law of social unity if we did not labor for the present and the future welfare of humanity.

Great teachers affect the world profoundly, not alone by their doctrines and example, but also by the impartation of the vital currents of nerve force. They become, in a literal sense, the life and soul of great movements. It is perfectly natural that the affections of the people should center in these leaders. But that affection and reverence must never be carried so far as to blind us to the great truths which these leaders represent. Truth is always greater than Persons. It reaches through the universe. It is the union of human lives that we are to seek ; not the substitution of one life for another. The glory of Jehovah is to be attained, not by the absorption of all lives into his life, but by the union of our lives with his, and by our exemplification of the divine image in our persons. Jehovah is not supremely selfish, seeking His own glory for its own sake. The same unselfish law of love that should rule man is also a part of the divine mind.

Our most secret thoughts and emotions extend their nerve—force to our fellow-beings, and affect them for good or ill. Whether we are conscious of it or not, the effects are as certain as those of gravitation. We cannot sever our relations with humanity. The good of one is in the good of all. To a great extent we must all rise or fall together.

We must directly seek to promote the welfare of others, in preference to our own. But as we are a part of humanity, and others are to be governed by the same rule, the benefits of our unselfish conduct are reflected back upon ourselves, not only by their direct personal actions, but in the vast results of concerted social activities.

When we thus directly seek to promote the good of others, our actions are not selfish, although we may know that the ultimate result will be the securing of our own happiness. Those actions are selfish which are planned without regard to the welfare of others.

The nerve-force from an attractive organ or group in one person may flow outward, and meeting the repulsive force from another person, it may neutralize the latter by equaling or exceeding it in quantity. This is according to a law which governs all of the forces in nature. Suppose, for example, that one person throws out a quantity of repulsive force from Destruction which would equal, we will say, $5x$, and another person meets this by enough attractive force from Love to equal $7x$, it is evident that the last will be sufficient to neutralize the first. In this way we may overcome evil with good. It is not by passively yielding to the evil, but by the active exertion of an opposite force; for the good person would be exercising the highest degree of Firmness and Self-control in connection with his organ of Love. This is a nobler way than to meet evil by evil, for this brings our own higher faculties in activity.

Transitions.—From the old forms of civilized society to the new methods of unitary life, the steps of transition may be taken in a very gradual manner. This will enable people to gain the required knowledge, and become adapted to the new order of things. The law of Phases furnishes a full guide for the successive steps in making this change, the law gives all the required forms of transition.

In the personal and the national growth of man, the more simple forms come first, and then those which are more and more complex. Following this great law of growth, it is not necessary to have the full complement of twelve groupates and twenty-six officers in order to commence a Band of Israel. Any persons who chose may unite and form a Band with only the seven following officers:

Recorder,	Rabbin,	Guard,
Curator,	Rabbiness.	Treasurer,
	Marshal.	

These officers represent the major axis of the brain, the line of forward movement. The brain itself begins its growth, with three vesicles on this line. These officers lead in the intellectual, the social, and the industrial work of the Town, as shown by their position in the table.

The following form of agreement is used in forming Bands, the names and dates being changed to suit each case:

BAND OF ISRAEL. We accept the plan, the life, and the laws of the Messianic Kingdom, and we organize the first Band of Israel, of London, this fifth day of September, in the year of the Exodus of Israel 3468.

This form is signed by the members and bound in at the end of the copy of the Sepherva kept in the hands of the Secretary.

Many bands of Israel will be formed for the preparatory work of intellectual culture, of learning the methods of the new life, and of spreading a knowledge of the new truths among the people.

They also will form the means of concerted action in securing a practical adoption of the new methods required in social or political life.

These Bands may hold conventions and act in unity with the fully formed Bands. They may organize their children into classes and groupets so as to form a school for daily or weekly training.

Whenever three-fourths of the members desire it, a band may enter upon its phase of practical life. As fast as expedient, it will then arrange its property and its employments on the unitary plan, as stated in this constitution.

Its buildings may be formed on the fundamental plan of the temple, but have a less number of rooms and amount of detail, and thus lessen the cost of building. These Bands at first have only the three departments, but when the number of members is sufficient, they may be divided up into the twelve groupates, and each of these have its leaders and assistants. Each Town will regulate these steps of growth according to its increasing amount of wealth, of vital culture, and of numbers.

The government of each State and Nation may be organized after the general plan given in the Model, long before the majority of the people are prepared to live in the high and unselfish condition of unitary homes.

The national or the state government, with that of each County, Town, are in twelve subdivisions or groupates, with two officers and an assistant over each one. The Towns might, however, retain the simpler form of only seven officers.

Within the State there might still remain more or less of the old sectional organizations, such as cnurches, lyceums etc., etc. But the true and natural work of these local societies could b much better done by the twelve groupates.

In this transition stage of government, the people, through the National, State and lower orders, would own and control all public lines of travel, commerce, and intercommunication. They would regulate Employment, Production, and Distribution. They would prevent the absorption of wealth by private monopolies.

The Nation would issue all money, consisting of notes redeemable in service or in labor-products, and equal in volume to the necessities of exchange. It would not allow money itself to be an object of speculative traffic, or to a bear a higher rate of interest than the average rate of increase of property in the country.

The expenses of government would be met by taxes, equalized according to the actual wealth of the people. The salaries of national officers must not exceed three times the average of a citizen's income, and that of the State and other officers must not exceed twice the same average.

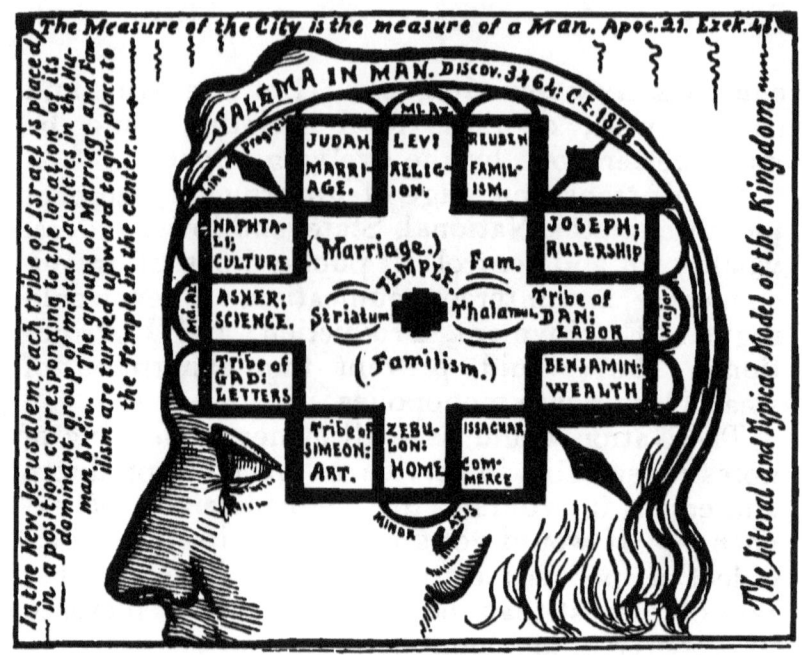

CHAPTER NINTH

SEALS OF TRUTH.

The great doctrines and ideas of the Hebrew Bible are represented by the Tree of Life and Garden of Eden; the Chosen People in twelve Tribes; the Promised Messiah and his reign; the Atonement and Judgment; the Resurrection; the Throne in Heaven with its twenty-four Rulers; and the New Jerusalem as the Capital of the Messianic Kingdom.

The writer of the Apocalypse saw, in a vision, a little book in which these doctrines were shown under seven seals. Christian writers and teachers have always regarded these doctrines and symbols as mysteries. But at the same time they have taught that the salvation of the world depends upon a full belief in these mysteries, before which the Catholic, the Greek, and the Protestant teachers have alike stood helpless, mute, and blind.

We shall here both prove and explain these doctrines, by the positive methods of science. and thus rend and remove this Veil of the Covering, once spread over all the nations.

Seventh Seal,—The sixth and Seventh seals will be explained first, because these two are the key to the rest.

When the Seventh seal was opened it was proclaimed that the kingdoms of this world had become the kingdom of the Messiah. The New Jerusalem was its capital. The Old and the New Testament focalize all their prophecies and promises in one burning picture, the resplendent image of the New Jerusalem.

The lower figure in our engraving shows the plan of the New Jerusalem, as described by the prophet Ezekiel, and as copied by John in the Apocalypse.

The great city was laid out four square, with twelve departments, twelve gates, and twelve foundations, three on each side. Each of its twelve departments was made up of members from a special one of the tribes, and its gates were named accordingly. Every part of the plan is full of important meaning.

The recent great discoveries of science, in regard

to these meanings. may be summed up in three propositions:—

First: The Plan of the New Jerusalem, is modeled after the plan of the Divine Mind. The arrangement, the number, and the character of all its parts, represent the attributes of Jehovah, and the relation of these attributes to each other.

Second: As man is in the image of the Deity, the plan of the New Jerusalem represents all the faculties of man, and the arrangement of these faculties in the human brain.

Third: The character of the twelve tribes of Israel, and the places occupied by each tribe in the plan of the City, corresponds precisely with that of the twelve groups of faculties, and the location of these groups in the brain. As man is the archetype of society, therefore the ancient nation of Israel, with its twelve tribes, was a type of that final and perfect organization of human society, described in the eighth chapter.

A simple comparison will bring into bold relief the proof of these propositions.

The people of the twelve tribes differed widely from each other in character. Those of each tribe had a special one of the groups of faculties as dominant traits in their character. These differences are strongly pictured in the blessings pronounced by Jacob on his twelve sons, and they are confirmed by the whole subsequent history of the separate tribes, as given in the Bible and by both Jewish and Christian historians. These characteristic traits are presented here in a table for convenient reference. The names of the tribes are marked in their appropriate groups in the Archetype of Society.

The engraved head at the beginning of this chapter must be laid down so that it will point north, because this polarizes it with the earth. The face turns to the west because this is the course which the development of civilization has taken.

The plan of the New Jerusalem is drawn on the head, so that the comparison may be direct and clear.

The groups of Art, Home, and Commerce form the base line, on the south side. Simeon is placed in the group of Art, and the Simeonites became the scribes and musicians of Israel. They represented literature and music, the only branches of art which were developed among the Israelites. Zebulon was located in the place where the Home group is, and he is the only one to whom Jacob assigns a definite home in the promised Land. The name Zebulon means Dwelling, and like all Hebrew names, it indicated the character of the bearer. Simeon means hearing or perception, the group that ruled in his tribe. Issachar is placed in the city in a position exactly corresponding with the group of Commerce in the brain. He is said to be a strong ass, crouching down between two burdens. This animal was the beast of commerce in Palestine. The name Issachar means hire, or one who is hired.

On the east side of the city are the tribes of Joseph, Dan, and Benjamin. Joseph is exactly where the group of Rulership is located, and he was made a ruler over all his brethren. The half tribe of his son Ephriam, stood at the head of the house of Israel when the ten tribes separated from Judah. They pushed with the horns of the unicorn. Dan is in the group of Labor, in which Justice is the leading masculine faculty. Dan means a judge, and it is said that Dan shall judge his people. Labor shall judge the world; it is a serpent by the path, it secretly strikes at the rulers, and they will fall backward out of power. Then shall follow the salvation of Yehovah, says the patriarch. Benjamin is placed where the group of Wealth is, in which are the defensive and acquiring faculties, and of Benjamin it is said that he shall raven as a wolf; in the morning he shall devour the prey and at night he shall divide the spoil. They were the most warlike of all the tribes.

The west side of the city contains Gad, Asher, and Naphtali. Gad is in the group of Letters or philosophy, of central truths, and he is said to be seated in a portion with the lawgivers. His group is the middle one of Intellect, the faculties which deal with laws. Asher is in the group of Science, and the Asherites, mixing with the Phenicians, became the most scientific of all the tribes. From them came the builders of Solomon's Temple. Asher shall have shoes of iron and brass, he shall dip his foot in oil, and as his days are, so shall his strength be. This prophecy has a most striking fulfilment in the modern triumphs of science. Its iron railways and brass-fitted machines of locomotion, are the shoes used in its swift lines of travel, and these must be constantly dipped in oil. Through these he brings royal dainties from foreign lands and makes them common in every household. Naphtali is in the group of Culture, and his goodly words and bland manners come from the faculties of this group. He is swift of foot, a hind let loose, and the group of Culture occupies the exact line of movement in walking and running, as explained by the law of polation.

The tribes of Judah, Levi, and Reuben are on the north side. Levi occupies the Religious group and the Levites had the priesthood, the religious care of Israel. His Urim and Thummim, his Lights and Perfections, were with the holy one. The twelve stones of the Breastplate represented, in their number, character, and arrangement, all the attributes of the human and the divine mind, the sum of all light and beauty. When these attributes are all balanced and complete, like their symbol in the breastplate, then the spirituals light and perfection of the mind is perfect. In order to leave a place for the temple in the center of the city, the two groups of Marriage and Familism had to be turned upward, on each side of Religion, with which they are still in line. Reuben's place is then in the group of Familism. Being the first born, he represented the family by the law of inheritance. Let not his men be few. The name Reuben means, see a son. Judah is in the group of Marriage, and the Lion of the tribe of Judah is to claim the redeemed Israel as his Bride. The number of Judah's name is 5x6, and it therefore means Law and Material perfection united in marriage. Again and again the prophets call the restoration of the nation, the union of the house of Judah with the house of Israel, a marriage. Thy land shall be married. In the New Life of the Kingdom, as shown in this Book, Marriage, or the pairing of the two sexes in all offices and employments, is made the high material pivot of the entire social structure.

THE MEASURE OF A MAN. 155

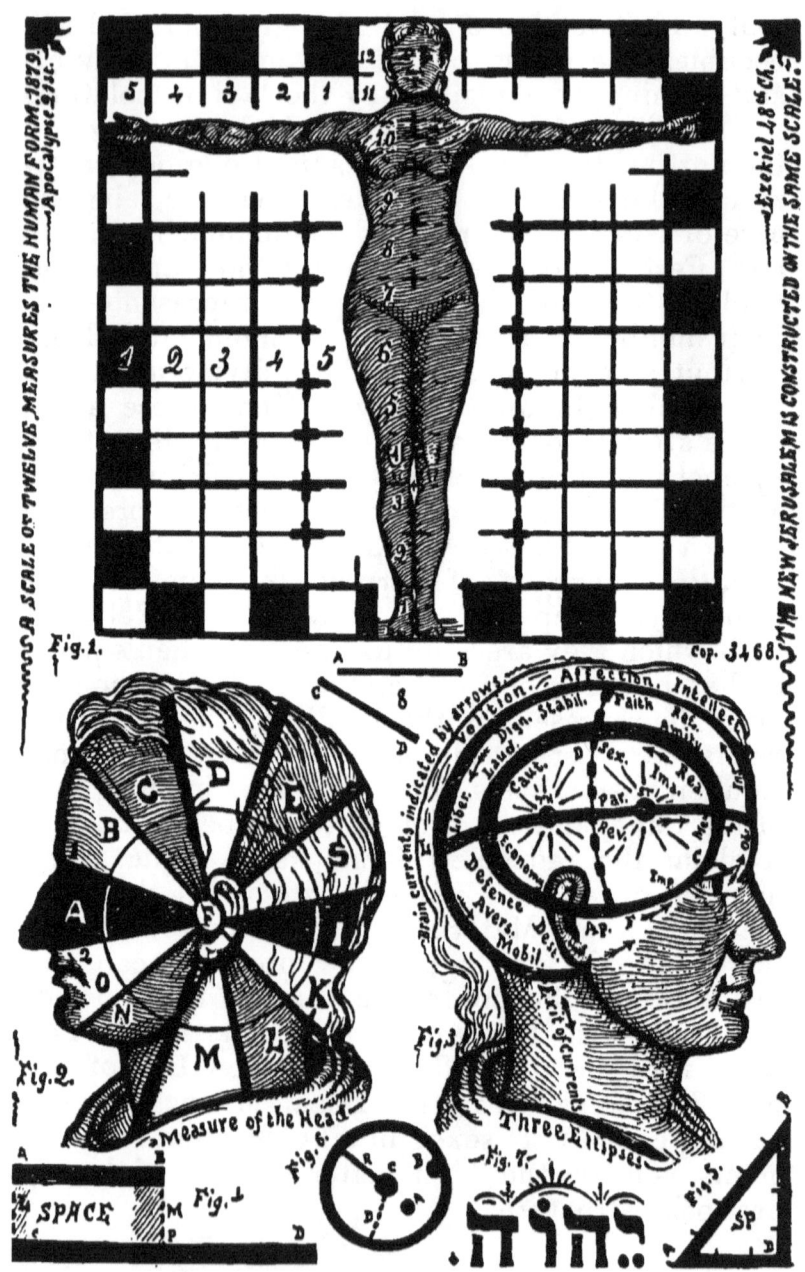

Here, then, we have the most marvelous fact that two objects, the Nation of Israel and the Human Brain, each made up of twelve widely differing parts, yet correspond to each other exactly in the whole character, the arrangement, and the number of these parts. This could not be the result of either accident or of coincidence. For let it be announced that in a certain place, unnamed, there are twelve things, having some certain arrangement, undescribed, and let the whole world set itself to guessing what the twelve things are, and how they were placed. The well known doctrine of mathematical chances proves that they might guess for a hundred centuries but could never solve the problem. We have then, the absolute proof of mathematics, that the parts and plan of the New Jerusalem, and the mental faculties of man as located in his brain and body, have the most fixed relations and adaptations to each other. They were both formed from one eternal model.

But the proof does not end here. If we turn to the Measure of Man, we shall see that a scale of twelve angles, arranged precisely in the order of the twelve squares of the New Jerusalem, is the only scale that will measure the human head. A scale of twelve measures the entire human form, and the angel said that the measure of the City is the measure of a man.

A perfect structure of society includes twelve groups of persons, each having one of the groups of mental organs dominant in its character. But the ancient nation of Israel presented just the same features. The twelve tribes were twelve different kinds of people, each marked by a dominant group of organs, and all united under one government.

Israel was therefore a true type of the final organization of human society. For this reason they were the Chosen People. But they had not discovered the laws of social harmony, and they never carried these laws into practical life. And because they were such a type, their record stands as the central fact in the world's history.

There is only one possible explanation of the facts in this case. Yehovah knew how the twelve groups of faculties are located in the human brain, for man is in his image. He selected Jacob, controlled the forming character of his twelve sons, so that each one had a different set of faculties dominant, and would transmit these characteristics to his descendants.

Yehovah also directed that the camp of the Israelites in the wilderness; the twelve stones in the High Priest's breastplate; and the twelve oxen under the brazen sea in Solomon's temple, should be arranged like the groups in the brain, and like the parts of the city. Teaching the same thing through many symbols during their national history, he at length gave to Ezekiel and to John the visions of the New Jerusalem, as a sublime type ef the everlasting kingdom to be established, and as the actual plan and model to be copied in building all the cities of the new and redeemed earth. The city was both a symbol and a reality.

Jehovah knew that of the twelve groups of the brain, five point downward, and seven point upward. They are not divided equally. That he knew this, is proved by this fact: In ancient Palestine, the twelve tribes were scattered about in irregular patches. But in the vision of Ezekiel, he saw them arranged in regular bands across

Palestine. as shown in the map at the beginning of this chapter. A square and band called the Oblation, was set apart for the city, the priests, and the prince. Then above this were placed seven tribes and below it were placed five, which represented the five lower groups of the brain in the plan of the city ; that is, the tribes of Benjamin, Simeon, Issachar, Zebulon and Gad.

The scientists who discovered and classified the organs of the brain had not the remotest idea that they were mapping out something which was in any way represented in the Bible. This is positively proved by the way in which their discoveries were made and published. Dr. Joseph Francis Gall began his discoveries by observing that his fellow-students, who were distinguished by verbal memory, had full and wide-set eyes. He proceeded step by step to note and compare the leading traits of character in his associates, or others, with their brain development, and thus located organs here and there over the human head. Gall's Works were published at Paris, in six volumes, and he died in 1828. Twelve years later, in 1841, Dr. Joseph Rhodes Buchanan corrected the errors in Gall's locations, and in 1854 published the full results in his "System of Anthropology." In none of these works or maps is there any trace or resemblance to any Bible symbols. Seventeen years later, the Author of this Book discovered that the organs were in twelve groups, a thing which Gall and Buchanan did not imagine. They had discovered the one mental law of Location, and part of another, that of Impressions. The Author discovered the remaining ten great laws, and published these from 1859 to 1866, Common

Era. But the Author's maps had been published nineteen years before he saw that the twelve groups had the same character and arrangement as the parts of the New Jerusalem.

All these facts prove that there was no intention on the part of these scientists to plan out something which should fit and explain the Bible. Any mistake in locating the groups would have spoiled the whole arrangement and resemblance. And if the Author had not discovered the true structure of a perfect Society, based upon the wants and faculties of man, then there would have been no practical value in the resemblance. The traits of character which marked each tribe of Israel were well known to Bible students. But none of these students suspected that if we put all these traits together they will exactly cover the twelve groups of faculties which make up the human mind.

The New Jerusalem was planned after the noblest model that the human mind can conceive. For man is the image of the Divine Being, and every one of his faculties and the proportion and relations of these, are faithful copies of the divine original.

The Messianic Kingdom is both material and spiritual. Everyone of its departments has its direct source and counterpart in some department of man's spiritual nature. Thus the department of Science, has its source in the Reasoning faculties ; that of Religion has its counterpart in the religious organs, and so of every part of the social structure, its foundation is in the spiritual nature of man. This was never before true of any system of government or national life.

This is the first form of civil society which has ever recognized reform and growth as normal and proper. Ample provision is made for these through its groupate of Culture.

It will never need to be changed for another form of society. For its constitution is in complete harmony with that of man, and it will permit of his unlimited advancement throughout coming ages.

Each tribe in the City is ruled by a male and female chief, and over these are the Prince and Princess, twenty-six rulers in all. Twenty-six is the number of the sacred name, Jehovah, and Ezekiel declares this name is embodied in the very plan of the City, and the Apocalypse declares the same thing.

Gathering the Tribes.—The work of organizing and locating the Bands of Israel, is the true work of gathering and sealing the twelve tribes of Israel. All nations, whether lineal descendants of Jacob or not, are to be thus sealed and gathered. They cannot have the name of Jehovah in their foreheads or in their hearts, unless they are in tribes, for the meaning of the tribes is in the number of his name, which represents the twenty-six rulers, two for each tribe and two centers.

Each band in society is like the ancient nation of Israel in miniature, and each state and nation presents the same features on a larger scale. The group of Religion is formed of members with dominant religious faculties; they are like the ancient Levites. Those with leading ambitious faculties are Josephites and go into the group of Rulership. And so of all the groups in society. By knowing what traits of character predominate in a person, we can tell at once to what groupate or tribe that person belongs.

When this work of grouping is established throughout the world, then all the lost tribes of Israel will be gathered and each person will be placed in his own tribe. We do not need to trace out his lineage, a thing which would be impossible now, for the genealogies are long since lost. We are guided by definite scientific knowledge, and require no miracle to direct us in the work of selection.

The tribe of Judah, mixed with that of Benjamin and part of Levi, are with us to-day as a distinct and easily recognized people, the modern Jews. The other ten tribes never returned after the Captivity, 720 B. C. They lost their distinctive name, but their descendants must still exist as a numerous people among the nations of the earth. There is a fairly proved chain of historical evidence which shows that the modern Anglo-Saxons are these ten tribes. But it is not necessary to prove this in order to fulfil the prophecies. We must not only be able to recognize the ten tribes as a whole but also exactly what tribe each person belongs to, in order to restore them to their true places. The work of identification would be useless without this definite knowledge.

The prophets declare that the Messianic Kingdom shall extend over the whole earth, and include all nations, with Palestine as their center. The great mass of the Jews will return to the land of their fathers. But many will remain in the countries where they are now, but the societies in which they live will be bands of Israel, with all the twelve tribes represented. The prophets say that many other people will be among the Israelites when they return, and that these shall have their inheritance with whatever tribe they may cast their lot.

Obeying the supreme law of Yehovah, the stick of Joseph is here joined with that of Judah, the long rent houses of Judah and Israel are united forever, and in them all the nations shall be blessed.

On the site of the ancient capital of Palestine a new City shall lift its magnificent domes toward heaven. The geographical center of the earth shall become the center of unity and power for all nations. And the ransomed of Yehovah shall return, and come to Zion with songs and everlasting joy upon their heads. The law of Yehovah go forth from Zion and the word of Yehovah from Jerusalem. For in the very plan of the New Jerusalem are embodied and illustrated the great laws of personal and national righteousness. The arrangement of its parts shows the balances and responses of the different parts and interests of society. Measuring in either direction across the city we will find parts which balance and respond to each other according to the laws of social polation. The Archetype of Society will illustrate these vital responses.

The front and back groups, on the same level, respond to each other, and their action pivots on the one between them. For example, the group of Art produces, and that of Commerce distributes, while both center upon the Home, or where their materials must be stored. Without material Wealth the group of Letters would not lead men to accumulate the records of knowledge, and without the family group between them, men would not perpetuate these records in families and communities. The group of Science discovers and invents, and then that of Labor applies these inventions in practical life. Both these have a high center in the vitally creative forces of marriage. The group of Culture leads us to improve and perfect our character, and then the group of Rulership impels us to take that rank in society which our culture merits. Both groups center upon Religion, for this includes in a comprehensive way, our relations to humanity and to the divine life.

In the New Life, the members of society make temporary exchanges of employment or of position with those who are their thirds, fifths, or octaves. For example, those in the department of Food-culture may exchange with those who are in the department of Luxuries; those in the groupate of Wealth may exchange with those in the groupate of Rulership. The different branches of labor are therefore related to each other by fixed and eternal laws of harmony.

Through these exchanges, the members secure a wide but systematic variety in their work and pleasures. And by thus calling all their faculties into activity, they prevent that partial development of personal character which would result from incessantly using a few faculties in one vocation. Such exchanges and harmonies were not possible in any of the societies of civilism.

The labors of society should succeed each other according to the law of mental responses. For example, the mind is rested and harmonized by passing from the work or amusements of the groupate of Art to those of Science; from that of the Family to that of Religion; from that of Wealth to that of Rulership. These groupates are thirds. The other responses up and down are Culture and Letters Marriage and Commerce.

The labor aud amusements of each day are to be arranged, as far as possible, in harmony with this law of alternation. These laws will exalt human labor to a noble kind of music, a rhythmic response of life to life.

In the new life, the division of the day should be based upon that of the mental classes, Intellect, Affection, and Expression. Each of these occupies about one third of the brain, and a corresponding division of the day would give four hours for intellectual culture and action; four hours for social relations; and four hours for physical labor and exercise. The social faculties include the sensitive group, and hence eating and the duties of the toilet come within the hours given to these faculties.

The whole structure of society is thus an exquisite piece of mechanism. From its three great departments down to its groupates, all of its parts are vitally responsive and interdependent, An imperative law of nature unites all the collective interests of society.

Such is the framework and form of society through which alone the new and perfect life of the redeemed earth can be expressed. And by the rigid, mathematic tests of science we have proved that this is identically what is represented by the great Bible promises of a Messianic Kingdom, and typified by the ancient nation of Israel.

It was to the founder of such a kingdom that every prophecy of a coming Messiah referred, in language not to be mistaken. That kingdom is both material and spiritual. Its duration is eternal, for it is based upon eternal laws. Its twelve foundations are these ; Art, Letters,, Science, Culture, the Home, the Family, Marriage, Religion, Rulership, Labor, Wealth, and Commerce. The laws governing these include the whole of a perfect life, for both persons and nations. And these laws are written in the constitution of man, in his inward nature, where Jeremiah says that the New Covenant should be found written. It should not be merely upon tables of stone, like the Mosaic law. All other systems of government have been the contrivances of man, but this is cut out of the mountain without men's hands. Although God had told man so emphatically where the New Covenant would be found, yet no one seemed to believe what he said and no one searched in the constitution of man to find it, until twenty years ago, when the successful explorations described in this book were commenced.

The Hebrew prophets speak of the government in the Messianic age as a Kingdom. But it is not a kingdom in the old sense of the term. It is not maintained by arbitrary decrees. It is a perfect Republic, for all of its rulers must be elected by a free choice of its members, and it recognizes no organic laws except those written in the very nature of man, and fully demonstrated by the fixed methods of science. With this understanding, we may still speak of it as a Kingdom but the proper title of its two chief rulers is in English, the Prince and Princess.

The Throne.—Both Ezekiel and John saw the vision of a great Throne. In our engraving of this throne of Israel, the central sun shows the two central rulers. The emerald bow represents Love and Wisdom, the uniting forces of society. Around this are the twenty-four rulers, two for each group or tribe. The Author painted these diagrams to represent the brain and the rulers of society, two years before he saw that they corresponded, even to the very colors. to the description of the throne in the Bible.

The major and minor axes divide the brain into four great lines of movement, and these are represented by the four living creatures around the throne, as shown in the engravings. The front lines includes the peculiar characteristics of man, These faculties measure, and the word Man means one who measures. The upward line of aspiration was typified by the eagle. The Ambitious and Defensive faculties unite on the backward line, and these give the traits which were supposed to be dominant in the character of the lion. The Sensitive, perceptive and impulsive groups center on the downward line, and their traits belong to the character of the ox.

Each creature had six wings, and each of these four regions contains six leading faculties, and these appear to spread out like wings, if we look at the drawings which show the plan of the brain. They were full of eyes, and the microscope shows these in the multitude of nerve cells, each an eye of the soul, in form and in use.

Second Seal.—When this was opened, one came forth on a red horse. The color of this determines that its place was in the group of Labor, just as the white horse and word Logos of the first seal placed that in the group of Science.

The second seal represents Labor, or the tribe of Dan, coming to execute judgment. Dan is a serpent by the path, and in Europe and America Labor was forced to organize in secret. It bites the horses heels, and the rulers fall backward, fall out of power and place. And then shall come salvation, said the Patriarch of Israel. For then organized Industry shall supplant civilized competition, Labor shall then no more be cursed. No longer a serpent. it walks erect in wisdom.

In vain may the rulers of earth seek to avert the blow, and to perpetuate their power. A greater power than theirs has opened the seal. Justice has long slumbered, but the hand that wields the sword is swift, mighty, and ubiquitous.

Third Seal.—This was represented by a rider on a black horse, with a pair of balances in his hand. It belonged to the group of Commerce and symbolizes the first form of the Atonement. This will lead us to consider and correct a great mistake which has been made in regard to nature of sacrifices. and their use among the ancients.

Nature of Sacrifices.—The Sacrifice was a feast offered by man to Yehovah. It was a feast expressing reconciliation, or goodwill, or gratitude. The entire Mosaic laws on this subject, the history of ancient Israel, as well as that of all nations, prove conclusively that this was the character and the import of all the sacrifices. This will appear very clear if we briefly consider the actual facts of the case.

First then, we must note that every object offerred in sacrifice consisted of some kind of food. It must be in a condition to be eaten before it could be accepted as a sacrifice. If of flesh, it must be cooked ; if of fruit, it must be ripe.

Among all eastern nations, the act of eating

with a person who has been offended, is regarded as an indication and a symbol of reconciliation. If man had offended the Deity, then he would offer him gifts of the best fruits and flesh just as he would to an earthly prince or a friend. If the man's offence had been great, he would not partake of the feast himself, but would stand meekly by and witness the "sweet smelling savor" ascend to Yehovah.

Hebraists inform us that the word *olah*, by which the burnt offering was commonly called, signifies that which ascends; the flesh is spoken of not as destroyed by burning, but rather as sent up in the fire like incense to Yehovah. The phrase "sweet smelling savor" is used so often, even in regard to the greatest of the sin-offerings, that there can be no possibility of mistaking that it was as food, as something to gratify the appetite, and to symbolize that life which we derive from food, it was for this that Yehovah accepted the sacrifice. It was a most appropriate and a most striking symbol that man's life, seperated by sin from that of God, was, through returning obedience, again united to its divine fountain. A token that man and God were again partaking of a common life. In most of the sacrifices, the priest, acting as the representative of the people, partook of the sacrifice, ate a part of it. And in the greatest of all the sacrifices, that of the Paschal Lamb or Passover, (see Exodus 12:27) the people ate the whole of it; not a morsel must be left.

We must next observe that the element of Pain, the shedding of blood and killing the animal, was never in any case, a part of the sacrifice, nor is it mentioned as such. There were directions about the way the animal should be killed, just as the Jews were then, and are at the present time, careful about how animals are to be killed for common food. And because the blood contains all the elements of life, all the materials out of which the living structures of the body are formed, therefore the blood was very properly used as a symbol. While it was yet warm and living, it was sprinkled upon the altar or upon the people, as a token of the interchange of life between man and Yehovah. If the blood became cold or coagulated, and thus showed any indication of death, then it could not be used. So careful was the Law to exclude the idea of death, of pain, or of punishment, from the sacrifice. These formed no part of its meaning.

The sacrifice represented a present fact, then and there accomplished. The reconciliation must take place before the sin offering could be made. It was not a prophecy of something in the future, it symbolized a fact already past. It was not a prophecy except in this sense; that in the Kingdom, man will yield a constant obedience and will enjoy an equally constant and conscious union with the divine life.

There have been nations so degraded as to eat human flesh as food. So, too there have been those who offered human sacrifices. But among the Israelites, this was forbidden under the most awful penalties and curses of Yehovah. And surely if this were so revolting in the symbol it could not be less shocking in the antitype. Neither Jesus nor any other man, could be offered as a sacrifice under the law. Surely the the law cannot be satisfied by violating both its letter and its spirit in the most flagrant manner.

If the law had allowed a human sacrifice, the body of Jesus must have been completely bled and then cooked, before it could be accepted. Well may our minds recoil from such a horrible picture. It is as far from the divine law as it was from the actual facts recorded in the gospel narrative. Crucifixion is a bloodless death. The nails were driven through the hands and feet at a place almost devoid of arteries and veins. Therefore the blood of Jesus was not shed on the cross. The two ounces, mixed with water, which came from his heart case, was dead blood and therefore could not be offered under the law. Christians have taught that the Paschal lamb was the chief type of Jesus, among the sacrifices. If this were true. then the people should have cooked and eaten his body.

The Apocalypse speaks of those "whose robes were made white in the blood of the Lamb". We must remember that this lamb, slain from the foundation of the world, can not be the individual man Jesus. For he was slain but once. But it does mean the lamb in man, or the spiritual side of his nature, which has always been persecuted, trampled down, and slain, by his lower nature, from the time of Abel down. Just as in Isaiah the lamb and the wolf were to dwell in harmony ; but this does not mean the lamb in the one man Jesus, it means the lamb and the wolf in every individual member of the Messianic kingdom. In this sense, the passage is broad as the redeemed race of man. And it is then more than a mere figure of speech, it has more than a spiritualized meaning. For the lower faculties when they rule are nourished by blood which is actually feverish and turbulent. When the higher faculties, the spiritual side, rule in the character, the blood that circulates in them is clear and pure, just as the radiated light from these faculties is white in color. The true doctrine thus comes directly home to the personal life and conduct of every man. It is in each of us that the blood of the lamb must purify the temple of life. The Messiah was a pre-eminent type of the Lamb, and the great leader of men in the work of overcoming the lower powers.

The Christian theory of the Atonement was based upon a total misconception of the nature of the divine laws and sacrifices. It contradicted alike the certain truths of history and of science.

The real truth of the Atonement is twelve hundred million times greater than was their misconception. For the law of the atonement is universal, uniting all men in the pulsating tides of a common spiritual life. It has been proved in the fourth chapter of this book that the currents of spiritual life constantly flow outward from every person and reach and effect other persons. In the selfish antagonism of civilized society these currents are the source of discord. But in the true life they are the source of the most intense and exalted pleasures. It is through these same currents that our lives are united with those of spiritual beings in higher realms of existence. It is impossible for us to escape from this law. Each of us gives and receives from the spiritual life of our associates. We live by perpetual interchange.

In this way the strong must help the weak, the virtuous must give moral life and power to the erring, and each man make atonement for his fellows. The good of one is through that of others. To give is to live.

To confine the atonement to one man and to one event, as the Christians have done, is to make the doctrine only a monstrous falsehood, thoroughly selfish in the motive it presents, and utterly opposed to all the laws of justice, of vital sympathy, and of causation.

Sacrifices Restored. — In our life in the messianic kingdom every meal will be eaten and regarded as a sacrifice. For we shall realize the fact that the life of our food, from which our own life is constantly supplied, has its central source in the life of Yehovah, and our union with his life will be conscious, full, and perpetual.

At the vernal and at the autumnal equinoxes will be the two great sacrificial feasts of the year. The two secondary feasts will be at the summer and the winter solstice. The third class of minor feasts will be every twelfth day. Over all these feasts the Pastor will preside. His office is the higher octave of Appetite.

In that life, Yehovah has promised that "He will dwell with men," he will not simply come as an occasional guest, to eat at a special table. Therefore there will not and need not be altars on which to offer the sacrifices. Every eating table be a consecrated altar in the true life.

When we urge a person to do right instead of wrong, telling him that he can reform if he will, our own nerve-force added to his may be sufficient to turn the scales of his mind in favor of the right. The earnest and true reformer should address the highest faculties, and enlist the sympathies of the public feeling, if he would open the most direct channel of influemce.

Obedience and Law. — Obedience brings Life,

in every sphere of existence. For the human constitution, the nature of our faculties and their laws of action, remain the same whether we exist in a physical or a spiritual world. We may fail to fulfill, but we cannot break or destroy a law. Thus it is a law of circulation that the finger must receive blood through its arteries and return this toward the heart through its veins, in order to maintain its life. Now if we cut off the finger, the law can no longer be obeyed, but it remains in existence all the same, and therefore the finger loses its life. If the law were really destroyed, if it ceased to be true, then very possibly the lfie of the finger might continue after the violation.

The violator in no case suffers individually the entire penalty. For by the laws of the nerve force a part of the evil results are invariably communicated to others. In a true constitution of society the incentives to wrong doing will be reduced to a minimum. Each person will see clearly that to do right will most certainly and directly lead to his pleasure. Society has often been so organized that it seemed to some of its members that wrong doing was the easiest and most direct way to secure private happiness.

The object of the physician is to cure the sick man of his disease, and not to destroy his life. And so in Messianism, the object of penal measures is social health. The motive of punishment is not vengeance, but restoration. The transgressor is still bound by social ties to the rest of society.

The same living organs, the same vital powers, are in action in states of disease as in states of health. In disease, these organs or powers have been interfered with, by bad conditions. The process of cure consists in restoring good conditions, and in adding such new ones as the altered states of the organs demand.

Length of life.—The amount of life is measured by the variety of powers, and the ability to resist those causes which tend to destroy the body. This quantity increases from infancy to maturity. Causes which would destroy the life of a child, seem scarcely to affect the health of an adult. There is no reason, that we have learned, why our physical existence might not be continued indefinitely, if all of the conditions of life were fully maintained.

The most eminent medical men in Europe and America are agreed that if the laws of health were obeyed there would be no disease, and in that case life might be as easily prolonged to a thousand years as to a hundred. The prophet, or rather Yehovah, promises that in the new heavens and new earth people shall live as long as a tree, that death itself shall be swallowed up in eternal life. A tree lives one or two, or even five thousand years. There certainly is nothing in science to oppose the idea of such a life for man.

Worth of Life. — But suppose that we were not assured of immortality, yet we can be absolutely certain that human life could be ushered in by a painless birth, that through long centuries it can be one scene of unalloyed happiness, that when old age should finally come, it would be a gradual fading out of life. We know that for generation after generation, human beings must live on this earth. And the possibility of removing the great evils of the race, is sufficient to move us to the mightiest efforts to transform the old conditions of human life, and banish the dark hosts of disease, of social wretchedness and of national discord, from the fair face of the earth. Life may be made eminently worth living.

With the higher development of the nervous system, the causes which influence the physical health of man become more and more of a spiritual nature, more and more dependent upon his intelligent obedience to higher laws of spiritual life.

Human life is not simply individual, each one independent of the rest. Our lives are so bound up in the lives of others, that as separate individuals we cannot yield a full obedience to the laws of life. There must be a collective obedience of society, before the life of any one of its members can be complete, or secure.

Fourth Seal.—The symbol of this was a pale horse, and it represents the reign of death through Appetite and the senses. This began in the Garden of Eden with the Tree of Life. It must end by opening the way of the Tree of Life, as we shall see in the following exposition.

The Cell.—The molecules of bioplasm arrange themselves in the form of Cells. The cell is usually microscopic in size, it may have an external cell-wall, and an internal circulation of its parts around the nucleus, N. The cell is the organic unit of structure. For all vegetable and animal tissues are formed by the evolution and action of these minute cells.

In the mineral or lifeless world, we find the unit of structure in the Crystal. The crystal is bounded by straight lines, and its poles, or lines of force, ipoint outside of itself, as seen at AB, CD, and EF, n t he initial engraving. The cell, on the other hand, also posseses circular polarity.

The cells are the units with which all living structures are built. But a pile of cells without any order would no more form a living organ than a pile of stones without order would form a stone house. There must be a definite plan for the arrangement of these units of life, and in the Leaf or Tree we find this plan perfectly exemplified.

Tree of Life.—The plan of the Leaf, as shown in our initial, essentially consists of a central tube or vein, with branches or subdivisions which terminate in minute cells, as seen at C. C. C. The reason why this plan is assumed, is found in a fundamental law of liquids. Both animal and vegetal tissues and organs, from the fragile nerve-substance to the dense, hard bone and wood, are formed from the plasmic blood and sap. About three fourths of both blood and sap consists of water. Wherever a circulation of water is established, it assumes the form of a tree. This is seen, for example, in all the rivers of the earth. If we gently pour water which has been thickened with paint, or otherwise, into a shallow dish of clear water, or, pour the thin into the thick liquid, then we shall see it spread out in the exact form of a leaf or tree.

In the cells of the leaf the vital changes take place. They convert the soluble materials, which have arisen through the stem of the plant, into gum, starch, and the substance of woody fibre. The tubes of the leaf are channels for the passage of liquids or of waves of force.

The leaf epitomizes the tree. Both have evidently the same plan. The trunk of the tree is a mass of tubes, like the midveins of the leaf. And the limbs of trees imitate all the forms of branching which we find in the veins of leaves.

If we dissect out the arteries, the veins, the lungs, the glands, the nerves, or any other organ of the animal body, we shall perceive that each one is formed on the plan of the leaf, and its parts exercise the same relative functions. We see this plainly in the tubes and aircells of the lungs, and in the various organs shown in the engraved plan of the physical organism.

The human brain is the highest and most perfect example of these tree-forms. The spinal cord is a vast bundle of nerve-tubes, and it passes upward, branching out through the striatum and thalamus toward the surface of the brain, where they terminate in the multitude of nerve cells, which compose the convolutions. This is shown in the engraved Plan of the Brain, and on the next page. This last is only idealized so far as to be taken out of the body and planted in the earth, and to have its cells enlarged so as to be visible to the naked eye. It is physiologically exact. The tree form is very evident in this drawing. We do not mean that the brain merely looks like a tree, or resembles one externally. But we do mean that it is an actual tree, and that by the most rigid scientific examination it is shown to fulfill the ideal type and plan of a tree more completely than any tree of the vegetable kingdom.

The spinal cord is the trunk of this great tree, and its roots are the nerves of feeling and motion, branching out over the body. It is a tree planted in the midst of many others, in a garden of Eden.

The brain of man is the great Tree of Life, spoken of by the ancient poets and seers of all nations. Its twelve groups of organs bear twelve kinds of fruit. And through the phases of childhood, youth, and maturity, it brings forth these fruits in succcession. In more than a hundred passages of the Bible, the conduct and feelings of man are spoken of as fruit. And through the language or literature of all nations are scattered abundant figures of speech based upon an instinctive sense of the great truth concerning this tree. In all ages, man has instinctively felt that in the tree was a type of himself. He gave expression to this perception in the Etz Hakeyim of Genesis, the Bo-Tree of Bhuddha, the Soma-Tree of the Persians, the Tooba-Tree of the Koran, the Olive of Minerva, the Oak of the Druids, the Ygdrasil of Scandinavia, and the sacred trees of other nations.

All that is sweet and noble and true, in human life and history, has been the fruit of this tree. Through past ages its lower branches have borne evil fruit, but in the New Life, the system of integral education will cultivate all of these in harmonic symmetry, and the institutions of society will embody them in all their fulness of immortal beauty.

The system of Education evolved in the next chapter was a direct deduction from the law we are now considering. The physical side of this law teaches us that each kind of food we eat, each grain or fruit, has a specific influence upon some special faculties of the brain, in either promoting or retarding their growth and action. On these important relations is founded the system of food and diet in the messianic life, as described in the twelfth chapter.

The leaves of the tree are for the healing of the nations. The lower branches of this tree point downward, and these ruled in the early ages of

THE TREE OF LIFE.

the world. They produce downward motions of the body, and hence it is said that Adam and Eve fell by eating their fruit. To them it was only a tree of the knowledge of good and evil. The fruit of the higher branches must be eaten with that of the lower ones, to produce perfect life.

The Bible does not say that Adam fell. It does not say that he was good, and pure, and wise, before eating of the tree. He was made in the divine Image with all of its parts and proportions, but he was not unfolded, either intellectually or morally. The Doctors of Religion taught, in this respect, what was never a part of the Bible or of its teachings.

On each side of the Tree of Life is the River of Life, the great artery and vein through which the currents of blood flow perpetually, The blood looks as clear as crystal when seen through the microscope, the eye of science. The blood is three fourths water, and through this are diffused the living materials which are to construct and maintain the bodily organs. The arteries and veins have the same plan as a river. In the garden of Eden the river parted from four heads. This is exactly true, for the heart is the head of this river and it has four chambers, or cavities, the two auricles and the two ventricles. In branching over the body, this river divides into four parts at seventeen different points. One branch of the river forms a network around the very trunk of the tree and spreads upward among its expanding limbs, as shown in the engraving. Thus, to the minutest details, the tree of life described in the Bible is proved to be a reality. We may look upon the great civilizations as springing directly from the different branches of this tree. The Messianic civilization will unite the lower and the higher branches in a perfect fruition.

Fifth Seal. — This covered the doctrine of the Resurrection, another name for the doctrine of Re-incarnation, accepted by so many ancient nations.

Among the Jews, many belived that the spirits of the ancients might come back and permanently occupy the bodies of persons who appeared to have been born in the usual way. Thus Jesus affirmed that John the Baptist was the old prophet Elijah, and some of the Jews thought that Jesus was an old prophet risen again.

According to the prophecies, this re-incarnation was to become frequent and common during the Messianic Age. Science now proves to us that when the human race passes fully into its great phase of Maturity, the spiritual faculties of the upper brain will rule in all the departments of life. The whole character of man will be transformed. For the first time, his character will be brought into complete unison with the spiritual forces and life of the universe. He will then be able to yield a full obedience to their high laws, and thus counteract all forces which tend to destroy his organism. He will then become himself a Master of Life, through perfect obedience. The duration of his life will be coextensive with his desires. As the days of a tree shall be the days of my people.

With that change in the body and mind of man will come that development called by Jesus the New or Spiritual Birth. Then the spiritual senses will be quickened and refined so much that all persons will see the nerve-spheres of their associates, and thus the high and intimate communion of souls will be established, and the body itself will be illumined and made beautiful by its indwelling and radiated light.

In the Resurrection, the men of ancient times will reappear with bodies and features of the face closely like those which they possessed when living on the earth before. Abraham, Jacob, and Joseph will recognize each other's faces as readily as two friends who meet day by day. Their likenesses have not been transmitted to us, and they may not bear the same names as before, but other names more fully expressive of their characters. But they themselves will certainly know who they are.

The resurrection is a re birth. And just as a tree planted in the ground has its life transmitted and comes up with a new body having the same character as the old, so are we to consider must be the manner of the resurrection. Resurrections will occur during the many years occupied in establishing the kingdom, as well as afterward.

Earthly and Heavenly.—The seven upward pointing groups form the heavenly side, and the five lower ones form the earthly side of man's nature. Each of these two sides has twelve great personal types in the Hebrew Scriptures. In this table the person who represents the earthly side is placed first in each pair.

Adam – Eve.	Ishmael–Isaac.	Caleb–Joshua.
Cain – Abel.	Esau – Jacob.	Eli–Samuel.
Japhet – Shem.	Reuben–Joseph.	David–Solomon.
Abraham–Sarah.	Moses–Aaron.	Aleyah-Alesha.

When the colors of the seven upper groups are mixed, they produce light or bright tints. Those of the five lower ones produce darkness. The upper ones are called the seven Lamps, the seven Eyes of God, the seven Spirits. Through them comes the spiritual light of the mind.

In prophetic writings as well as in common language, the power of the lower faculties and back brain are symbolized by the Beast, the Dragon, the wolf, the lion, the serpent and other lower animals, in which these lower faculties are ruling elements. The gentle qualities of the lamb, the horse, and the dove, led to the adoption of these as symbols of the higher parts of man's nature.

The lion and the ox, the wolf and the lamb, the serpent and the dove, represent the polar organs of the human brain. In the engraved head of the Reign of Peace, the names of these animals are placed in their appropriate localities, and around these are the organs with underscored lines.

In the early ages of the world, and up to the time of writing this Book, the base and back brain, the lion and the wolf in man, have always devoured the lamb and its work. The Lamb in man, in all men, has been slain from the foundation of the world. But the prophets declare that in the age of the Messiah these shall be at peace, the wolf and the lamb, the lion and the ox, shall dwell in unity, and a little child shall lead them.

The child belongs to the Family group, where the parental, filial, and patriotic faculties are located. We see on the head that its location is midway between the animals which are to be reconciled. The prophetic language is in a high degree figurative, yet to an equally high degree it is also scientifically exact and literal.

In the New Life of Israel, the organism of society is so planned that the lower faculties must always be subordinate to the higher ones. The once conflicting interests of the society are adjusted and balanced by fixed and natural laws of harmony. The fierce and selfish passions which led to war and oppression can no longer rule the nations. The whole character of these lower passions will be changed, softened, and directed to new objects, by the higher powers.

The great Battle with the Beast is already begun. It is the conflict of both spiritual and material forces, of both institutions and nations. And woe to the statesman who puts on his followers the " mark of the Beast." And he does put this mark on them if he says that selfinterest, or in other words, the beastly faculties, must rule in politics or in social life. The Cotton and Rail-Road Kings, the Merchant Princes and Bankers of Christian Civilization, have the same brand of darkness on their right hands.

The Seer of Patmos saw the word Mystery, in Greek, Mysterion, written on the forehead of the great image of Babylon. The forehead is the seat of the understanding, the intellect, the eye of the mind. Hence a mark on the forhead must mean a mark on the understanding, in our intellectual conceptions or knowledge. The lower faculties specially delight in mystery, in secret methods, in great swelling words of vague import, in things which perplex our reason, and foil philosophy. In deliberately affirming and teaching " that the Doctrines of Religion are Essential Mysteries" not to be penetrated by the reason of man, in teaching and beliving this, the Protestant, the Catholic, and Greek Churches have alike branded themselves on the forehead with the accursed mark of the Beast and of Babylon. There is no other possible interpretation to this mark of darkness.

Law of Symbolism. — The process of Construction or growth always involves a succession of steps, taken in a definite order. Thus in the construction of a house, there must first be a foundation, and then the framework, the walls, the roof, floors, plastering, and finally the finish of paint and paper. In the growth of a plant, there is the succession of the seed, the plumule and radicle, the stem, branches, leaves, flowers, and fruit. But conversely, the process of Destruction requires no regularity. We may destroy a house or a tree in a hundred irregular ways. We may burn it, or cut it down, or tear it in pieces, or let it perish by natural decay.

This great law, governing constructive and destructive processes, must apply fully to prophetic symbolism. Those symbols which refer to the formation of new institutions should be fulfilled with exactness of form and order. But those which refer to the destruction of old institutions and modes of life need never be fulfilled with any precision. In the latter class of symbols there are many monstrous objects, such as never had or will have a literal existence. The Great Red Dragon, the Beast with seven heads and ten horns, and such monstrous images, do not require an exact fulfillment. For they represent destructive things or events. In vain may commentators exert their wits to make these and similar figures fit the events of history with any sort of exactness. The law does not require it. These destructive symbols occupy four fifths of the Apocalypse. The remaining fifth describes the Throne in Heaven, the People sealed in twelve Tribes, the New Jerusalem, and the Tree of Life. These have been explained in the present chapter.

Nature of Deity.—It is necessary to notice and to correct some grave errors into which philosophers have fallen, concerning the Deity, Infinite Space, and a First Cause.

We will use the figures of the engraving "Chart of Space," to illustrate the argument. The scientists tell us that Form, or shape, is an essential property of matter. Every object must possess form. But every form, a circle or a triangle, for instance, must have outlines, limits, or boundary lines. Suppose that in the triangle, we take away the limiting lines AB, BC and AC. There will be no triangle or form left. In the circle, if we remove the circumference or limit, the form disappears. As no object can be deprived of form, so no object can be deprived of limits. As no single object can be without limits, so the universe, or all objects collectively, must have limits.

Take the squares, 1, 2, 3, in the engraving. Now if we start from the outer border of square 1, and pass toward B, we shall see that the last limit or edge of 1 is the first limit of square 2. Passing across this square, we see that its last limit is the first limit of the third square. And so on forever. The last limit of one object is always the first limit of the next. What we always discover in passing from one object to another is the fact, the existence of Continuity. It is not the absence of Limits. The objects are in absolute contact. There is no difficulty whatever in conceiving of the continuity of the universe. Wherever we might go in the universe, we should find on reaching the last line of any one thing that we had reached the beginning of the next thing. This idea is just as simple and clear, when applied to objects a million, or a trillion miles in extent, as it is when applied to squares only an inch across.

We cannot describe the extension of the universe by the negative word Infinite, meaning without limits, or bounds. For that would be to deprive the whole of a property belonging to each of its separate parts. That would be to plunge ourselves into a sea of foolish absurdities.

The mistake of the philosophers was in regard to the nature of Space itself. For they attempted to conceive of space as something which did or could exist separate from matter.. They tried to think of space as an immense Nothing, into which all things have been stuffed. Their abortive conception was as far as it is possible to get from the truth.

Space is an inherent, inseperable property of matter and spirit. No person ever measured any space, or had any distinct cognition of it, except as a part of some object. We have shown, above, that forms can not exist without limits, and this is equally true of space. Suppose we take figure 6, and ask ourselves how we know that there is a difference between the line AB and the line CD. We know it because that if we lay AB on CD, the limit B will not coincide in position with the limit D. The limits of the two lines are not alike, and therefore the space of the two lines is different. Conceal the limits, and then we could not discover the difference between the lines. A line is space having direction. The limits of an object always have position, a definite relation to other parts. Without *limit, direction,* and *position,* no Space can exist, either in fact or in imagination. Extension is the element of space which is described by these three terms. When we have named these, we have included all that belongs to the idea of Space. There is nothing else in the idea to explain. But all these are inseparable from our conception of matter. They are as much a part of the inherent properties of matter as the element of form. No one tries to conceive of Form as separable from objects, and neither can they conceive of Space as separable. In either case, the attempt to form such a conception must end in utter confusion.

There is no such thing as Infinite Space, any more than there is such a thing as Infinite Form. Both terms are as devoid of truth as words can be made. We must substitute a positive conception in place of the old negative notion. For space is the most central and the most positive of all the properties of matter and spirit. The science of Space and Form is Geometry, and this was the first one of all the sciences to be developed. Its propositions are the clearest, and they appeal the most directly to the common consciousness of men. They are the most comprehensible.

As all objects are in absolute contact with adjacent ones, we cannot move any object without moving others. This is proved by the most exact and conclusive experiments of science. Suppose that we take the figure of the three circles to illustrate this truth. For convenience we use the triangle E to indicate the earth, and around this the Water, Air and Ether will represent the whole universe, or all that we can conceive of it. Now if we revolve this circle from the first to the second and third positions, we see that the Water, the Air and Ether all change places with each other; they change their relative position. When one moves the others must move also. There are no blanks between them, no spaces without anything in them. The water, the air and the ether, each keeps all the space it had, all of its magnitude or dimension. The element in which the change takes place, is that of position, the relative direction of the object is no longer what it was at first.

In our common experience, the senses only partly inform us of the actual fact of the case A man walks into a room, and does not see that in order to do so, he had to push a quantity of air, equal to the size of his body, out of the room. He swings his hand in the air, without seeing that he must move the air in order to move his hand. If the air and the ether had been visible to the human eye, then the philosophers would never have thought of forming such an absurd and incomprehensible theory of Space, as that which so long disgraced their works. Upon a vast and vague basis of nothingness they sought to build up the mysteries of theology, and by an impenetrable wall of Infinitude to shut man away from any definite knowledge of his divine Father.

The Universe would be much better named the Totoverse, the All-turning, instead of the One-turning. It is all-extended, not infinite. The terms *finite* and *infinite* can have no place in a system of exact truth. They have served well as bugaboos with which pseudo-philosophers and priests might frighten their timid followers. They have taught the people that as the Deity is infinite, therefore the finite mind of man cannot comprehend him, but must blindly and trustingly accept God and Religion as sublime mysteries. Such teachings are directly opposed to the demonstratious of science and to the plain declarations of the Bible. The prophets say that in the Messianic age all persons shall have a knowledge of Yehovah, from the least to the greatest. But where knowledge fills the mind, there mystery cannot exist.

It is absurd to speak of Yehovah as infinite, to attempt to describe his greatness by a term which altogether excludes the idea of extension. But we can readily understand that Yehovah may be a conscious center of the universe, just as the brain of man may be conscious of all parts of the body. The processes of world growth and of universal motion are all in harmony with the attributes of the Divine Mind, the great centre of all the acting forces.

The Deity is a personal being, and man is in his image. Man has the same number and kind of attributes, but differs in their degree of development. Through a study of man's nature, we may obtain a true knowledge of the Divine Original from which it was copied. An obedience to the laws of Yehovah is only a fulfilment of the true laws of the human constitution. Our affection for him may, and should be, direct, conscious, and reciprocal. Our entire nature, every faculty of our minds, must find its perpetual and complete response in his all-perfect life.

In the Mosaic account, God is represented as creating the world. We must now consider the import of the terms used in that account. The first word used there is Bereshith. Its factors, by analysis, are +2, and 2×26×10. If we translate these sacred numbers, we get this statement: In the primary conception of all things, spirit existed along with matter. These two acted and reacted upon each other according to, or guided by, the twenty-six attributes of Yehovan, until these attributes became expressed in material objects and laws, placing man as the crown of the organic series. No scientist can now speak of the beginnings of world-growth in more exact terms.

The word Bara, translated "create," does not mean to produce from nothing. Its number is 203. This number means that at first there are two things, and these, left free to act upon each other, produce a third thing. Now this is precisely true in every act of making or formation. It must have been as true 6000 years ago as it is to day. The phrase "Vayomer Elohim," "and God said," is used in the account nine times. The number of this phrase is 7×7×7. As 7 means spiritual force or dynamic energy, this phrase means that spiritual force was used three times, or to the fullest possible extent, as the creative factor. It does not mean that God simply uttered the sounds "Vayomer."

It has been supposed that God has a right to rule the world because he made it. But he is not the God of the dead, but of the living. His rulership depends upon his now being the center of all spiritual forces.

Another error of many philosophers was in regard to a first Cause. A single example will illustrate this. The chemical change of combustion in a lamp is a cause of light. But this light, in turn, causes an impression or effect in the eye. And this effect in the eye, is in its turn the cause of an impression on the brain; and this in turn becomes the cause of a succession of thoughts or of emotions. Now in this case the motion is transferred from one object to another, and what is an effect at one end of each step is a cause at the other end. Cause and Effect are therefore simply terms to designate the different points of the steps in a line of changes, and that line may always be a circle, because all forces are convertible. Hence it is evident that there cannot be a First Cause of all things, anymore than a beginning to the universe.

In all paths of investigation, science teaches that when a new body is formed, the materials have come from the decomposition of some other body. So far as we know at present, one world or solar system may be forming while another is dissolving. The universe, as a whole, never had a beginning, but renewal and decay repeat the cycles of its perpetual activity.

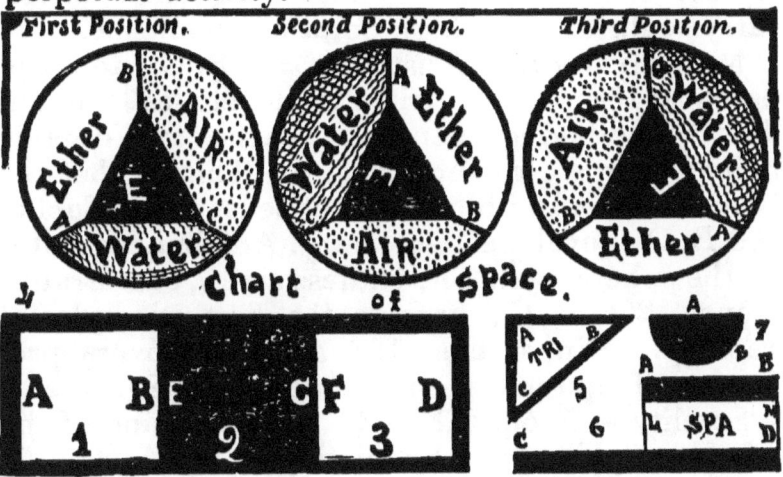

PHASES OF GREEK MENTAL LIFE.

Infancy.—From Homer, 800, B. C., to Thales, 636, B. C. They believed the earth to be flat, and full of dragons, monsters, and marvels.

Childhood.—From Thales to Socrates, 469 B.C. Opening of Egyptian ports, 636 B. C., stimulates Greek thought. Thales teaches that the First Principle is water, and the world has a soul. Anaximander, B. C. 610, discovers obliquity of ecliptic, teaches that the earth is a cylinder; that the sun acts on the miry clay, producing filmy bladders, with a prickly rind, and from these, animals come forth. Pythagoras believes that all things are constituted by the laws of Sacred Numbers.

Youth.—From Socrates, 469 B. C., to Epicurus, 342. Socrates says that mathematics and physics lead to vain conclusions, and Plato thinks that the senses are illusory. He believes that God, Matter, and Ideas are the three primal principles. Epicurus believes in pleasure through temperance, but rejects immortality. Phidias and other artists carry sculpture to a high point of excellence.

Maturity.—From Aristotle, 384, B. C., to Hipparchus, 168 A. C. Aristotle developes the Inductive method in science. Teaches that organic beings form a connected chain. Thinks that the brain is devoid of blood and of sensation. Euclid, 300 B. C., developes Geometry. Archimedes writes on the sphere, cylinder, endless screw, etc. Eratosthenes, 276 B. C., unfolds the first principles of geology. Hipparchus, 168 A. C., discovers precession of equinoxes, and catalogues 1080 stars.

Senility — From 213 B. C. to the closing of the schools of philosophy by Justinian, 529 A. C. It produced mystical and impractical speculations.

WORDS OF THE TEACHERS.

Thou shalt love Yehovah with all thy heart, and thy neighbor as thyself. MOSES, 1571, B. C.

To those of a noble disposition, the earth itself is but one family. Religion is tenderness toward all creatures. HESTOPADES, VISHNU SARMAN. B. C. 1000.

The wise man avengeth his injuries with benefits. LAO-TZE, 604 B.C.

If thine enemy hunger, give him bread to eat; if he be thirsty, give him water to drink. SOLOMON, 1000 B. C.

Hatred does not cease by hatred at any time. Hatred ceases by love. This is the eternal law. DHAMMAPADA, 600 B. C.

The true doctrine consists in having the heart right, and in loving one's neighbor as one's self. Reciprocity is the one rule of practice in life. What you wish done to yourself, that do to others. KONG FU-TSE, 551 B. C. in Lun Yu, 15, 23.

All things whatsoever ye would that men should do to you, do you even so to them, for this is the law and the prophets. JESUS OF NAZARETH, 31 A. C.

The love of all to all, is the moral rule of life. PYTHAGORAS, 500 B. C.

He who commits an injustice is ever made more wretched than he who suffers it. It is never right to return an injury. PLATO, 387 B. C.

As for the Truth, it endureth and is always strong; it liveth and conquereth forever more. It is the strength, the kingdom, the power and the majesty of all ages. ZERUBBABEL, 520 B. C.

To live, is not to live for one's self alone, let us help one another. MENANDER, 293 B. C.

Nature har inclined us to love men, and this is the foundation of the law. Justice devotes itself wholly to the good of others. CICERO, 30 B. C.

The moral condition of the world depends upon three things—Truth, Justice and Peace. RABBI SIMON, 150 B. C.

NERVO-SYSTEM. 195

Brain.
  Mentorgans—Rad. Fibres, Cells, Converg. Fibres.
  Centers—Striatum, Thalamus, Ucenter,
  Commissures—Ucefalon, Callosum Tuberum.

Nutro nerves.
  Fibres—Distributed to all the Organs.
  Ganglions—Cardicus, Gastricus, Pelvicus.
  Bands—Fibres, con. ganglia and Spinal Cord.

Sensi-motors.
  Sensors—Special and Spinal Nerves.
  Centers—Medulla Spinalis, Encephalon.
  Motors—Special and Spinal Nerves.

NUTRO-SYSTEM.

Genitals
  Femorgans—Vulva, Ovary, Uterus.
  Flower—Pistil, Ovary, Stamen.
  Mascuorgans—Penis, Testis, Vesiculus.

Alimentors.
  Ingesters—Mouth, Salivators, Throat.
  Digesters—Stomach, Glands, Intestines.
  Egesters—Anus, Kidneys, Skin.

Circulators.
  Arteries—Pulmonics, Capillaries, Systemics.
  Heart—Auricles, Valves, Ventricles,
  Veins—Pulmonates, Lymphatics, Recursors.

MOTO-SYSTEM.

Muscles.

Flexors,	Head,	Voluntary,	Striated.
Sphincters,	Trunk,	Mixed,	Elastic tis.
Extensors,	Limb,	Involuntary,	Non-Stri.

Body.
  Head—Face, Corona, Neck.
  Trunk—Thorax, Abdomen, Pelvis.
  Limbs——Manupes, Arms, Legs.

Bones.
  Head Bones—Cranium, Nasum, Maxillæ
  Trunk Bones—Ribs, Sternum, Vertebræ..
  Limb Bones—{ Shoulder, Arm, Hand.
                     { Thigh, Leg Foot

CHARACTER OF THE TWELVE TRIBES OF ISRAEL.

As Described in the Bible and by Jewish Historians.

(See Genesis xlix. and Milman's and Benisch's History of the Jews.)

In a perfect structure of Society, the members are in twelve groups, each having a dominant group of mental organs, and devoted to corresponding pursuits. The twelve Tribes of Israel were marked by just these same differences, and hence ancient Israel was a true, though an undeveloped type, of the final Social Organism. The grouping of the members in society is the real work of "sealing in tribes" spoken of in the Apocalypse. The names of the tribes, below, are followed by their ruling mental groups, in SMALL CAPITALS, and by the meaning and number of their Hebrew names, in *italics*. In the Breast Plate and New Jerusalem the tribes have the same arrangement as the mental groups in the brain.

JUDAH. MARRIAGE. Heb.—*Praise.* 5x6. A lion; loving, faithful, and strong. The kingly bridegroom of New Jerusalem and Palestine.

LEVI. RELIGION. Heb.—*Joined or unity.* 46=5x8+6. Religious, zealous and intense. The priests of this tribe held up the Lights and Perfections of Religion.

JOSEPH. RULERSHIP. Heb.—*Adding or Increase.* 6x26. A ruler crowned over his brethren; ambitious, dignified and aspiring; pushing with the horns of the unicorn.

NAPHTALI. CULTURE. *Wrestling.* 570. Swift of foot, bland in manners, speaking good words; his group is in the Line of Progress.

ASHER. SCIENCE. *Bringer of Happiness.* 10x10x5+1. Mixing with the Phœnecians, they became the most scientific of the tri   . The railway, locomotive, and engine are the shoes of iron and brass, bringing luxuries to us all.

DAN. LABOR. *Judging.* 6x9. Shrewd and keen; a swift judge against the oppressors of the poor; striking unjust rulers in secret.

GAD. LETTERS. *A Troop or Multitude.* 7. His seat was with the law-givers, and the multitude of facts he at last gathers into order.

REUBEN. FAMILISM. *See a Son.* 259. Paternal kindness, pious care. Let not his men be few. As the eldest born, he represented the family.

BENJAMIN. WEALTH. *Son of the right hand.* 5x19. Bold, warlike, and acquisitive. A wolf going to the prey and dividing the spoil.

SIMEON. ART OR PERCEPTION. *Hearing or Perception.* 470. The Simeonites became the scribes and musicians, the artists of Israel.

ZEBULON. HOME. *Dwelling.* 178. Love of home and its comforts, of sensuous pleasures, of landscape and waterscape.

ISSACHAR. COMMERCE. *A hire.* 830. A strong ass, bearing two burdens, the beast of Hebrew commerce; a worker for hire

CHAPTER TENTH.

THE PROPHECIES.

The Old Testament or Hebrew Scriptures contains more than four hundred verses which either Jewish or Christian writers have referred to the Messiah and his Kingdom. In order to form a true estimate of what we have a right to expect in that Kingdom, and of how little has been already fulfilled, we shall in this chapter, first present those passages which no one can claim have been fulfilled up to the year 1860; and then these will be followed by verses which were believed to have had a fulfillment before the Christian Era.

These prophecies have been the subject of so many intemperate controversies, that it now requires a sober and careful study to learn the meaning of their important promises. In reading the comments which follows them in this chapter, the reader must not form a hasty judgment from any single paragraph.

THE KINGDOM OF THE MESSIAH.

Its Character as Foretold and Described by the Prophets.

Proof Texts.

Ezek. 1: 15 to 28.
Isa. 25: 6 to 9.
Isa. 11: 1 to 16.
Isa. 32: 1, 2, 17, 18.
Dan. 7: 9 to 16.
Dan. 2: 31 to 45.
Jer. 31: 31 to 40.
Isa. 60: 1 to 21.
Gen. 49: 1 to 28.
Exod. 28: 15–21.
Isa. 65: 17 to 25.
Isa. 35: 1 to 10.
Isa. 49: 1 to 12.
Isa. 4: 1–6.
Isa. 55: 1 to 13.
Isa. 66: 6 to 12.
Gen. 2: 8 to 16.
Ezek. 47: 7 to 12.
Jer. 33; 15 to 22.
Jer. 34: 1 to 15.
Ezek. 34: 10 to 16.
Isa. 11: 10 to 16.
Ezek. 28: 21–26.
Ezek. 36: 28.
Ezek. 37: 15 to 28.
Ezek. 48: 1–35.
Isa. 62: 1–7.
Micah 4: 1–5.
Isa. 43: 1–6.
Ezek. 38: 1 to 23.
Ezek. 39: 1 to 29.
Isa. 28: 16–21.
Isa. 52: 1–12.
Joel 3: 2–13.
Zech. 14: 6–16.
Isa. 19: 18–25.
Mal. 3: 1–5.
Mal. 4: 1–6.

336 verses. These were unfulfilled in 1881. It is claimed that some 60 verses (not any of these) were fulfilled 1800 years since. But that 60 verses is only one-sixth part of the whole number of Messianic verses in the Prophets.

The splendors of the Messianic Kingdom were described by the Hebrew Prophets in all the glowing wealth of Oriental imagery.

They proclaimed that the Veil of Mystery which had so long concealed the realm of spiritual laws from the vision of man shall be rent and removed through the hand of the Messiah. His surpassing wisdom shall establish a perfect system of Life and Government. One which shall forever unite the laws of spiritual with those of physical harmony, the internal with the external worlds. The solid and enduring framework of its laws shall be a reflected part of the Divine Mind itself, and be imaged forth in the very structure of man, an inherent part of his constitution. Its twelve departments were represented by the twelve tribes of Israel, as an undeveloped type. They correspond to every part of man's nature, and provide for every human want.

The beneficent power of that Kingdom shall glorify the earth with universal wealth, physical health, and domestic happiness. No tears shall stain private life, no disease invade and mar our bodily pleasures. and no wars or crimes shall blacken national history. The very face of nature shall be changed and renewed under the molding hand of man.

One clear Standard of Truth shall guide all men with equal safety, so that even the wayfaring man shall not mistake in the way. Under one system of government and with one common language, all nations shall be united in a vast composite life.

In that day, the very age of the Messiah's appearance, the mighty hand of Yehovah shall stretch forth and gather the Twelve Tribes descended from his ancient people of Israel. He shall plant them forever, in the land of Palestine, as the central nation of the world. From its capital, the New Jerusalem, shall go forth the political and moral laws of Yehovah to guide the united nations of the world.

Such was the kingdom to be established by the Messiah, and such are the prophecies unfulfilled in this year 1881 or Hebrew year 5642.

The plan of this Kingdom has now been discovered, and its details demonstrated, through the positive methods of Science. It involves New Institutions of Society. It is NOW READY for adoption, by all nations. And, under divine direction, man must be the instrument to effect its spiritual growth and its material construction.

DESCRIPTION OF THE KINGDOM.

The following description of the Kingdom is given in the exact language of the prophets. It is from the foregoing proof texts and some others, but still does not include all of the Messianic verses.

The reader must bear in mind that by the "House of Israel, or Ephraim," the prophets mean the ten tribes who revolted under Jereboam, and by "House of Judah," or simply Judah, they meant the tribe of Judah with that of Benjamin, and part of Levi. These are now mixed together as the modern Jews.

The New Earth. For behold I create a New Heavens and a New Earth. And the former shall not be remembered nor burden the mind.

But be ye glad and rejoice forever in that which I create, for behold I create Jerusalem a rejoicing and her people a joy, and the voice of weeping shall no more be heard in her.

Duration of Life. Infancy shall no more be reckoned by days, nor old age by years; for a person dying an hundred years old shall be called a child. And they shall build houses, and inhabit them; they shall plant vineyards and eat the fruit of them. They shall not build and another inhabit, they shall not plant and another eat, for as the days of a tree shall be the days of my people, and mine elect shall long enjoy the work of their hands. They shall sit every man under his vine and under his fig-tree, and none shall make them afraid.

They shall not labor in vain, nor give birth to children for trouble; for they are the seed of the blessed of Yehovah, and their offspring with them. And it shall come to pass that before they call I will answer, and while they are yet speaking, I will hear.

Universal Peace. The wolf and the lamb shall feed together, the leopard shall lie down with the kid, and the calf and the young lion together, and a little child shall lead them. They shall not hurt, nor destroy in all my holy mountain, for the earth shall be full of the knowledge of Yehovah, as the waters cover the sea.

The people shall beat their swords into plowshares and their spears into pruning hooks. And nation shall not lift up sword against nation, neither shall they learn war any more.

Yehovah's House. And it shall come to pass in the last days, that the mountain of Yehovah's house shall be established in the top of the mountains, and shall be exalted above the hills, and all nations shall flow unto it. And many people shall go and say, "Come ye, and let us go up to the mountain of Yehovah, to the house of the God of Jacob, and he will teach us of his ways, and we will walk in his paths : for out of Zion shall go forth the Law, and the word of Yehovah from Jerusalem. And he shall judge among the nations, and shall rebuke many people.

The Feast and Veil.—In this mountain shall Yehovah of hosts make unto all people a feast of fat things, a feast of wines on the lees, a feast of fat things full of marrow, of wines on the lees well refined.

And he will destroy in this mountain the face of the Covering cast over all people, and the Veil that is spread over all nations. He will swallow up death in victory! and the Lord Elohim will wipe away the tears from off all faces, and the rebuke of his people shall he take away from off all the earth, for Yehovah hath spoken it. And it shall be said in that day, Lo this is our God, we have waited for him, and he will save us. For Yehovah alone is the Saviour, the Redeemer of Israel.

The City.—Awake, awake, put on thy strength O Zion ; put on thy beautiful garments, O Jerusalem, the holy city ; for herceforth there shall no more come unto thee the uncircumcised and the unclean. Shake thyself from the dust, arise, and sit down, O Jerusalem, loose thyself from the bands of thy neck, O captive daughter of Zion. For thus saith Yehovah, Ye have sold yourselves for naught, and ye shall be redeemed without money.

How beautiful upon the mountains are the feet of him that bringeth good tidings, that publisheth peace and salvation ; that saith unto Zion, Behold thy God reigneth! The watchmen shall see eye to eye, when God shall restore Zion.

Who are these that fly as a cloud, and as the doves to their windows? Surely the isles shall wait for me, and the ships of Tarshish first, to bring thy sons from far, their silver and their gold with them, unto the name of Yehovah thy God, and to the Holy One of Israel, because he hath glorified thee. And the sons of strangers shall build up thy walls, and their kings shall minister unto thee ; for in my wrath I smote thee. Therefore thy gates shall be open continually; they shall not be shut day nor night ; that men may bring unto it the forces of the Gentiles, and that their kings may be brought.

Whereas thou hast been forsaken and hated, so that no man went through thee, I will make thee an eternal excellency, a joy of many generations. Thou shalt also suck the milk of the Gentiles, and shall suck the breasts of kings : and thou shalt know that I Yehovah am thy Savior and thy Redeemer, the mighty one of Jacob. For brass I will bring gold, and for iron I will bring silver, and for wood brass, and for stones iron. I will lay thy stones with fair colors, and thy foundations with sapphires. And I will make of rubies thy battlements, and thy gates into carbuncle stones, and all thy borders into precious stones. I will make thy officers peace, and thine exactors righteousness.

Violence shall no more be heard in thy land, wasting nor destruction within thy borders · but thou shalt call thy walls Salvation, and thy gates Praise. The sun shall be no more thy light by day ; neither for brightness shall the moon give light unto thee ; but Yehovah shall be unto thee an everlasting light, and thy God thy glory. Thy sun shall no more go down ; neither shall thy moon withdraw itself : for Yehovah shall be thine everlasting light, and the days of thy mourning shall be ended.

Thy people shall be all righteous ; they shall inherit the land forever, the branch of my planting, the work of my hands, that I may be glorified. A little one shall become a thousand, and a small one a strong nation : I Yehovah will hasten it in his time.

The Covenant.—And when Abram was ninety years old and nine, the Lord appeared to Abram, and said unto him, I am the Almighty God ; walk before me, and be thou perfect. And I will make my covenant between me and thee, and will multiply thee exceedingly.

And Abram fell on his face, and God talked with him saying, As for me, behold, my covenant is with thee, and thou shalt be a father of many nations. And thy name shall be called Abraham, for a father of many nations I have made thee. And I will make thee exceeding fruitful, and I will make nations of thee, and kings shall come out of thee.

And I will establish my covenant between me and thee and thy seed after thee in their generations, for an everlasting covenant, to be a God unto thee and to thy seed after thee. And I will give unto thee, and to the seed after thee, the land wherein thou art a stranger, all the land of Canaan, and I will be their God. And God said unto Abraham, As for Sarai thy wife, thou shalt not call her name Sarai, but Sarah shall her name be. And I will bless her, and give thee a son also of her ; yea, I will bless her, and she shall be the mother of nations ; kings of people shall descend from her.

The Land Promised.—And the Lord said to Joshua, Moses my servant is dead, now therefore, go over this Jordan, thou, and all this people, unto the land which I do give to them, even unto the children of Israel Every place that the soul of your foot shall tread upon, that I have given unto you, as I said unto Moses. From the wilderness and this Lebanon even unto the great river, the river Euphrates, all the land of the Hittites, and unto the great sea toward the going down of the sun, shall be your coast.

And Jacob dreamed, and behold a ladder set up on the earth, and the top of it reached to heaven ; and behold the angels of God ascending and descending upon it. And, behold, the Lord stood above it, and said, I am the Lord God of Abraham thy father, and of Isaac ; the land whereon thou liest, to thee will I give it, and to thy seed, And thy seed shall be as the dust of the earth ; and thou shalt spread abroad to the west, and to the east, and to the north, and to the south ; and in thee and in thy seed shall all the families of the earth be blessed.

Yehovah showed to Ezekiel in a dream how the Land should be divided in the Restoration ; and it shall come to pass, that ye shall divide it by lot for an inheritance unto you, and to the strangers that sojourn among you, which shall beget children among you ; and they shall be unto you as born in the country among the children of Israel ; they shall have inheritance with you among the tribes of Israel. And it shall come to pass that, that in what tribe the stranger sojourneth, there shall ye give him his inheritance, saith the Lord God.

And these are the going out of the city on the north side, four thousand and five hundred measures. And the gates of the city shall be after the names of the tribes or Israel; three gates northward, one gate of Reuben, one gate of Judah, and one gate of Levi. And at the south side four thousand and five hundred, and three gates, one gate of Simeon, one gate of Issachar, one gate of Zebulon ; and on the east side four thousand five hundred; and three gates, one gate of Joseph, one gate of Benjamin, and one gate of Dan.

At the west side four thousand and five hundred, with their three gates ; one gate of Gad, one gate of Asher, and one gate of Naphthali. It was round about eighteen thousand measures; and the name of the city from that day shall be, the Lord is there, Yehovah Shammah.

The Land Renewed. — The wilderness and the solitary place shall be glad for them; and the desert shall rejoice, and blossom as the rose. It shall blossom abundantly, and rejoice even with joy and singing: the glory of Lebanon shall be given unto it, the excellency of Carmel and Sharon: they shall see the glory of the Lord, and the exeellency of our God.

Strengthen ye the weak hands, and confirm the feeble knees. Say to them that are of a fearful heart, Be strong, and fear not; behold, your God will come with vengeance even God with a recompense; he will come and save you.

Then the eyes of the blind shall be opened, and the ears of the deaf shall be unstopped. Then shall the lame man leap as a hart, and the tongue of the dumb sing: for in the wilderness shall waters break out, and streams in the desert. And the parched ground shall become a pool, and the thirsty land springs of water; in the habitation of dragons, where each lay, shall be grass with reeds and rushes. So shall ye know that I am the Lord your God dwelling in Zion, my holy mountain: then shall Jerusalem be holy, and there shall no strangers pass through her any more. And it shall come to pass in that day, that the mountains shall drop down new wine, and the hills shall flow with milk,, and all the rivers of Judah shall flow with waters, and a fountain shall come forth from the house of the Lord, and shall water the valley of Shittim.

Egypt shall be a desolation, and Edom shall be a desolate wilderness, for the violence against the children of Israel, because they have shed innocent blood in their land. But Judah shall dwell forever, and Jerusalem from generation to generation. For I will cleanse their blood that I have not cleansed: for the Lord dwelleth in Zion.

And the Lord God planted a garden eastward in Eden; and there he put the man whom he had formed. And out of the ground made the Lord God to grow every tree that is pleasant to the sight, and good for food, the tree of life also in the midst of the garden, and the tree of knowledge of good and evil.

And a river went out of Eden to water the garden; and from thence it was parted and became into four heads. The name of the first is Pisorn, that is it which compasseth het whole land of Havilah, where there is gold: and the gold of that land is good: and there is bdellium and the onyx stone.

And the name of the second river is Gihon : the same is it that compasseth the whole land of Ethiopia. And the name of the third river is Hiddekel: that is it which goeth toward the the east of Assyria. And the fourth river is Euphrates.

And the Lord God took the man, and put him into the garden of Eden to dress it and to keep it. And the Lord God commanded the man, saying, Of every tree of the garden thou mayst freely eat; but of the tree of the knowledge of good and evil, thou shalt not eat of it, for in the day that thou eatest thereof thou shalt surely die.

Now when I had returned, says Ezekiel, behold, at the bank of the river were very many trees on the one side and on the other. Then said he unto me, These waters issue out towards the east country, and go down into the desert, and into the sea: which being brought forth into the sea, the waters shall be healed. And it shall come to pass that every thing that liveth, which moveth, whithersoever the rivers shall come, shall live ; and there shall be a very great multitude of fish, because these waters shall come thither; for they shall be healed; and everything shall live whither the water cometh. And it shall come to pass that the fishers shall stand upon it from Engedi even unto Eneglaim; they shall be a place to spread forth nets ; their fish shall be according to their kinds, as the fish of the great sea, exceeding many.

But the miry places thereof and the marshes thereof shall not be healed; they shall be given to salt. And by the river upon the bank thereof, on this side and on that side shall grow all trees for meat, whose leaf shall not fade, neither shall the fruit thereof be consumed ; it shall bring forth new fruit according to his months, because their waters they issued out of the sanctuary ; and the fruit thereof shall be for meat, and the leaf thereof for medicine.

Thou, O king, sawest, and behold a great image. This great image, whose brightness was excellent, stood before thee, and the form thereof was terrible. This image's head was of fine gold, his breast and his arms of silver, his belly and his thighs of brass, his legs of iron, his feet part o iron and part of clay.

Thou sawest till that a stone was cut out without hands, which smote the image upon his feet that were of iron and clay, and brake them to pieces. Then was the iron, the clay, the brass, the silver, and the gold, broken up together, and became like the chaff of the summer threshing floors; and the wind carried them away, that no place was found for them: and the stone that smote the image became a great mountain, and filled the whole earth.

This is the dream; and we will tell the interpretation thereof before the king. Thou, O king, art a king of kings: for the God of heaven hath given thee a kingdom, power and strength, and glory. And wheresoever the children of men dwelt, the beasts of the field and the fowls of the heaven hath he given into thine hand, and hath made thee ruler over them all. Thou art this head of gold.

And after thee shall arise a kingdom inferior to thee, and another third kingdom of brass, which shall bear rule over all the earth, and the fourth kingdom shall be strong as iron; for as much as iron breaketh in pieces and subdueth all things, and as iron that breaketh all these, shall it break in pieces and bruise.

And whereas thou sawest the feet and toes. part of potters' clay, and part of iron, the kingdom shall be divided; but there shall be in it of the strength of the iron, forasmuch as thou sawest the iron mixed with miry clay. And as the toes of the feet were part of iron, and part of clay, so shall the kingdom be partly strong, and partly broken. And whereas thou sawest iron mixed with miry clay, they shall mingle themselves with the seed of men; but they shall not cleave one to another, even as iron is not mixed with clay.

And in the days of these kings shall the God of heaven set up a kingdom, which shall never be destroyed; and the kingdom shall not be left to other people, but it shall break in pieces and consume all these kingdoms, and it shall stand forever.

Blessings of Jacob and Moses.—And Jacob called unto his sons and said, Gather yourselves together, that I may tell you that which shall befall you in the last days. Gather yourselves together. and hear ye sons of Jacob; and hearken unto Israel your father.

Reuben, thou art my first born, my might, and the beginning of my strength, the excellency of dignity, and the excellency of power: Unstable as water, thou shalt not excel; because thou wentest up to thy father's bed; then defiledst thou it; he went up to my couch. Let Reuben live, and not die, and let not his men be few.

Simeon and Levi are brethren; instruments of cruelty are in their habitations. O my soul, come not thou into their secret; unto their assembly, mine honor, be not thou united; for in their anger they slew a man, and in their self will they digged down a wall. Cursed be their anger, for it was fierce; and their wrath, for it was cruel; I will divide them in Jacob, and scatter them in Israel. And of Levi, Moses said, Let thy Thummim and Urim be with thy holy one, whom thou didst prove at Massah, and with whom thou didst strive at the waters of Meribah; who said unto his father and to his mother, I have not seen him; neither did he acknowledge his brethren, nor knew his own children; for they have observed thy word, and kept thy covenant. They shall teach Jacob thy judgments, and Israel thy law; they shall put incense before thee, and whole burnt sacrifice upon thine altar. Bless, Lord, his substance, and accept the work of his hands: smite through the loins of them that raise against him, and of them that hate him, that they raise not against him.

Judah, thou art he whom thy brethren shall praise; thine hand shall be in the neck of thine enemies; thy father's children shall bow down before thee. Judah is a lion's whelp: from the prey, my son, thou art gone up; he stooped down, he couched as a lion, and as an old lion, who shall rouse him up? The sceptre shall not depart from Judah, nor a lawgiver from between his feet, until Shiloh come, and unto him shall the gathering of the people be. Binding his foal unto the vine, and his ass's colt unto the choice vine, he washed his garments in wine, and his clothes in the blood of grapes. His eyes shall be red with wine, and his teeth white with milk.

Zebulon shall dwell at the haven of the sea; and he shall be for a haven of ships; and his border shall be unto Zidon.

Issachar is a strong ass, crouching down between two burdens; and he saw that rest was good, and the land that it was pleasant: and bowed his shoulder to bear, and became a servant unto tribute.

Dan shall judge his people as one of the tribes of Israel. Dan shall be a serpent by the way, an adder in the path, that biteth the horse heels, so that his rider shall fall backward. I have waited waited for thy salvation, O Lord.

Gad, a troop shall overcome him; but he shall overcome at the last. And of Gad he said, Blessed be he who enlargeth Gad: he dwelleth as a lion, and teareth the arm with the crown of the head. And he provided the first part for himself, because there, in a portion of the lawgiver was he seated; and he came with the heads of the people, he executed the justice of the Lord, and his judgments with Israel.

Out of Asher his bread shall be fat, and he shall yield royal dainties. Let Asher be blessed with children ; let him dip his foot in oil. Thy shoes shall be iron and brass, and as thy days, so shall thy strength be.

Naphtali is a hind let loose : he giveth goodly words. O Naphtali, satisfied with favour, and full with the blessing of the Lord, possess thou the west and the south.

Joseph is a fruitful bough, even a fruitful bough by a well, whose branches run over the wall. The archers have sorely grieved him, and shot at him, and hated him ; but his bow abode in strength, and the arms of his hands were made strong by the hands of the mighty God of Jacob; (from thence is the shepherd, the stone of Israel:) Even by the God of thy father, who shall help thee; and by the Almighty who shall bless thee with blessings of heaven above, blessings of the deep that lieth under, blessings of the breasts and of the womb. The blessing of thy father have prevailed above the blessings of my progenitors unto the utmost bound of the everlasting hills : they shall be on the head of Joseph, and on the crown of his head that was separate from his brethren. His glory is like the firstling of the bullock, and his horns are like the horns of unicorns ; with them he shall push the people together to the ends of the earth : and they are the ten thousands of Ephraim, and the thousands of Manasseh.

Benjamin shall raven as a wolf, in the morning he shall devour the prey, and at night he shall divide the spoil. The beloved of the Lord shall dwell in safety by him ; shall cover him all the day long, and he shall dwell between his shoulders.

All these are the twelve tribes of Israel : and this is it that their father spake unto them, and blessed them ; every one with an appropriate blessing.

Now these are the generations of Ishmael, Abraham's son, whom Hagar the Egyptian, Sarah's handmaid, bare unto Abraham; and these are the names of the sons of Ishmael, by their names, according to their generations : the firstborn of Ishmael, Nebajoth ; and Kedar, and Adbeel, and Mibsam, and Mishma, and Dumah, and Massa, Hadar, and Temah, Jetur, Naphish, and Kedemah. These are the sons of Ishmael, and these are their names, by their towns, and by their castles ; twelve princes according to their nations.

And these are the years of the life of Ishmael, a hundred and thirty and seven years ; and he gave up the ghost, and died, and was gathered unto his people. And they dwelt from Havilah unto Shur, that is before Egypt, as thou goest toward Assyria: and he died in the presence of all his brethren.

Joining the Sticks.—The word of the Lord came again unto me, (Ezekiel) saying, Moreover, thou son of man, take thee one stick, and write upon it, for Judah, aud for the children of Israel, his companions; then take another stick, and write upon it, For Joseph, the stick of Ephraim, and for all the house of Israel, his companions; and join them one to another into one stick: and they shall become one in thine hand.

And when the children of thy people shall speak unto thee saying, Wilt thou not shew us what thou meanest by these? Say unto them, Thus saith the Lord God: Behold I will take the stick of Joseph, which is in the hand of Ephraim, and the tribes of Israel his fellows, and will put them with him, even with the stick of Judah, and will make them one stick, and they shall be one In mine hand.

And the sticks whereon thou writest shall be in thine hand before their eyes. And say unto them, Thus saith the Lord God; Behold, I will take the children of Israel from among the heathen, whither they be gone, and will gather them on every side, and bring them into their own land; and I will make them one nation in the land upon the mountains of Israel; and one king shall be king to them all, and they shall be no more two nations, neither shall they be divided into two kingdoms any more at all; neither shall they defile themselves any more with their idols, nor with their detestable things, nor with any of their transgressions; but I will save them out of their dwelling-places, wherein they have sinned, and will cleanse them; so thall they be my people, and I will be their God.

And David my servant shall be king over them; and they all shall have one shepherd: they shall also walk in my judgments, and observe my statues and do them. And they shall dwell in the land that I have given unto Jacob my servant, wherein your fathers have dwelt; and they shall dwell therein, even they and their children, and their children's children forever: and my servant David shall be their prince forever.

Moreover I will make a covenant of peace with them; it shall be an everlasting covenant with them: and I will place them, and multiply them, and will set my sanctuary in the midst of them for evermore. My tabernacle also shall be with them; yea, I will be their God, and they shall be my people. And the heathen shall know that I the Lord do sanctify Israel, when my sanctuary shall be in the midst of them for evermore.

The word of the Lord came unto me again, saying, What mean ye, that ye use this proverb concerning the land of Israel, saying, The fathers have eaten sour grapes, and the children's teeth are set on edge? As I live, saith the Lord God, you shall not have occasion any more to use this proverb in Israel.

Yet say ye, Why? doth not the son bear the iniquity of his father? When the son hath done that which is lawful and right, and hath kept all my statues, and hath done them, he shall surely live. The soul that sinneth, it shall die. The son shall not bear the iniquity of the father, neither shall the father bear the iniquity of the son; the righteousness of the righteous shall be upon him, and the wickedness of the wicked shall be upon him.

But if the wicked will turn from all his sins that he hath committed, and keep all my statutes, and do that which is lawful and right, he shall surely live, he shall not die. All his transgressions that he hath committed, they shall not be mentioned unto him; in his righteousness that he hath done he shall live.

The Gathered Tribes.—Thus saith Yehovah, the God of Israel, I will cause the captivity of Judah and the captivity of Israel to return, and will build them as at the first. Again in this place, which is desolate and without man and without beast, and in all the cities thereof, shall be a habitation of shepherds, causing their flocks to lie down. Behold the days come, saith the Lord of Hosts, that I will perform that good thing which I have promised to the house of Israel and to the house of Judah. In those days, and at that time, I will cause the Branch of righteousness to grow up unto David, and he shall execute judgment and righteousness in the land.

In those days shall Judah be saved, and Jerusalem shall dwell safely; and this is the name wherewith she shall be called, the Lord our Righteousness. For thus saith the Lord; There shall not be cut off from David a man to sit upon the throne of the house of Israel; neither shall the priests the Levites want a man before me to offer burnt offerings, to kindle meat offerings, and sacrifice continually.

And the word of the Lord came unto Jeremiah, saying, Thus saith the Lord; If ye can break my covenant of the day, and my covenant of the night, and that there should not be day and night in their season ; then may also my covenant be broken with David my servant, that he should not have a son to reign upon his throne ; and with the Levites the priests; my ministers. As the host of heaven cannot be numbered, neither the sand of the sea measured ; so will I multiply the seed of David, my servant, and the Levites that minister unto me.

For the children of Israel shall abide many days without a king, and without a prince, aud without a sacrifice, and without an image, and without an ephod, and without teraphim. Afterward shall the children of Israel return, and seek the Lord their God, and David their king ; and shall fear the Lord and his goodness in the latter days.

Therefore, behold the days come, saith the Lord, that they shall no more say, The Lord liveth, which brought up the children of Israel out of the land of Egypt ; but the Lord liveth which brought up and which led the seed of the house of Israel out of the north country, and from all countries whither I had driven them ; and they shall dwell in their own land.

Woe be unto the pastors that destroy and scatter the sheep of my pastures, saith the Lord. Therefore thus saith the Lord God of Israel against the pastors that destroy my people : ye have scattered my flock and driven them away, and have not visited them : behold I will visit upon you the evil of your doings. saith the Lord.

And I will gather the remnant of my flock out of all countries whither I have driven them, and will bring them again to their folds ; and they shall be fruitful and increase. And I will set up shepherds over them which shall feed them : and they shall fear no more, nor be dismayed, neither shall they be lacking, saith the Lord.

For thus saith the Lord God ; Behold I, even I, will both search my sheep, and seek them out. As a shepherd seeketh out his flock in the day that he is among his sheep that are scattered ; so will I seek out my sheep, and will deliver them out of all places where they have been scattered in the cloudy and dark day. ·And I will bring them out from the people, and deliver them from the countries, and will bring them out from the people, and gather them from the countries, and will bring them to their own land, and feed them upon the mountains of Israel by the rivers, and in all the inhabited places of the country.

I will feed them in a good pasture, and upon the high mountains of Israel shall their fold be : there shall they lie in a good fold, and a fat pasture shall they feed upon the mountains of Israel. I will feed my flock, and I will cause them to lie down, saith the Lord God. I will seek that that which was lost, and bring again that which was driven away, and will bind up that which was broken, and will strengthen that which was sick : but I will destroy the fat and the strong, I will feed them with judgment.

And in that day when the Branch appears, there shall be a root of Jesse, which shall stand for an ensign of the people : to it shall the Gentiles seek; and his rest shall be glorious. And it shall come to pass in that day when the Branch appears, that the Lord shall set his hand again to recover the remnant of his people, which shall be left, from Assyria, and from Egypt, and from Pathros, and from Cush, and from Elam, and from Shinar, and from Hamath, and from the Islands of the sea.

And he shall set up an ensign for the nations, and shall assemble the outcasts of Israel, and gather together the dispersed of Judah from the four corners of the earth. The envy also of Ephraim shall depart, and the adversaries of Judah shall be cut off; Ephraim shall not envy Judah, and Judah shall not vex Ephraim.

But they shall fly upon the shoulders of the Philistines toward the west, they shall spoil them of the east together : they shall lay their hands upon Edom and Moab ; and the children of Ammon shall obey them. And the Lord shall utterly destroy the tongue of the Egyptian sea ; and with his mighty wind shall he shake his hand over the river, and shall smite it in the seven streams, and make men go over dryshod. And there shall be a highway for the remnant of his people, which shall be left from Assyria ; like as it was to Israel in the day that he came up out of the land of Egypt.

In those days the house of Judah shall walk with the house of Israel, and they shall come together out of the land of the north, to the land that I have given for an inheritance to your fathers.

But Zion said, Yehovah hath forsaken me, and my Lord hath forgotten me. Can a woman forget her sucking child, that she should not have compassion on the son of her womb?

Yea, they may forget, yet will I not forget thee. Behold I have graven thee upon the palms of my hands, thy walls are contiuually before me.

Thy waste and desolate places, and the land of thy destruction, shall even now be too narrow, by reason of the inhabitants, and they that swallowed thee up shall be far away. The children, which thou shalt have, after thou hast lost the other, shall say again in thine ears, The place is too strait for me, give place to me that I may dwell.. Then shalt thou say, Who hath begotten me these, seeing that I have lost my children, and am desolate, a captive, and removing to and fro? and who hath brought up these? Behold, I was left alone; these. where had they been?

Thus saith the Lord God, Behold, I will lift up my hand to the Gentiles, and set my standard to the people: and they shall bring thy sons in their arms, and thy daughters on their shoulders. And kings shall be thy nursing fathers, and queens thy nurnsing mothers; they shall bow down to thee with their faces toward the earth, and lick up the dust of thy feet. And thou shall know that I am Yehovah; for they shall not be ashamed that wait for me.

Turn, O backsliding children, saith Yehovah, for I am married to you; and I will take you, one of a city, and two of a family, and will bring you to Zion. And I will give you pastors according to mine heart, which shall feed you with knowledge and with understanding.

A voice of noise from the city, a voice from the temple, a voice of the Lord that rendereth recompense to his enemies. Before she travailed, she brought forth; before her pain came she was delivered of a man child. Who hath heard such a thing? Who hath seen such things? Shall the earth be made to bring forth in one day? or shall a nation be born at once? for as soon as Zion travaled she brought forth her children.

The New Covenant.—Behold, the days come, saith the Lord, that I will make a new covenant with the house of Israel, and with the house of Judah; not according to the covenant that I made with their fathers, in the day that I took them by the hand to bring them out of the land of Egypt; which my covenant they brake, although I was a husband unto them, saith the Lord.

But this shall be the covenant that I will make with the house of Israel: After those days, saith the Lord, I will put my law in their inward parts, and write it in their hearts.

And they shall teach no more every man his neighbor, and every man his brother, saying know the Lord ; for they shall all know me, from the least of them unto the greatest of them, saith the Lord; for I will forgive their iniquity, and will remember their sin no more.

Thus saith the Lord, which giveth the sun for a light by day, and the ordinances of the moon and stars for a light by night, which divideth the sea when the waves thereof roar ; the Lord of hosts is his name. If those ordinances depart from before me, saith the Lord, then the seed of Israel also shall cease from being a nation before me for ever. Thus saith the Lord : If heaven above can be measured, and the foundations of the earth searched out beneath, I will also cast off the seed of Israel for all that they have done, saith the Lord.

Behold, the days come, saith the Lord, that the city shall be built to the Lord from the tower of Hananeel unto the gate of the corner. And the measuring line shall yet go forth against it upon the hill Gareb, and shall compass about Goath. And the whole valley of the dead bodies, and of the ashes and all the fields unto the brook of Kidron, unto the corner of the horse gate toward the east, shall be holy unto the Lord ; it shall not be plucked up nor thrown down any more for ever.

And a highway shall be there, and a way, and it shall be called the way of holiness ; the unclean shall not pass over it ; but it shall be for those : the wayfaring men, though fools, shall not err therein. No lion shall be there, nor no ravenous beast shall go up thereon, it shall not be found thereon ; but the redeemed shall walk there.

And the ransomed of the Lord shall return, and come to Zion with songs and everlasting joy upon their heads : they shall obtain joy and gladness, and sorrow and sighing shall flee away.

Wherefore hear the word of the Lord, ye scornful men, that rule this people which is in Jerusalem. Because ye have said, We have made a covenant with death, and with hell are we at agreement ; when the overflowing scourge shall pass through, it shall not come unto us ; for we have made lies our refuge, and under falsehood have we hid ourselves.

Therefore, thus saith the Lord God, Behold, I lay in Zion for a foundation stone, a tried stone, a precious corner stone, a sure foundation ; he that believeth shall not make haste. Judgment also will I lay to the line, and righteousuess to the plummet ; and the hail shall sweep away the refuge of lies, and the waters shall overflow the hiding place. And your covenant with death shall be annulled, and your agreement with hell shall not stand . when the overflowing scourge shall pass through, then ye shall be trodden down by it. From the time that it goeth forth it shall take you: for morning by morning shall it pass over, by day and by night: and it shall be a vexation only to understand the report.

For the bed is shorter than that a man can stretch himself upon it : and the covering narrower than that he can wrap himself in it. For the Lord shall rise up, as in Mount Perazim, he shall be wroth as in the valley of Gibeon, that he may do his work, his strange work ; and bring to pass his act, his strange act.

The Messenger.—Behold, I will send my messenger, and he shall prepare the way before me : and the Lord, whom ye seek, shall suddenly come to his temple, even the messenger of the covenant, whom ye delight in ; behold, he shall come, saith the Lord of hosts. But who may abide the day of his coming? and who shall stand when he appeareth ? for he is a like a refiner's fire, and like fuller's soap. And he shall sit as a refiner and purifier of silver: and he shall purify the sons of Levi, and purge them as gold and silver, that they may offer unto the Lord an offering in righteousness. Then shall the offering of Judah and Jerusalem be pleasant unto the Lord, as in the days of old, as in former years. And I will come near to you to judgment ; and I will be a swift witness against the sorcerers, and against the adulterers, and against false swearers, and against those that oppress the hireling in his wages, the widow, and the fatherless, and that turn the stranger from his right, and fear not me, saith the Lord of hosts.

For behold, the day cometh that shall burn as an oven ; and all the proud, yea all that do wickedly shall be stubble ; and the day that cometh shall burn them up, saith the Lord of hosts, that it shall leave them neither root nor branch. But unto you that fear my name shall the Sun of Righteousness arise with healing in his wings ; and ye shall go forth, and grow up as calves of the stall ; and ye shall tread down the wicked ; for they shall be ashes under the soles of your feet in the day that I shall do this, saith the Lord of hosts. Remember ye the law of Moses my servant, which I commanded unto him in Horeb for all Israel, with the statutes and judgments Behold, I will send you Elijah the prophet before the coming of the great and dreadful day of the Lord, And he shall turn the heart of the fathers toward the children, and the heart of the children to the fathers, lest I come and smite the earth with a curse.

The Messiah.—And there shall come forth a rod out of the stem of Jesse, and a Branch shall grow out of his roots; and the spirit of Yehovah shall rest upon him, the spirit of wisdom and understanding, the spirit of counsel and might, the spirit of knowledge and of the fear of the Lord; and shall make him of quick sagacity in the fear of Yehovah, and he shall not judge after the sight of his eyes, neither reprove after the hearing of his ears; but with righteousness shall he judge the poor, and reprove with equity for the meek of the earth; and he shall smite the earth with the rod of his mouth, and with the breath of his lips shall he slay the wicked. And righteousness shall be the girdle of his loins, and faithfulness the girdle of his reins.

The wolf also shall dwell with the lamb, and the leopard shall lie down with the kid; and the calf and the young lion and the fatling together; and a little child shall lead them. And the cow and the bear shall feed; their young ones shall lie down together; and the lion shall eat straw like the ox. And the sucking child shall play on the hole of the asp, and the weaned child shall put his hand on the cockatrice' den. They shall not hurt nor destroy in all my holy mountain: for the earth shall be full of the knowledge of Yehovah as the waters cover the sea.

Behold, the days come, saith the Lord, that I will raise unto David a righteous Branch, and a King shall reign and prosper, and shall execute justice and judgment in the earth. In his days Judah shall be saved, and Israel shall dwell safely: and this is his name whereby he shall be called, THE LORD OUR RIGHTEOUSNESS, YEHOVAH—TSIDKENU.

Behold, a king shall reign in righteousness, and princes shall rule in judgment, and a man shall be as a hiding place from the wind; and a covert from the tempest; as rivers of water in a dry place, as the shadow of a great rock in a weary land. Then judgment shall dwell in the wilderness and righteousness remain in the fruitful field. And the work of righteousness shall be peace: and the affect of righteousness, quietness and assurance forever. And my people shall dwell in a peaceable habitation, and in sure dwellings, and in quiet resting-places.

Thus saith the Lord, It is a light thing that thou shouldst be my servant to raise up the tribes of Jacob, and to restore the preserved of Israel; I will also give thee for a light to the Gentiles, that thou mayst be my salvation unto the end of the earth. For the Lord promised unto Abraham, saying, In blessing I will.bless thee, and in multiplying I will multiply thy seed as the stars of heaven, and as the sand which is on the seashore. And thy seed shall possess the gates of his enemies. And in thy seed shall all the nations of the earth be blessed, because thou hast obeyed my voice.

The Thrones.--I, Danield, behel till the thrones were cast down, and the ancient of days did sit, whose garments were white as snow, ane the hair of his head like the pure wool; his throne was like the fiery flame, and his wheels as bnrning fire. A fiery stream issued and came forth before him; thousand thousands ministered unto him, and ten thousand times ten thousand stood before him; the judgment was set and the books were opened.

I beheld then because of the voice of the great words which the horn spake; I beheld even till the beast was slain, and his body destroyed and given to the burning flame.

As concerning the rest of the beasts, they had their dominion taken away; yet their lives were prolonged for a season and a time.

I saw in the night visions, and, behold, one like the son of man came with the clouds of heaven, and came to the ancient of days, and they brought him near before him. And there was given him dominion, and glory, and and a kingdom, that all people, nations, and languages should serve him; his dominion is an everlasting dominion, which shall not pass away, and his kingdom that which shall not be destroyed.

Now as I, Ezekiel, beheld the living creatures, behold one wheel upon the earth by the living creatures, with his four faces. The appearance of the wheels and their work was like unto the color of a beryl; and they four had one likeness; and their appearance and there work was as a wheel in the middle of a wheel. When they went, they went upon their four sides, and they turned not when they went.

As for their rings they were so high that they were dreadful; and their rings were full of eyes round about them four. and when the living creatures went, the wheels went by them; and when the living creatures were lifted up from the earth, the wheels were lifted up.

And above the firmament that was over their neads was the likeness of a throne, as the appearance of a sapphire stone : and upon the likeness of the throne was the likeness as the appearance of a man above upon it And I saw as the color of amber, as the appearance of fire round about within it, from the appearance of his loins even upward, I saw as it were appearance of fire, and it had brightness round about.

As the appearance of the bow that is in the cloud in the day of rain, so was the appearance of the brightness round about. This was the appearance of the likeness of the glory of the Lord.

The True Saviour.—Thus saith Yehovah the King of Israel, and his Redeemer Yehovah of hosts : I am the first, and I am the last, and beside me there is no God. I, even I, am Yehovah, and beside me there is no savior. I have declared, and have saved.

And Yehovah shall be King over all the earth ; in that day shall there be one Yehovah, and his name one.

Thus saith Yehovah, your Redeemer, the Holy One of Israel ; for your sake I have sent to Babylon, and have brought down all their nobles and the Chaldeans.

One shall say, I am Yehovah's ; and another shall call himself Jacob ; and another shall subscribe with his hand unto Yehovah, and surname himself with the name of Israel. The God of Israel, Yehovah of hosts is his name. O Jacob, my called one; I am the first, and I am the last.

The Great Battle.—And at that time shall Michael stand up, the great prince which standeth for the children of thy people, and there shall be a time of trouble, such as there never was since there was a nation even to that same time : and at that time thy people shall be delivered, every one that shall be found written in the book.

And many of them that sleep in the dust of the earth shall awake, some to everlasting life, and some to shame and everlasting contempt. And they that be wise shall shine as the brightness of the firmament ; and they that turn many to righteousness, as the stars forever and ever.

But thou, O Daniel, shut up the words, and seal the book, even unto the time of the end ; many shall run to and fro, and knowledge shall be increased. Then I Daniel looked, and behold, there stood other two, the one on this side of the bank of the river, and the other on that side of the bank of the river. And one said to the man clothed in linen, which was upon the waters of the river, How long shall it be to the end of these wonders? And I heard the man clothed in linen, which was upon the waters of the river, when he held up his right hand, and his left hand unto heaven, and sware by him that liveth forever, that it shall be for a time, times, and a half; and when he shall have accomplished to scatter the power of the holy people, all these things shall be finished.

Gog and Magog.—And the word of Yehovah came unto me, saying, Son of man, set thy face against Gog, the land of Magog, the prince of Rosh, Meshech and Tubal, and say, Thus saith the Lord God, behold I am against thee, O Gog, prince of Rosh, Meshech, and Tubal; and I will turn thee back, and put hooks into thy jaws, and I will bring thee forth, and all thine army, horses and horsemen, all of them clothed with all sorts of armour, a great company with bucklers and shields, all of them handling swords. Persia, Ethiopia, and Phut with them, Gomer with his bands, the house of Togarmah of the north quarters, and all his bands and many people.

Surely in that day there shall be a great shaking in the land of Israel, so that the fishes of the sea, and the fowls of heaven, and the beasts of the field, and all the men that are on the face of the earth, shall shake at my presence, and the mountains shall fall down and the towers shall fall. And I will call for a sword against Gog throughout all my mountains, every man's sword shall be against his brother. And I will plead against him with pestilence and with blood; and I will rain upon him, and upon his bands, and upon he many people who are with him, an overflowing rain, and great hail-stones, fire and brimstone. Thus will I magnify myself, and sanctify myself, and I will be known in the eyes of many nations, and they shall know that I am Yehovah.

And they that dwell in the cities of Israel shall go forth, and set on fire and burn the weapons, both the shields and the bucklers, the bows and the arrows, and the javelins and spears, and they shall make a fire of them seven years, Thus saith the Lord God, Speak unto the fowl of every wing, and to every beast of the field, Assemble yourselves, from every side, to my slaughter that I sacrifice for you, even a great sacrifice upon the mountains of Israel, that ye may eat the flesh of the mighty and drink the blood of the princes of the earth, of rams, of bullocks, all of them fatlings of Bashan.

MESSIANIC PROPHECIES.

The Battle at Jerusalem. For Yehovah will gather all nations against Jerusalem to battle, and the city shall be taken, and the houses rifled, and the women ravished, and half of the city shall go forth into captivity, and the residue of the people shall not be cut off from the city. Then shall Yehovah go forth, and fight against those nations, as when he fought in the day of battle. And his feet shall stand in that day upon the mount of Olives, which is before Jerusalem on the east, and the mount of Olives shall cleave in the midst thereof towards the east,, and towards the west, and there shall be a great valley, and half of the mountain shall remove toward the north, and half of it toward the south. And ye shall flee to the valley of the mountains; for the valley of the mountains shall reach unto Azal; yea, ye shall flee, like as ye fled before the earthquake in the days of Uzziah king of Judah: and the Yehovah my God shall come, and all the saints with thee.

And it shall come to pass in that day, that it shall be evenly light over the parts of the earth. And living waters shall go out from Jerusalem; half of them toward the Eastern sea, and half of them toward the hinder sea; in summer and in winter it shall be.

And the land shall be turned as a plain from Geba to Rimmon south of Jerusalem; and it shall be lifted up, and inhabited in her place, from Benjamin's gate unto the place of the first gate, unto the corner gate, and from the tower of Hananeel unto the king's winepresses. And the men shall dwell in it, and there shall be no more utter destruction: but Jerusalem shall be safely inhabited. And this shall be the plague wherewith the Lord will smite all the people that have fought against Jerusalem; their flesh shall consume away while they stand upon their feet, and their eyes shall consume away in their holes, and their tongues shall consume away in their mouth. And it shall come to pass in that day, that a great tumult from the Lord shall be among them; and they shall lay hold everyone on the hand of his neighbor, and his hand shall rise up against the hand of his neighbor. And Judah also shall fight at Jerusalem; and the wealth of all the heathen round about shall be gathered together, gold and silver, and apparel in great abundance.

And it shall come to pass that everyone that is left of all the nations which came against Jerusalem, shall even go up from year to year to worship the Kintne Yehovah of hosts, and to keep the feast of the tabernacles.

The Christian teachers claim that the following verses were fulfilled by Jesus of Nazareth eighteen hundred years since.

The Seed of Woman.—And I will put enmity between thee and the woman, and between thy seed and her seed, it shall bruise thy head, and thou shalt bruise its heel.

The sceptre shall not depart from Judah, nor a law-giver from between his feet; until the coming to Shiloh, and unto him shall the gathering of the people be.

I will rise them up a prophet from among their brethren, like unto Moses, and I will put my words in his mouth; and he shall speak unto them all that I command him. And it shall come to pass that whosoever will not hearken unto my words which he shall speak in my name, I will require it of him.

But thou, Bethlehem, Ephratah, though thou be little among the thousands of Judah, yet out of thee shall he come forth that is to be ruler in Israel.

Therefore the Lord himself shall give you, Ahaz, a sign; Behold, a young woman, almeh, shall conceive and bear a son, and shall call his name Immanuel. Butter and honey shall he eat that he may know to refuse the evil and choose the good.

(And Mary brought forth a son, and they called his name Jesus or Saviour.

When Israel was a child, then I loved him, and called my son out of Egypt. As they called them, so they went from them; they sacrificed unto Baalim, and burned incense to graven images.

Thus saith the Lord; A voice was heard in Ramah, lamentation, and bitter weeping; Rachel weeping for her children, refused to be comforted for her children, because they were not.

The voice of him that crieth in the wilderness, Prepare ye the way of the Lord, make straight in the desert a highway for our God. Every valley shall be exalted, and every mountain and hill shall be made low; and the crooked shall be made straight, and the rough places plain. And the glory of the Lord shall be revealed, and all flesh shall see it together; for the mouth of the Lord hath spoken it.

Behold, I will send my messenger, and he shall prepare the way before me: and the Lord, whom ye seek, shall suddenly come to his temple.

Behold I will send you Elijah the prophet before the coming of that great and dreadful day of Yehovah.

And I will shake all nations, and the desire of all nations shall come: and I will fill this house with glory, saith the Lord of hosts.

Behold my servant whom I uphold; mine elect, in whom my soul delighteth; I have put my spirit upon him: he shall bring forth judgment to the Gentiles. He shall not cry, nor lift up, nor cause his voice to be heard in the street. A bruised reed shall he not break, and the smoking flax shall he not quench; he shall bring forth judgment unto truth.

The spirit of the Lord God is upon me, because Yehovah hath anointed me to preach good tidings to the meek, he hath sent me to bind up the brokenhearted, to proclaim liberty to the captives and the opening of the prisons to them that are bound.

Then the eyes of the blind shall be opened, and the ears of the deaf shall be unstopped. Then shall the lame man leap as a hart, and the tongue of the dumb sing.

Many are the afflictions of the righteous: but the Lord delivereth him out of them; he keepeth all his bones, not one of them is broken. They pierced my hands and feet, they part my garments among them and cast lots upon my vesture,

For thou wilt not leave my soul in hell, neither wilt thou suffer thine holy one to see corruption. Thou wilt show me the path of life; in thy presence is fulness of joy; at thy right hand there are pleasures forever more.

Rejoice greatly, O daughter of Zion; shout, O daughter of Jerusalem; behold, thy king cometh unto thee: he is just, and having salvation; lowly, and riding upon an ass, and upon a colt the foal of an ass.

Seventy sevens are determined upon thy people, and upon the holy city, to finish the transgression, and to make and end of sin, and to make reconciliation for iniquity, and to bring in everlasting righteousness, and to seal up the vision and prophecy, and to anoint the Most Holy. Know therefore, and understand, that from the going forth of the commandment to restore and to build Jerusalem, unto the

Messiah the Prince, shall be seven sevens, and threescore and two sevens; the street shall be built again, and the wall even in troublous times. And after three score and two sevens shall Messiah be cut off, and nothing remains to him; and the people of the prince that shall come shall destroy the city and the sanctuary; and the end thereof shall be with a flood, and unto the end of the war desolations are determined. And he shall confirm the covenant with many for one week; and in the midst of the week he shall cause the sacrifice and the oblation to cease, and for the overspreading of abominations he shall make it desolate, even unto the consummation, and that determined shall be poured upon the desolate. Dan. 9.

The following passages are the ones usually referred to Jesus: General ones declaring the coming of a Messiah, Gen. 3. 15; Deut. 18. 15; Ps. 89. 20; Is. 2. 2; 9. 6;—the nation, tribe, and family he was to descend from, Gen. 12. 3; 49. 8; the time when he was to appear, Dan. 9. 24; Mal. 3. 1; the place of his birth, Mic. 5. 2; that a messenger should go before him, Is. 40. 3; Mal. 3. 1; 4. 5; that he was to be born of a virgin, Is. 7. 14; that there should be a massacre at Bethlehem, Jer. 31. 15; that he should be carried into Egypt, Hos. 11. 1; that he should be hated and persecuted, Ps. 22. 6; 35. 7. 12; 109. 2; Is. 49. 7; 53. 3; that the Jews and Gentiles should conspire to destroy him, Ps. 2. 1; 22. 12; 41. 5; that he should ride triumphantly into Jerusalem, Ps. 8. 2; Zech. 9. 9: that he should be sold for thirty pieces of silver, Zech. 11. 12; that he should be betrayed by one of his own familiar friends, Ps. 41. 9; 55. 12; that his disciples should forsake him, Zech. 13. 7; that he should not plead upon his trial, Is. 53. 7; that he should be scourged, Is. 50. 6; that he should be crucified, Ps. 22. 14, 17; that they should offer him gall and vinegar to drink, Ps. 22. 15; 69. 21; that they should part his garments, and cast lots upon his vesture, Ps. 22. 18; that he should be mocked by his enemies, Ps. 22. 16; 109. 25; that his side should be pierced, Zech. 12. 10; also his hands and his feet, Ps. 22. 16; Zech. 13. 6; that he should be patient under his sufferings, Is. 53. 7; that a bone of him should not be broken, Ps. 34. 20; that he should die with malefactors, Is. 53. 9, 12; that he should be buried with the rich, Is. 53. 9: that he should rise again from the dead, Ps. 16. 10: that the potter's field should be bought with the purchase money. Zech. 11. 13.

The Contrast.—By the side of the magnificent descriptions of the New Heavens and New Earth, the universal kingdom of happiness and peace, we have now placed the tragical pictures of sorrow and failure which the Christian world has applied to Jesus of Nazareth, and his career eighteen hundred years since. We have to inquire whether the fulfilment of such a very small proportion of the prophecies was sufficient to establish his claim to the Messiahship at that time; and also to consider the question of a second coming.

The fulfilled passages number less than the one sixth part of the whole messianic prophecies. For every verse claimed as fulfilled, there are five verses which no one would have the hardihood to claim were in any manner fulfilled. But the case is much worse than the mere comparison of numbers would indicate. For not one of these claimed verses contains the promise of any thing good for mankind. A large part of them refer to such persecutions as have been the common lot of those who attempted to reform the institutions of men. They were not one whit more true of Jesus than they were of a hundred other men. No one can read history and remain blind to this fact.

And where the prophecies seemed to be definite and circumstantial, examination shows they were not so. To name a child Jesus, is not to fulfil a passage which says he shall be called Emanuel, for the two names are not equivalents, they do not mean the same thing at all. The Roman soldiers cast lots upon his vesture, but so they did upon other criminals which they executed. They gave him vinegar to drink. That also was their practice with others. If the passage "Out of Egypt I called my son," applied to Jesus, then he offered sacrifices to graven images, for this is affirmed in the next verse. Such things as these could not possibly serve to distinguish the Messiah from other men.

The whole of the 53rd chapter of Isaiah has been referred to Jesus. But the beginning of that passage says that it is speaking of some one who is styled "My servant." And seven times in the chapters just preceding this, Yehovah has declared that the nation of Israel is his servant. To say that this chapter refers to the Messiah, is to contradict the direct words of Yehovah himself.

It is true that two hundred years after the time of Isaiah, through another prophet, Zechariah, we are told that the Branch (Zemach) is my servant. But Zechariah also says that this Branch is Joshua the son of Josedak the high priest. He therefore could not be the great Messiah.

The Jewish people in themselves, have fulfilled the 53rd chapter of Isaiah to the very letter. But Jesus did not. For it says that after his sufferings he should see his children and prolong his days. But Jesus never had any children, and he died at the early age of thirty three. It has been pretended that his children means the church, that is, while the suffering were literal and real, the blessings were only figurative!

At the end of his life, Jesus seemed to realize that he could not fulfil the messianic prophecies, for he declared that his kingdom was not of that age, but that he would come to establish it in power. Whatever may have been the cause of his failure, the facts of the history can not be traversed. We must explain it by saying that his mission was to offer the kingdom to that generation before their long dispersion, but that the Jewish mind could not then accept the terms and conditions which he proposed. The Jews could not see that a disconnected collection of moral precepts, and the healing of a few sick people, would deliver them from the hard yoke of Roman power, and from the multiform evils that cursed their social and political life.

And so, guided by fanatical bigotry and blind hate, they put him to the horrible death of crucifixion. He died because he was true to the spiritual light within him, a light which could not penetrate or dissipate the darkness of that age.

A little further on we shall consider the question of a Second Coming. We must here notice how Christians have turned aside the obvious meaning of the prophets. For they claim that the prophecies apply to the Church; that it is the true Israel.

How false this claim has always been, is seen from the direct words of Yehovah. For he says that in the day that the Messiah appears, in that very age, and not eighteen hundred years afterward, he will set forth his hand and gather the twelve tribes of Israel, the ten lost tribes as well as the tribes of Judah and Benjamin; and plant them forever in the land in which their fathers have dwelt, upon the mountains of Israel, and that he will there establish them as at the first, and that they shall no more be two nations, and they shall not again be plucked up, but shall dwell in safety forever. If this language has not a literal meaning, then it would be impossible for God to find words in the whole compass of human language, by which a literal meaning could be expressed. The promise is repeatedly expressed in the strongest terms. Indeed, to use the words of another, those who assent to the true laws of language and of symbols, will no more deny or doubt that the prophecies teach that the Israelites are to be actually restored, than those who assent to the definitions and axions of geometry will deny the demonstrations founded on them.

Jesus choose twelve apostles, to rule over the twelve tribes of Israel. But they did not gather the tribes, they never ruled them, they did not organize the church into twelve departments after the one divine model; six of them sunk out of sight without leaving a trace of their history or of their personal character; and since the days of the apostles the church has never had twelve departments, twelve doctrines, twelve rulers, twelve symbols, or indeed twelve anything.

If the restoration of the people of Israel has only a spiritual sense, and means the Christian church, then the carrying away of Israel to Babylon was only in a spiritual sense, and not literal. For the some prediction speaks of both the dispersion and the restoration. If Shalmaneser and Nebuchadnezzar only took the Christian Church, and not the literal cities of Samaria and Jerusalem, then and only then, may we interpret the prophecies to mean that the Church is to be enlarged and restored, instead of the literal people of Israel, and the literal cities of Palestine.

The church has persistently done all of the things which Jesus forbade in his followers.

The prophets assert in the most positive manner that the kingdom of Messiah shall be one of universal peace. Nation shall not lift up sword against nation, neither shall they learn war any more. But every Christian Nation, without exception, has engaged in repeated wars, and its priests have sanctioned these wars. Christian nations still fight with the skill of demons, and Christian sects still quarrel with malignant hate, in this year after Christ 1881. In the light of these facts, to call the Christian Church the kingdom of the Messiah, is to utter an atrocious falsehood.

Nor does the Christian religion, as explained by its teachers, contain the foundations upon which the Kingdom is to be laid. For it does not contain any provisions, or principles, or laws, which could be formulated into a system and applied in a literal kingdom as its constitution. All things must be made new. The confused Babel of Christian sects can not be patched up into the New Jerusalem.

It is as easy to distinguish between the figurative and the literal language of the prophets, as it is to distinguish these in the common speech of every day life. When the prophets speak of a great day of burning, against the wicked, they no more mean a fire like that of wood and coal, than when we now speak of "burning hate," "fiery passions," "getting into hot water." The figure of speech means that a force would be used sufficient to destroy the evil referred to.

The True Messiah.—The prophets have a great deal to say about the coming Kingdom, and but a very little to say about the King who was to be its great founder. And we have a right to think that this shows that the kingdom was much more important than the king. In contradiction to the prophets, the Christain world centered all of its hopes in a person, and has cared little for the omnipotent and immortal system of truth and life which he was to establish.

In all the Hebrew prophets, there is not even a hint that the Messiah was to be a God, or anything more than an extraordinary man, excelling all other men in his wisdom, his loftiness of purpose, and the enduring benificence of his government. Had the prophets foretold that God himself was to come as the Messiah, the Jews could not have failed to read it; but they had no such expectation.

If we are told that the Divinity of the Messiah was not to be revealed until his appearance, then we ask how could God come and live here in a body, and yet not say one single thing which men did not know before? Is so God much more ignorant than any one of the ten thousand scientific men who are living to-day? He, the Creator of the World, stands thirty years among men, speaking familiarly three languages, and yet does not so much as explain how a single plant grows, or a single pebble is formed. How could he have avoided displaying his superior knowledge, when he so constantly used these natural objects to illustrate his discourses?

Healing a few sick people by miraculous power was a poor substitute for great sanitary systems, which should banish disease, and its causes from the world.

A few noble precepts about love and unselfishness have proved powerless against the organized injustice of governments and aristocracies of wealth, which have ground down the life and fed on the spoils of the people.

The command to be perfect, even as your Father in heaven is perfect, was a poor substitute for a system of integral education, which should secure to every child the glory of a mind and body trained and developed in perfect symmetry.

To bless little children, and say "Of such is the kingdom of Heaven," seems like a dreadful mockery in a Christian civilization which allows one half of the children to die before the age of five years, from easily preventible causes of disease.

The spasm of conversion and the hope of escaping hell, was but a sad substitute for the spiritual unity of mankind and the conscious and perpetual communion with the angelic world. The scope of religion is immensely broader and deeper than the Christian definition and example.

No system of doctrines and of life was formulated by Jesus. Cut off while his mission was scarcely begun, the work was left to other hands. Christianity was molded into form by monastic teachers, who substituted impractical and false dogmas for the simple precepts of their professed master. These impostors put forth the dogmas expressed in the phrases "Saved by the blood of Christ," "Justified by Faith," "By the deeds of the law no flesh shall be justffied," "Vicarious Atonement," "Christ our substitute," "Imputed Righteousness," "Mystery of Godliness." Not one of these formed any part of the teachings of Jesus. Not one of them belonged to the character of that Messiah who was foretold by the prophets. There is not a single passage in the old Testament which says that the Messiah should be offered as a sacrifice for the sins of men, and that through this substitution they were to gain admittance to heaven. According to christian teaching, their master preached three years without once stating the central doctrine on which the Plan of Salvation rests.

The writer of the first fourteen Epistles of the New Testament sums up his own teachings in these words: "We know that a man is not justified by the works of the law, but by the faith of Jesus Christ, for by the works of the law shall no flesh be justified. For through the law I am dead to the law. If righteousness come by law, then Christ is dead in vain. Christ is the end of the law for righteousnes, to every one that believeth. Ye are become dead to the law and delivered from it. A man is justified by faith without the deeds of the law. If ye are led by the spirit, ye are not under the law. The law was a schoolmaster to bring us to Christ, but after that faith is come, we are no longer under a schoolmaster. Ye are not under the law, but under grace. We are justified by the blood of Christ, who is our propitiation, and who bore the curse of the law for us. Without the shedding of blood there is no remission of sins." Such are the doctrines which that writer attempts to support through his Epistles by a series of the most amazing sophistries and false quotations that ever found expression in words. Upon these doctrines the Christian theology was founded and by these texts it was defended. We must remember that the writer of these epistles spoke wholly by his own authority, that he did not claim and did not show the authority of inspiration. And against his teachings stand the express and unequivocal declarations of Jesus, in these words: " Think not that I came to destroy the law, but to fulfil. For truly I say unto you: Till heaven and earth pass away, not one jot or tittle shall pass from the law, till all things be accomplished. Whosoever shall do and and teach the commandments of the law, shall be called great in the kingdom of heaven. If thou wilt have eternal life, obey the commandments given by Moses, these do and thou shalt live. Ye must obey the law more fully and more in its spirit, then even the strict Pharisees.

It is impossible to reconcile these teachings of Jesus with those of the Epistles. For a law can not be destroyed or set aside by being obeyed. The law of seeing requires that light should enter the eye. We do not set the law aside by going into a room which is full of light. We have obeyed the law, but it still remains in force. The spiritual laws are as much a part of man's spirit, as the laws of vision are inseparable from the eye. Take away the laws, and our spirits would have neither action, power, or even existence.

But long before the time of Jesus, we find that Yehovah himself had declared the truth, through Ezekiel, in these words:

"Yet say ye, Why? doth not the son bear the iniquity of the father?

When the son hath done that which is lawful and right and hath kept all my statutes, and hath done them, he shall surely live. The soul that sinneth, it shall die. The son shall not bear the iniquity of the father, neither shall the father bear the iniquity of the son: the righteousness of the righteous shall be upon him, and the wickedness of the wicked shall be upon him.

But if the wicked will turn from all his sins that he hath committed, and keep all my statutes, and do that which is lawful and right, he shall surely live, he shall not die. All his transgressions that he hath committed, they shall not be mentioned unto him : in his righteousness that he hath done he shall live."

And David says "The Law of Yehovah is perfect, giving peace to the soul, the commandment of Yehovah is clear, enlightening the eyes. They are sweeter than honey, and in keeping them there is great reward.

The Christians have coolly rejected the teachings of Yehovah and of Jesus, and put in their place the opposite doctrines of the Epistles.

Justice demands that those who have sinned shall be punished. But says Dr. Hodge, an eminent theologian, " Unless the Redeemer was a sacrifice on whom our sins were laid, who bore the penalty we had incurred, it is no atonement. He suffered the penalty of the law in our stead." The punishment of all our guilt was absolutly and actually borne by Christ," says another equally distinguished Christian preacher. To this it must be answered that, The satisfaction by substitution is impossible. If the law had said that either we *or* a substitute should die, this might be, but it said no such thing. The law is before us, and we see with our own eyes that it contains no such clause. If I cut off my finger, than it will be my finger that will perish, it will not be the finger of my neighbor. It is true that indirectly my neighbor may suffer, just as other parts of my own body might suffer, from the loss of the finger.

It has been supposed that all the sacrifices were types of the Messiah. But the Old Testament does anywhere say or hint such a thing. From the very nature of sacrifices it has been proved, in the ninth chapter of this Book, that the Messiah could not be a sacrifice.

We must judge of the character of the Messiah by the nature of the government which he was to establish. It involves the unfolding of new forms of knowledge as the basis of a new life. It has been falsely taught that Love was the one distinguishing element in his character. But Yehovah himself has declared differently. Through Isaiah he names four intellectual qualities of the Messiah. These are Wisdom, Sagacity, Counsel, and Knowledge. With these he mentions only one quality of Love or feeling, and this is the fear of Yehovah, with one of Will, the spirit of might or strength.

A perfect character must have as much wisdom as love, and as much of will as of either the others. The three are equal parts of the mind, bound together by inseparable laws of action and dependence.

The expectation of the Jews at the present time, (1880) is in harmony with the teachings of the prophets, and with the deductions of science. In the words of a leading Jewish Journal " The Messiah is to be, according to our belief, but a man of marvellous intelligence and power of influence and organization. There is no reason why the prophecies, in which the vast majority of us devoutly believe, may not be fulfilled in an apparently natural and consequent manner." The prophets do not predict the exertion of any miraculous power in connection with the establishment of the kingdom. If it required a miracle to introduce it, then a perpetual miracle would be required to sustain its activities. The truth is far from such a notion. For the Kingdom and its laws are a part of a plan which was eternal in the Divine Mind.

The desolation of Palestine was brought about by the acts of men. It must be restored by the labor of man. But in doing this, man must work after the divine model and then he will have divine assistance.

The idea and the hope for a Messiah were of very gradual development among the ancient Israelites. The word Messiah means one who is anointed, like the King or the Highpriest. David calls himself the Messiah, and Solomon applies the same term to himself. So did others who could not be regarded as in any way types of the great Deliverer. After the Captivity, the Jews came at length to use the term in an exclusive sense.

All human history displays the fierce and continued conflict between the lower and the higher powers, between the spheres of darkness and of light in man. At last the great final struggle comes, and the leader of the hosts of light is the Messiah. He must organize the higher faculties and attributes of man into the permanent institutions and structure of society, or his triumphs will be as unstable as the sand, as transitory as a summer vapor.

Only in this Book of Israel is such a high structure set forth. Only in the Hebrew prophets and nation are its magnificent symbols and types foreshown with completeness. Yet the hope of a Messiah was equally a part of the religious creeds f China, of India, Persia, and Arabia. Thus Kong-fu-tse, in the Tshoung Young, says, "A great Holy One shall appear in the latter days, to whom nations look forward as fading flowers thirst for rain. His all penetrating spirit, his prudence, virtues and counsel, shall govern the world without the prestige of power. The nations seeing him will prostrate themselves before him; and hearing him they shall be convinced, and with one voice praise his works. China shall see the rays of his glory approaching, which shall penetrate even to the savage nations, and to the unapproachable wilderness."

In the Persian Zend Avesta, we find Zarathustra saying, " In the last time a man shall appear who will adorn the world with religion and righteousness, Kings shall obey him, and all his undertakings shall prosper. He shall give victory to true religion. In his time rest and peace shall prevail, all dissensions cease, and all grievances be done away.

The Bhuddists of India believe that the next coming will be an incarnation of Bhudda, the same person who founded their religion.

The Moslems exspect that the Messiah, El Medi, will appear in 1882, the 1260th year of the Hegira. Then, or in 1885, the false prophet, El Dajal, will appear to oppose him, but will be overcome.

A Second Coming. — The Hebrew prophets say nothing whatever about a second coming of the Messiah, and the Christian expectations concerning it are based wholly upon the New Testament predictions.

While Christians accuse the ancient Jews of falsely understanding the prophecies of the first coming to be all literal and material, the Christians themselves do the same thing in regard to the New Testament predictions of a second coming. They have not seen that certain figures which are used must be spiritual and can not be material or physical.

Four times it is declared "He shall come in the clouds of heaven." One of these times it is said that it shall be in the same manner as the disciples saw him ascend from the Mount of Olives. But that was in the daytime and in plain sight of all Jerusalem, and if the clouds were of watery vapor, if the light was material light, then it must have been wittnessed by thousands of Jews. Yet no one saw it except the disciples. And therefore they saw it spiritually just as they saw the transfiguration, and not physically; even as the prophet Daniel saw the same clouds in a vision. A cloud of light guided the Israelites at the time of the Exodus; but it seemed only darkness to the Egyptians, like an ordinary cloud. If he comes again in that way, then no one will see him unless their spiritual sight is opened. That the clouds are spiritual clouds, such as we have proved to exist, in the fourth chapter, is conclusively shown by the declaration that "He shall come like a thief in the night." This is also repeated four times, and must be just as true as the other. The peculiarity of a thief's coming is its secrecy, we do not know that he has come until afterwards. If Jesus should come conspicuously in shining rain-clouds, then it would not be like a thief. But if the clouds are composed of spiritual light, then only a few will see them when he comes, yet after the kingdom is established, all the nations will both see and realize its glory. That would be coming like a thief.

It is certain that we cannot know in what manner the kingdom will come unless we know its plan, its constitution, and its methods of life. Without this knowledge we can not know what means are necessary for its establishment.

We have proved in the eighth chapter that the plan and laws of that kingdom are now, and always have been, a part of the constitution of man, and that they can only be learned by the methods of science. They are not to be revealed and taught and applied by a miracle. A great spiritual growth, carried on now through long centuries, has prepared the minds of multitudes to work in that new creation. Its central impulse and sustaining power is spiritual, its external form is physical and literal.

That the second coming is to be in the name and authority of Science, is proved by the direct and positive testimony of John in the Apocalypse. Under the first seal he saw one come forth on a white horse, the symbol of pure reason in a living form. His name (or Noma, law) was the Logos. Three hundred years before the time of John's vision, the writings of the Greek Plato had fixed the meaning of this word Logos. It signified the divine Reason and Law, incarnated in men, and embodied in the works of creation. In modern times, this meaning has been still further intensified. The word logos forms the syllable *logy*, in the termination of English words, and is thus used in naming the many subdivisions of modern science. For example, the Greek word *Ge*, means earth, and *Logos* means science. United they form the word *Geology*, meaning science of the earth. It was in this name that the Rider on the white horse fought and won the great battle with the

Beast. The Beast, himself we are told, believed in miracles and used them, his conqueror believed in science.

The Apocalypse declares that the second coming will be with a "new name." Therefore, He will not come with the name of Jesus or Christ.

The writer of this Book of Israel privately believes that the same person who appeared eighteen centuries since as Jesus of Nazareth was to reappear as the Messiah. That he was to be born and grow up, apparently in the same manner as other men, but that he himself would be distinctly conscious of having pre-existed. His claim to Messiahship would not and could not rest upon the question of his pre-existence, for that is not now capable of scientific demonstration in his case. There is no personal description of Jesus, and if there were, he did not then fulfill enough of the prophecies to establish his claim. In the present age that claim must rest upon the question of the surpassing clearness of his knowledge of the plan, the laws, and the methods of the kingdom; his unity of feeling and purpose with its divine life; and his entire and life-long consecration to the work of its establishment.

The Messiah will not be distinguished for his tact and skill in managing men. For all the arts of diplomacy, the ability to make others believe that which we do not believe ourselves, all these arts of political dexterity can have no part in a kingdom based upon and conducted by the purest truth. They are not to be used to maintain its life and stability, nor must they be used in ushering in its existence. But he will show all the attractiveness of noble and delicate personal manners, the outward index of that pure heart and clear intellect that must belong to a Sun of Righteousness.

His authority will be the truth itself, which is greater than any person. He will not seek to secure the worship and adulation of the world. His consciousness of personal supremacy will be entirely subordinate to the great work of building the institutions of the new life, and securing their perpetual observance.

The New Covenant.—The Bible gives a very careful description of the kingdom, and represents it by types which have mathematical exactness. And Yehovah tells us, through, Jeremiah, where the laws of the kingdom may be found, as we see in the following passages:

"Thus saith Yehovah, 'Behold I will bring back again the captivity of my people Israel and Judah and will cause them to return to the land of their fathers, and they shall possess it. And the city shall be rebuilt upon her own heap of ruins, and the palace shall be inhabited after its ancient manner. Behold I will bring the remnants of Israel from the north country, and I will gather them from the farthest ends of the earth. With weeping shall they come, and with supplications will I bring them in. I will lead them by brooks of water in a straight way, where on they shall not stumble, for I am become a father to Israel, and Ephraim is my first-born.

When that day comes, saith Yehovah, I will make with the house of Israel and with the house of Judah, a new Covenant. Not like the covenant that I made with their fathers in the day that I took hold of them by tneir hand to bring them out of the land of Egypt, which my covenant they have broken, although I was become their husband, saith Yehovah. That Mosaic covenant was written upon tables of stone, but this is the covenant that I will make with the house of Israel, I will place my law in their inward nature, and upon their hearts will I write it. And they shall not teach any more every man his neighbor, and every man his brother, saying, 'Know ye Yehovah,' for they all shall know me, from the least of them, even unto the greatest.'"

Here we have the express declaration of Yehovah himself that the laws of the Kingdom are to be discovered in the constitution of man. In the eighth chapter of this Book these laws are elaborately given. All other plans of government and society, ever yet proposed. were the inventions and devices of men. No man had ever before searched in the inner nature of man for the plan and laws of society. No one could therefore show a divine authority for the plan he proposed. Measured by this final and true test, all the past systems and professed attempts to fulfil the Messianic prophecies, are proved to have been vain delusions or impositions. And if any person claims he is the Messiah,, and yet cannot prove that the plan and laws of society which he proposes are a part of the very constitution of man, and therefore a transcript of the divine laws, and equally adapted to the people of all nations ; if he can not prove this, then we may be certain that he is either self-deceived, or an impostor.

The laws and plan of the great kingdom must have the character of universality. They must be equally adapted to the European, the Chinamen, the Hindoo, the Semite, and the African. If its laws and plans bear the mark of local prejudices and customs, if they are the outgrowth of particular phases of the feeling and thought of some one nation, then they cannot be the guide and standard for the common and universal conduct of the human race. The prophets assert with emphasis that the Kingdom will be universal and will take the place of all others. It must therefore possess the qualities of universal adaptation. It must equally satisfy the rigid scientific analysis of the Englishman, the subtile speculation of the German, the delicate precision of the Frenchman, the expanding enterprise of the American, and the warm imagination of the Asiatic mind.

The constitution of man, or the faculties of the human mind, are the same among all men. It is only in the degree to which these faculties are developed that men differ from each other in different nations and ages. The laws and plan of the kingdom, are a true statement of that constitution, and therefore will never need to be changed, they will permit of the continued development of man through all coming times.

The Mosaic Polity undertook to establish the unity and fatherhood of God, and the rule of his laws; the unity of national and domestic life; civil liberty and political equality; an elective magistracy, with all officers responsible to their constituents; universal education with an enlightened public opinion; the sacredness of the family relation; and the inviolability of private and public property, sustained by universal industry.

It was for human good, for their own welfare that Yehovah made the provisions of the law. He declares of his own character that he is merciful and gracious, long-suffering and abundant in goodness; keeping mercy for thousands; forgiving iniquity, transgression and sin, and that will by no means clear the guilty.

In that age, and with the small degree of knowledge which then existed in the world, the Mosaic laws were as well adapted to secure these ends, as any which could have been given. At their conclusion, Moses declared that their binding force arose from their being found in the very very hearts of the people, Deuteronomy, 30. 19. The Messianic kingdom aims to secure the same great ends. It is not a contradiction or setting aside of the Mosaic laws it is only that fuller and complete statement of them which is made possible by the enlarged spiritual growth, and the precise scientific knowledge of the present age. It is Yehovah himself who has said, through Jeremiah, that a new covenant should be given. And this word is as true as what he spake through Moses. It will be new in its fulness, its completeness, and its practical results. The Rabbis have taught that the 365 positive and the 248 negative precepts of the Mosaic law, corresponded to the same number of parts which compose the human body. We know this is not the exact number of parts. Yet the chosen people themselves, in the number of their tribes and rulers, and their great national symbols, contained the identical numbers which are now proved by mathematics to constitute the framework and measure of the body and mind of man. The truth is even greater and deeper than the Rabbis imagined.

The Divine mind is three-fold, it consists of

Wisdom, Love and Will, just as the human mind is constituted. We may be certain that this trinity of powers exists, for man is in the divine image, and these form the mind of man.

The nature of the Divine Mind fits it for a system of government with parts and officers like those best adapted to the wants of human beings. We must reason here from analogy, for the names of the divine rulers who are directly under Yehovah are not revealed in the Bible. The four angels, Michael, Phanuel, Gabriel, and Raphael, were and will be, especially interested in the establishment of the Kingdom of Israel.

We may believe that the Messiah was to be the person who is the masculine head of this Earth, of this division of the physical and moral universe. In this sense, he is a representative of Yehovah, with the duty of administering the divine government on the earth. We may be certain that he will never assume to be God himself; he will never claim or consent to receive divine honors. The spontaneous love and the intelligent obedience of the world will be given him, and his response will be in his unselfish devotion to all human interests.

Rites of the Law.—In the ninth chapter the restoration of the sacrifices has been described. The rite of circumcision was a sign of the Covenant made with Abraham. That covenant engaged that the posterity of Abraham should forever inherit and occupy the land of Palestine, and that in them all nations of the earth should be blessed. When the Restoration of Israel takes place, and the Kingdom is set up, then that rite will be no longer required or be practiced, any more than we would continue to give the presents which were used to witness the title-deed, after we had taken possession of the property. The rite of circumcision mutilated the person, and so in being faithful to that covenant, the Jews have been physically mutilated by their enemies, through numberless persecutions, down to the time of this writing, 1880.

Destiny of Nations.—A large part of the Jewish people will return to Palestine within the next twelve years. With them will go a large number of people from England, from the United States, from Scandinavia, and from Germany. These will all accept the laws and the life of the kingdom. The throne of David will be established in its ancient seat. Three kings ruled Israel while it was a united people; these were Saul, David, and Solomon. David was regarded as the best type, and hence the Jews still say " David melek Israel havekim,—David ever rules as king of Israel."

We must notice that Ephraim and Manasseh were reckoned as half tribes, and only counted as one; except in enumerations and allotments, where the tribe of Levi was given a special work, or was distributed among the other tribes. In laying out the land in the New Palestine, the half-tribe of Manasseh takes the place of Levi. In the city, however, Levi takes his regular place, while Ephraim and Manasseh, are united as the tribe of Joseph. The tribe of Levi has the principal charge of the Oblation and Portion for the Prince. The divine laws require that there should never be more than twelve tribes, with twelve princes, twelve places, and twelve symbols.

Both America and England will take a direct part in the restoration of Israel. This is indicated by Isaiah : Ho! land spreading wide the shadow of thy wings ; (America) Go, as a swift messenger, to a people wonderful from the beginning hitherto, a nation expecting and hoping, and trampled under foot, whose lands the river have spoiled. And all the inhabitants of the world shall see the uplifting of the banner upon the mountains, and shall hear the sound of the trumpet. At that time shall be brought unto Yehovah a present of that pulled and torn people, to the place of the name of Yehovah of Hosts, the mount of Zion.

The children of Ishmael were also in twelve tribes. They also are children of promise and of the seeed of Abraham, as well as their cousins, the Israelites. They have been equally taught to look for the Great Deliverer. Under the same political constitution they will be arranged in tribes and will occupy northern Africa from Morocco to the Red sea along with Arabia. The visions of the prophet of Mecca will be fulfilled with a higher truth than he foresaw.

Ishmael represented the material line, and Isaak the spiritual line of inheritance. So far, in all history, the material and the spiritual have warred with each other. In the Messianic kingdom, the two are forever united in harmony. The children of Isaak shall dwell in peace with the children of Ishmael. The rule of discord sundered the Israelites into two nations in ancient times. One hand and one law will unite all the children of promise, and through them, the whole race of man.

With the new basis of unity, the Turkish people, the Persians, and the Armenians and Circassians, will form three parts of the new Assyrian nation.

Great Britain, the United States, Russia, Germany, France, Italy, Spain and Portugal, China, Japan, Mexico and the South American states, will, in the order here named, accept the Messianic constitution and form an international unity, within the coming forty years.

The Negro race of Africa will be arranged in three Nations, the Eastern, Western, and Southern.

When all nations have the same political and social constitution, the jealousies and quarrels which have so long divided them will come to an end. The common interests and common knowledge of all nations will demand a universal Language as its symbol and instrument of expression In the next chapter it will be show how such a language must be founded upon the same natural laws of thought and feeling that will give form to the composite and united life of the nations.

It has been well said that Palestine is so remarkably situated, that it forms the bridge between two continents and a gateway to the third. Were the population and wealth of Europe, Asia, and Africa condensed at central points, Palestine would be the center of their common gravity. And with the amazing facilities of modern intercourse, and vast extent of modern traffic, it is not easy to estimate the commercial grandeur to which a kingdom may attain, placed on the apex of the world, with three continents spread out beneath its feet. It pas a part of divine wisdom to ordain this land as both the mart of nations and the spiritual center of the human race.

Historic Numbers.— It has been proved by Mahan, Guinness, and others, that the periods of history are measured by certain uumbers. These are the very numbers which enter into the structure of man and of the universe.

If we classify the events of history according to their different kinds, then we shall see that each kind is divisible by a certain number. For example, those events which relate to Renewal or new life, have eight as a prominent factor in their dates. Those which relate to the display of spiritual power, have seven as a factor. Six is a prominent factor of periods of secular or earthly power, like the Roman and Mohamedan. The 1260 in their dates resolves into the factors, 6x6x5x7. From the end of Cyrus to the final Dispersion of the Jews is 666 years. The year of the Flood 1656, is 6x6x46. The destruction of Jerusalem, 4194, is 6x699. The nines are numbeas of Judgement. From Nabonassar to Romulus Augustulus, the last of Roman Emperors, is 1260 lunar years.

Forty is eight times five, the number of *covenanted probation*. It occurs twelve timee in the history of encient Israel.

The "Seventy Weeks" of Daniel is 490 years, counted by the year-day theory. This measures from Exodus to Samuel; from Samuel to the Babylonian captivity by Nebuchadnezzar; and from Nehemiah's Commission and its execution in rebuilding the Temple, 418 B. C., to its Destruction under the Roman Titus, is 490 years.

Thirteen is a number of discord or division, and is a factor in periods of this kind, like the Ishmaelitic and Mohamedan. When the thirteen is a pivot, then it is a number of structural unity.

HISTORIC DATES.

In the first column are the dates from Adam. After the Exodus, the first column gives the years from the Exodus, and the second marked B. C., gives the years before the Common Era, or the 27th year of Augustus. "C. E.," stands for Common Era.

B. C. E. 4124. ADAM PLACED IN EDEN, AND EATS OF THE TREE OF LIFE.

1056—Noah born, ninth descendant from Adam.

1656—Noachian Flood. Noah 600 years old. His three sons, Shem, Ham, and Japheth, people the earth.

2008—Abraham born, ninth descendant from Noah.

2583 & 2108—Covenants made with Abraham, 490 years before Exodus.

2073—Birth of Ishmael, son of Abraham and Hagar.

21 08—Birth of Isaac, son of Abraham and Sarah.

2158—Death of Shem, father of the Semitic race, aged 600.

2168—Birth of Esau and Jacob, sons of Isaac and Rebekah.

2234—Babylon founded by Nimrod.

2244—Jacob marries Leah and Rachel, his cousins.

2252—Birth of Judah, fourth son of Jacob and Leah.

2258—Birth of Joseph, first son of Jacob and Rachel.

2448—Birth of Moses, of the tribe of Levi.

2298—Jacob's family go into Egypt.

2538—March 21st, EXODUS OF ISRAELITES UNDER MOSES, FROM EGYPT. This was 1586 before the Common Era, and 3468 before 1882. And 430 years after covenant with Abraham.

Years of Israel.

46—Israelites led into Promised Land, by Joshua. EJSODUS.

46 to 424—Era of Twelve Judges, ends with Samson.

444—Samuel anoints Saul king, rules 40 years. 400 after Joshua.

445—David born. Becomes king 474; rules Israel 40 years.

514—Solomon king rules 40 years. Dedicates first Temple 524.

554—Rehoboam rules Judah. Ten Tribes revolt under Jeroboam, forming the House of Israel or Ephraim.

689—Alesha takes the place of Aleyah.

755—or 776 B. C. Beginning of the Greek Olympiads. This was 780 years after the founding of Athens.

779—or 752 B. C. Founding of Rome by Romulus.

784—or 747 Beginning of Babylonian Empire. B. C. Era of Nabonassar. End of 1st Asssrian Empire Feb. 26.

816—or 720 B. C. HOUSE OF ISRAEL CAPTIVE, Shalmaneser king of Assyria carries away the Ten Tribes. 255 years after Division.

817—or 721 B. C. Total eclipse of the moon March 19th, 4½ hours before midnight at Babylon, (Sargon, or Shalmaneser, king).

926 or 606 B. C. House of Judah captive in Babylon, 468 after David, 338 after Division, and 134 after Israel's captivity.

245 or 587 B. C. Temple destroyed by Nebuchadnezzar.

952 or 580 B. C. Jeremiah and Baruch escaping with king Zedekiah's daughter, are supposed to reach Ireland.

821, or 713 B. C. Time of Isaiah's Prophecies.

930, or 602 B. C. Beginning of Daniel's prophecy.

572 B. C. Ezekiel's vision of Temple and New Jerusalem.

996, or 536 B. C. End of Judah's 70 years of captivity. First year of Cyrus the Great of Persia. He sends back 42,360 people of the tribes of Judah, Benjamin and Levi.

HISTORIC DATES. 257

1125, or 457 B. C. March 20th. Ezra returns authorized by Artaxerxes to rebuild the Temple. Reaches Jerusalem July 16th.

490 B. C. Greek power rises; battle of Marathon.

1126 or 458 B. C. Queen Esther procures favors for the Jews.

444 B. C. Brilliant age of Greece. Pericles, Apelles, and Herodotus.

1174 or 410 B. C. Malachi the last of the prophets.

1200 384 B. C. Birth of Aristotle; he founds Inductive Science.

334 B. C. Alexander the Great, Battle of Granicus.

1273 323 B. C. Alexander's kingdom divided. Ptolemy takes Egypt, Antigonus rules Syria. Lysamichus rules Asia Minor, and Cassander rules Greece. The "four horns" of Daniel.

182 312 B. C. Era of the Seleucidae.

291 B. C. Simon the Just, last of the Great Synagogue. Close of the Hebrew Canon.

247 B. C. Ptolemy Philadelphus founds Alexandrian Library.

1418 168 B. C. Antiochus Epiphanes sets up the Abomination of Desolation in the Temple.

1421 165 B. C. Temple purified by Judas Macabeus.

50 B. C. Julius Cesar crosses the Rubicon.

1559 27 B. C. February 14th Augustan Era Begins.

1561 25 B. C. Herod begins to rebuild the Temple.

1580 6 B. C. Birth of Jesus of Nazareth, or Yeshua.

1586 1. BEGINNING OF COMMON ERA, 27th OF AUGUSTUS.

1614 28 C. E. Crucifixion of Jesus, aged 33.

1656 70 C. E. 10th of 5th month, Destruction of Jerusalem by Romans under Titus. 1,100,000 people perished.

1721 135 C. E. Barochab claims Messiahship, and is defeated by Romans. Jews dispersed, 580,00 perished.

Rabbi Yehuda forms the Mischna about 170.

1909 323 C. E. Constantine makes Christianity national in Rome.

1981 395 C. E. Roman Empire divided into Eastern and Western.

410 C. E. Sacking of Rome by Alaric the Goth.

2038 452 C. E. Hengist and Horsa with the Saxons arrive in Britain.

2062 476. End of Western Roman Empire. 1260 lunar years from Nabonassar, 1222½ solar years.

2119 533. Justinian Edict makes Bishop of Rome the head of all the Churches. Thence to 1755 is 1260 lunar years.

2176 590. Gregory the Great. He Latanizes the Church.

2193 607. Phocas decrees Headship of the Roman Bishop. Thence to flight of Pope in 1848 is 1260 lunar years.

2208 622. JULY 16th HEGIRA OR MOHAMMEDAN ERA. From Jehoakiam 1260 solar years. Hegira is 1260 solar years from 1882 C. E.

2223 637. Saracens take Jerusalem, and build Mosch of Omar, 1260 lunar years after Burning of Temple by Nebuchadnezzar, 588 B. C. Thence to 1882 is 2520 years.

2286 800. Charlemagne rules Germany, France, and Spain.

800 C. E. Haroun Al Raschid, Caliph of Bagdad.

861 Russian monarchy founded by Ruric.

871 Alfred the Great king of England.

1017· Canute the Dane, monarch of England.

1076. Soliman, a Seljukian Turk takes Jerusalem.

2542 1066 William the Norman conquers England.

HISTORIC DATES.

2572 1096 First Crusade, 1260 solar years from cleansing of Temple by Judas Macabeus, 165 B. C.
2575 1099. Jerusalem taken by Crusaders, July 15th, 490 lunar years or "seventy weeks" from Hegira.
2667 1187 Saracens under Saladin retake Jerusalem.
1204 King John of England, massacres the Jews.
1399 C. E. The Ottoman Turks march westward from the upper Euphrates, led by Ortoghrul.
1374 Wickliffe publishes the Pope as Antichrist.
3024 1438 Printing invented by Faust, Guttenberg and Schaeffer
3039 1453. Turks under Mahommed 2nd, take Constantinople
3078 1492 America discovered by Columbus, Oct. 19th.
1492-4 The Jews banished from Spain, Portugal, and France.
1498 Vasco De Gama sails to India by Cape of Good Hope.
3105 1519 Luther begins Protestant Reformation.
3129 1543 Copernicus teaches the modern Astronomy.
3162 1576 Kepler discovers three planetary laws.
3206 1620 Pilgrims settle at Plymouth in America.
3268 1682 Peter the Great Czar of Russia.
3232 1610 Gallileo invents the Telescope.
3278 1685 Newton discovers the law of Gravitation.
3361 1775 American Colonies revolt from England.
1558 Elizabeth of England ascends the throne.
3379 1793 French Revolution, 1260 Solar years from Justinian Edict. Dethrones the Pope in 1798, from Seige of Samaria 2520 solar years,—"Seven Times." The Revolution's incitement began in 1755.
3390 1804 Napoleon Emperor of France, falls 1815.
3394 1808 to 1828 Gall discovers Functions of the Brain.
3420 1834 The Author of Sepherva came into the world.—1700—
3427 1841 J. R. Buchanan completes Map of Brain Organs.
3429 1843 William Miller sets time of the Millennium.
3430 1844 Turkish Edict of Toleration for Jews and Christians in Turkey, 2520 lunar years from 606 B. C.
3430 391 years or "a day, a month, and year" from 1453.
3430 1844 May 29th. First Magnetic Telegraph line.
3445 1859 Discovery of the Science of Society.
3447 1861 The Tree of Life discovered.
3447 1861 Civil War in the United States; ends in 1865.
3456 1870 Victor Emanuel deprives Pope of temporal power, September 20th, 1260 years solar years from death of Phocas,.
3464 1878 Plan of the New Jerusalem and of Messianic Kingdom discovered. Anglo-Turkish Convention secures protection to Jews in Palestine.
1878 C. E. was the 2625th year from the era of Nabonassar.
3464 1878 October 30th, Millennial Conference in New York.
3468 1881 a Transition Date from Old to New.
3468 or 1882 from March 21st. First Band of Israel formed.
1894 is 2500 years after the captivity of Judah 606 B. C.

Periods of Judgement have nine as a factor. The date 1881 contains twice 9 in the century, and 9x9 in the year, making it eminently the turning point as a year of Judgement. It reads the same backward or forward, it looks equally toward the past and the future. It is the 19th century of the common era, and 19 signifies Humanity come to judgement.

Time is a dynamic element, and therefore 5, 7, 9 and other odd or dynamic numbers are found more frequently than the even or structural numbers, in the dates in history.

Transition Periods. — Every event in history is the result of a growth, and that growth must occupy time. There must always be a period or phase of preparation, more or less extended. The critical point of change, from one to another, may be very clear; but we can trace each phase back for years or centuries, into the preceding age. There may be several points with apparently almost equal claims to be concidered as the turning points of a phase of history.

Solar Cycles—The revolutions of the earth, the moon and the sun, have a direct and well marked effect not only on the physical growth and life of plants and animals, but also upon the social or historic life of men. The great events on the dial plate of history synchronize with these cosmical revolutions.

The day contains 24 hours, and is measured by one revolution of the earth on its axis.

The month extends between one new moon and another, the time of one revolution in its orbit, or 29 days, 12 hours, 44 minutes, and three seconds.

The year or apparent course of the sun around

the earth, from any given point in its orbit to the same point again, occupies 12 months, 10 days and 21 hours; or 365 days, 5 hours, 48 minutes, and 49 seconds.

These three periods taken singly will not measure each other without a fraction. Calling the year 365 days, there is almost one day of excess every fourth year, hence Julius Ceasar proposed to intercalate one day every fourth year as Leap year. But the slight excess of 11 minutes and 11 seconds by this method, amounts to an entire day, or 23 hours, 50 minutes, and 50 seconds, in every 130 years.

Omar the Persian, (1079 C. E.) proposed to interpolate a day, as in the Julian system, every fourth year, only postponing to the 33rd year the intercalation, which on that system would be made on the 32nd. This is equivalent to omitting the Julian intercalation altogether in each 128th year (retaining all the others). To produce an accumulated error of a day on this system, would require a lapse of 5000 years.

A cycle is a period which brings into harmony different celestial revolutions, containing a certain definite number of each, without a remainder or factor.

The period of 1040 years is a cycle at once *secular*, *lunar*, and *diurnal* or terrestrial, of the most perfect accuracy. Now this period of 1040 years, is exactly the difference between the 1260 and the 2300 year periods named in the book of Daniel and in the Apocalypse, as prophetic times.

Each of these latter periods has played an important part in the past history of nations. These past phases belong to transition, disorder, and development; and consequently the prevailing factors in them are dynamic and earthly, and not spiritual and constructive.

Future Measures. — In future history, from the beginning of the Kingdom of Israel, the constructive, or factors of of organization, will rule. Then 1260 and 2300 will disappear as measures of eras, while 1040, with its factors and aliquot parts, will become the standard of division in historic periods. 1040 is 7 times 144 plus 36, or 3 times 12. It will be subdivided into 7 periods of 144 years each, a great Week of Years, with a period of 36 years in which to prepare for the next age. The factors of 1040 are $4 \times 26 \times 10$. It contains 4 the first number of organization, with 26, the number of the Human and the Divine Attributes: of the great Name; and of the Rulers on the Thrones. Its last factor, 10, is the number of material and spiritual law and power.

In the Kingdom of Israel, the year is divided into 12 month of 30 days each. This leaves five transdays at the end of each year. These transdays are used in making the annual change of office, employments, and studies. The year commences on the 21st of March, or the Vernal Equinox.

The day begins in the morning, measured from sunrise on the vernal equinox, and the 24 hours of the day are numbered consecutively from the morning hour of one day to that of the next. This avoids the awkwardness of being obliged to add A. M. or P. M. to each hour before we can know whether it is an hour of the day, or of the night. The hour itself is divided into twelve parts, (five minutes each, by Old Style) called horines, and each horine into twelve parts or minims (25 seconds)

Each minim contains twelve parts or timets; forming the smallest required units of time.

The hours from morning till night are given to the interests of the twelve groups of faculties, in orderly succession. The religious faculties come in the seventh or the twelfth hour of the day, by this arrangement.

The week contains twelve days, and the twelfth has three hours for the Religious group, this having united with it the groups of Rulership and Culture. The year contains 30 of these weeks. The Mosaic week of seven days was based alone upon the seven upper groups of faculties, without recognizing the five lower ones. That week with its Sabbath was sufficient as a type of the coming Age of Peace. But that Age is based upon *twelve* and not upon *seven* foundations. Seven alone is only a dynamic number. Twelve includes both dynamic and structural numbers. It is necessary that the elemement of time or movement, and that of structure should be in harmony in the true life. But with twelve departments and only seven divisions of time, the two elements cannot be made to agree.

The Turning.—The great law of the Phases of Life is now sweeping the human race upward across the line that divides the lower from the upper spheres of the brain. That great transition will occupy from 1880 to 1887, of the Common Era. To this period all the great dates of prophecy point. And the actual growth and discoveries of the present time indicate the same thing in a not less decisive manner. After that time, the higher faculties will exert their beneficent sway over the earth. A great spiritual growth has been proceding through past ages. But it could not have an external form, it could not be embodied in social life or political institutions, until the plan and laws of the Kingdom were discovered and demonstrated. Since that was done in 1878, C. E., the whole path before us is clear. Our own hands must be instruments in building the magnificent structure of the new heavens and the new earth. We are to work after the divine and eternal pattern. And whenever we do this, the whole spiritual force of the angelic world will work with us, until success crowns our labors.

The Kingdom does not rest wholly upon Prophecy and interpretation. If all prophecies were swept away, its foundations would remain eternal and unshaken. For they are fixed in the constitution of man, they reach to the centre of the universe, and are proved by the sure tests of science.

A mistake in these dates can therefore only change our knowledge of the methods and means by which we must reach the great consummation

The Books of the prophets and the Apocalypse of John are the only parts of the Bible which distinctly claim to be inspired. And that claim we have removed from the historic to the scientific ground. All that is now necessary is to prove that it was written previous to the year 1840 A. C., in order to prove that its great Symbols and Types actually represent a true Scheme of Life, given through inspiration.

In the life of the Kingdom, inspiration will exist among all classes in society, it will not be sporaic and infrequent, as it was in ancient times.

Seven Teachers.—Confucius and Lao-Tse were the two great religious founders produced by the

Mongolian race. The Aryan race produced Gautama, the founder of Buddhism, and Zoroaster, who founded the Persian religion. Among the Semitic races, there were likewise two, Jesus and Mohammed. To lead the present age, the seventh great teacher must be cast in a more composite mould. He must be great as a master of exact science, as a spiritual seer, and as the organizer of a new life for humanity. On entering the phase of maturity it is perfectly natural for the nations to produce a great mind, able, through the high methods of science, to discover the interior laws of man's nature, and through these to organize anew the thought, the life, and the conditions of all society.

The six great teachers all taught noble precepts and seemed inspired by lofty motives. But none of them saw clearly how the doctrines of religion must be expressed through every department of knowledge and every form of industry, not less than through the perpetual fountain of human emotions. All this was reserved for the growth of a later age.

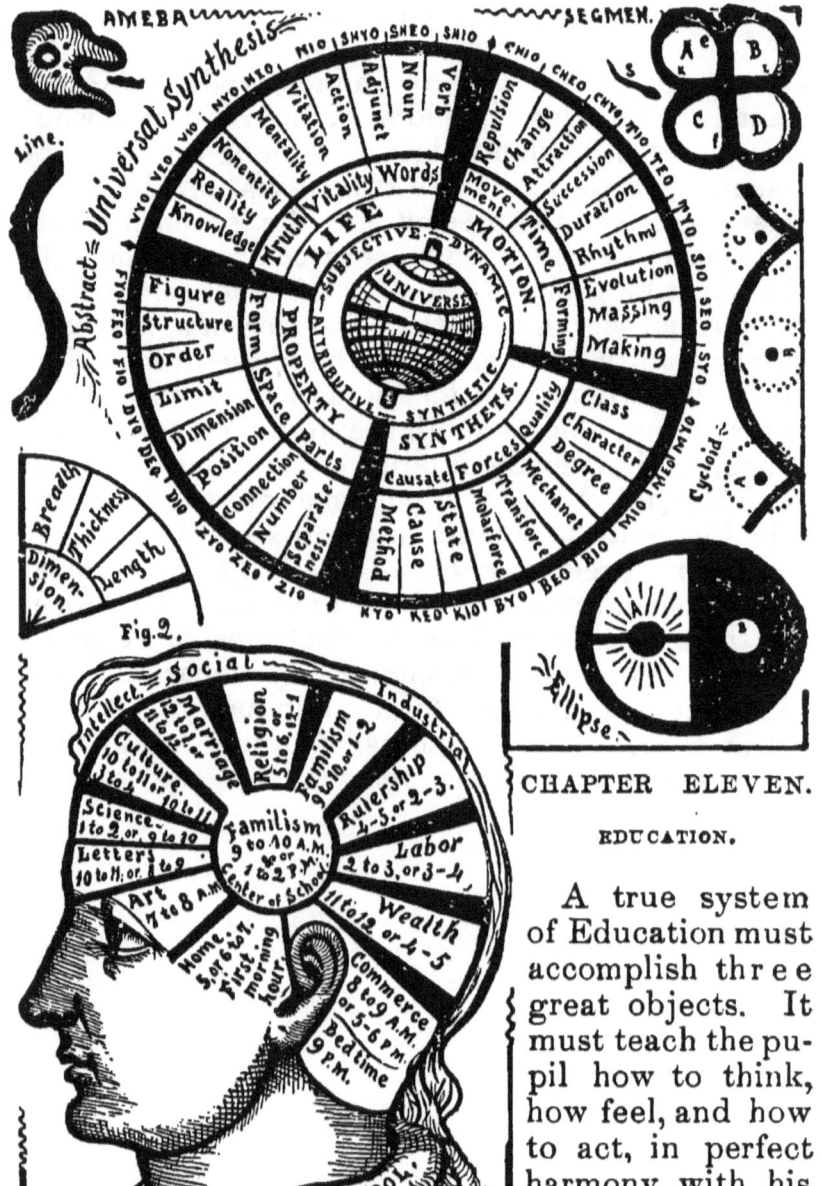

CHAPTER ELEVEN.

EDUCATION.

A true system of Education must accomplish three great objects. It must teach the pupil how to think, how feel, and how to act, in perfect harmony with his own constitution and with that of nature and society around him. To express this in a more formal statement ;—

First. It must impart a good and practical knowledge of the various branches of art, philosophy, and science.

Second. It must cultivate and develop all of the mental faculties in a systematic manner.

Third. It must devolop the body in connection and in harmony with the mind.

The plan of every school must be so arranged that it will secure these objects with directness and certainty.

The purpose of the school is to fit the child to become a member of society. In doing this we must conform to the natural laws of development and of action which belong to the mental constitution of childhood. It is the natural tendency of children to attempt in play and in a rude manner, to do those things which they are going to do in earnest when they reach mature life. As child-life imitates and prepares for maturity, so the school must be modelled on the same plan as society itself.

Plan of School.—The general plan of the school is shown in the circular diagram at the head of this chapter. This applies to the Home School, the College, and the University.

In each society, the children under ten years of age form three groupets of Art, Home, and Commerce. The youths from ten to fifteen form three groupets of Letters, Family and Wealth. Those from fifteen to twenty-four form the six groupets of Science, Culture, Religion, Marriage, Rulership, and Labor. The groupets thus duplicate the groupates of the parent society, and have the same names. Like them, they are in three departments, Intellectual, Social and Industrial.

As some children develop faster than others of the same age, the above limit of years cannot be rigidly observed.

Like the adults, the children are grouped as far as possible in harmony with their characters.

The school is presided over by the Teacher and Nurse, assisted by the members of the Family groupate, and these become the twelve sub-teachers of the school.

The College—In each county one entire society may be devoted wholly to education, and it is then called a College. Its twenty-six officers all become its theoretic and practical teachers, and it s members become the assistants of these teachers.

The two central officers of the College are called the Master and Mistress.

The University.— This is the highest af all the grades. Students may be admitted to the Universities who have only passes through the Colleges. The average age of entering the College would be twenty-one years, with a three-years' course for those who were preparing for the University, and an aditional year for those those who go directly from the College into the duties of practical life.

The central officers of ihe University are called the President and Presidess.

Course of Study.— The analytical tables furnish a classified view of the great circle of human knowledge and its chief subdivisions. These tables are made the guides for the course of study in the schools of all grades.

The general relation of all these studies to the divisions of the faculties has already been mentioned. Each branch of study, whether theoretical or practical, tends by its influence on the mind to develop or stimulate the action of a special part of the faculties. The following analysis is intended to show these more special relations. For example, the Perceptive group of faculties is stimulated and developed by the study of form, space, color, number, and so forth.

Order of Study.—The cultivation of the groups should be taken up and carried forward in a methodical manner.

The order in which the studies succeed each other is given in the following table. Every group of faculties is stimulated and developed by a special kind of studies, and this truth is the basis of our classification of studies. These hours of culture are also shown in the initial engraving of this chapter.

The order in the table takes up, in succession, groups of faculties which are polar thirds. Every third, or every sixth day, this may be varied as shown on the Head.

By this plan of giving an hour to each group, we are certain that every faculty has been brought daily under systematic training. And no other plan can secure integral culture with certainty.

This plan gives four hours a day for intellectual, four for social, and four for industrial culture. The four groups of Expression govern the muscular system, and their culture belongs to physical education, although more or less labor is used as a means of teaching other groups.

A less elaborate plan for a school could be adopted as a preparation for the perfect form.

PLAN OF STUDIES IN THE SCHOOL.

NORMAL METHODS, SYSTEMATIC CULTURE, PHYSICAL TRAINING.

In the schools of all ranks, one nour is given, each day, to the direct culture of each group of mental faculties, through appropriate studies, as shown in this table. This order may be varied so as to take, in succession, the groups of Art, Letters, Science, Culture, Marriage, Religion, Familism, Rulership, Labor, Wealth, and Commerce.

Group of Home 5 to 7 o'clock. ART OF DRESSING—bathing, toilet and costume. ART OF EATING—flavors, odors, and digestion. HOUSE AND FIELD—house-care, messages, and field culture.

Art Group, 7 to 8 o'clock. MATHEMATICS—geometry, arithmetic, and measuring. GRAPHICS—drawing, painting, and penmanship. OBJECT LESSONS—geography, botany, and zoology.

Commerce Group, 8 to 9 o'clock. ENGINEERING—civil, mechanical, and locomotive. FERTILITY—textile culture, fertilzers, and stock-raising. COMMERCE—distribution, travelling, and transportation.

Familism, 9 to 10 o'clock. LEARNING—obedience, guidance, and study. AMUSEMENTS—plays, festivals, and work. SERVICE—waiting, altruism, and patriotism.

Letters. 10 to 11 o'olock. HISTORY—civilization, biography, and chronology. LANGUAGE—grammar, speaking, and music. PUBLICATION—books, newspapers, and correspondence.

Wealth, 11 to 12 o'clock. FACTORIES—order in work, tools and machinery, fictiles and textiles. ECONOMICS—expenses, ownership, and exchanges. STORAGE—providence, warehouses, harvesting.

Marriage, 12 to 1 o'clock. DUALISM—sex-structure, floration, and rites. HEREDITY—transmission, permanence, and variation. LUXURIES—recreation, caressing, and pleasures.

Science, 1 to 2 o'clock. LAWS—Logic, mentology, and rules. BEAUTY—esthetics, symbolism, and adornment. SCIENCE—mechanics, cosmology, and dynamics.

Labor, 2 to 3 o'clock. JUSTICE—rights, duties, and penalties. UTILITY—Labor groups, industrial plays, and trades. ENVIRONS—climate, forestry, and horticulture.

Culture, 3 to 4 o'clock. HOSPITALITY—entertainment, conversation, and freindship. REFORM—discoveries, teaching, and adoption. MANNERS—mimetics, morality, and elocution.

Rulership, 4 to 5 o'clock. LEADERSHIP—authority, training, and ranks. ELECTIONS—voting, grouping, and transferring. DISPLAYS—standards, exhibitions, and processions.

Religion, 5 to 6 o'clock. WORSHIP—ceremonies, spirituality and belief. UNITY—philanthropy, interchanges, and discipline. ENTERPRISES—reclamation, improvements, and undertakings.

would have three departments, intellectual, social, and industrial, instead of twelve groupets; and would give two hours to the culture of each of these departments. It might have one, two, or three teachers.

Method of Study.— All truth exists in things, it is concrete. We never see it walking around without a body. From the beginning to the end of teaching, we must never lose sight of this fact. As far as possible, each faculty should be cultivated through its own proper objects of action and not simple through word instruction.

Thus the Friendship of a child is cultivated by its doing friendly deeds; its Integrity by showing it how to treat its fellows justly; and its Construction by teaching it to make articles of use and play. A child learns naturally by seeing others do thtngs, as well as by the trial of its own powers.

Object lessons, conversations, and industrial plays are the chief instruments used during the first ten years. When we are in the act of reading, the intellect is chiefly exercised. But when listening to a lecture, the voice of the speaker naturally excites our social faculties—the hearer and speaker are in social sympathy; and the gestures and experiments excite our volition. This form of instruction therefore is the highest, for it addresses all three classes of faculties. From the tenth to the fifteenth year, the child may also study lessons from text-books. The series of text-books used during this period must embrace such truths of science, philosophy, and art as are required for use by every person, in every sphere of life.

This primary series of text-kooks, giving the

elementary principles, would include separate treatises on Geometry, Spacics, Arithmetic, Chemistry, Cosmology, Dynamics, Mentology, Physiology, Botany, Language, Esthetics, and Hand-Art. The Sepherva, abridged or complete, is used as the text-book on Mentology.

In childhood the lower faculties are dominantly active, and then successively higher ones come into prominent activity. But there are truths belonging to the higher faculties which are so simple that a child may understand them without difficulty, and other truths which may make a vivid impression through their symbols and ceremonies. It is through these that the higher faculties of the child must be first cultivated.

For example, the symbols of religion may impress the mind of a child, at three years, and at seven he may form an idea of his relation to the human family from that which he bears to his brothers, sisters, and parents. He would learn the laws of sex at first from the study of flowers and fruits.

At the age of fifteen the character and tastes of the youth have been well studied by his teachers, he has learned the use of various tools in the work-shops and on the farm, and hence he is ready to choose his profession for life. Having made this choice of a profession, or trade, he takes up the special and elaborate studies which belong to it, and follows these until his graduation at twenty-one. During this time he is under the direct practical instruction of the leaders in that group of the society to which his profession belongs.

From the fifth year onward, the life of the child is more or less productive to the society. Its industries are so organized that they are in every way attractive to the unfolding mind and the developing physical system.

The education of the brain and the body can be conducted in harmony with each other only by observing the definite connections of these with each other, as described and illustrated in the second chapter and in the table of mental chords.

Following these indications, the muscles of the arms and shoulders are exercised while cultivating the group of Rulership ; the muscles of the thighs and legs are used while training the group of Commerce ; and so of the rest. Strong muscular labor would be wrong while cultivating the social faculties, for these are related to the organs of nutrition in the body, and not to the muscles.

The sympathy of each part of the brain and body is direct and constant. They were formed to work together. But the systems of gymnastics always violate this fundamental law of physiology. They are aimless so far as the mind is concerned. We reject all these systems. The mind and the body must exert their force in the same direction at the same time. We substitute real labor for the fictions of gymnastics, aud make these labors attractive by arranging them in accordance with the laws of mental harmony.

The best plans of schools in civilism only cultivated the Perceptive, Retentive, and Parental groups, or less than one fourth of the faculties. They left the other three fourths to develope as best they might under the influence of accidental and variable causes. They could never secure integral culture, even under the most skillful teachers. The plan proposed in this Book secures the highest grade of intellectual training, along with the complete developement of the social faculties and of the physical character.

Culture in maturity. — After the youth has left school, he still finds the means of integral culture around him during life. The school furnishes a model for the orderly succession of daily employments among the adult members of society. They also give an hour of each day to each one of the groupates, taking up their labors or employments in the same order as shown in the diagram of the school, or else in some polar order. In every society regular courses of lectures and discussions are held, in which systematic explanations are given on art, philosophy, and science, with all the new discoveries. The school is a home, and the home is a school. Our education is perpetual.

The Sabbath of the Israelites was a type of this arrangement. They set apart a special time for the culture of the religious group of faculties. The law given above, completes the ancient type, for it gives a special hour to each group of faculties, and makes each day a consecrated Sabbath of work, rest, and unity.

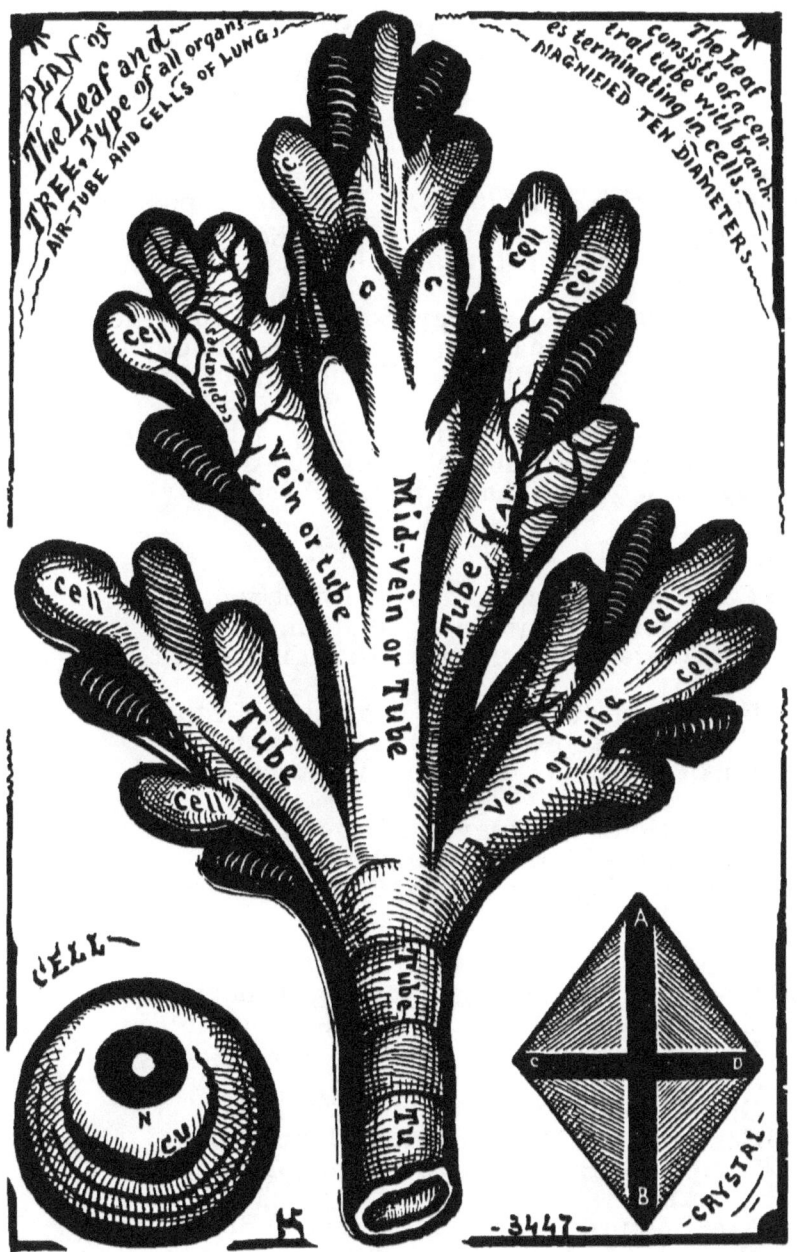

ANALYSIS OF KNOWLEDGE.
SCIENCE.
MATHEMATICS.
  Geometry—Formology, Engineering, Topography.
  Spacics—Trigonometry, Surveying, Mensuration.
  Arithmetic—Algebra, Book-keeping, Calculus.
BIOLOGY.
  Mentology—Psychology, Sociology, Economics.
  Physiology—Anatomy, Vitology, Sanatology.
  Botany—Morphology, P. Vitology, Floralogy.
HYSICS.
  Cosmology—Geography, Geology, Astronomy.
  Chemistry—Morphation, Cuisine. Analysis.
  Dynamics—Mechanics, Statics, Vibratics.

LETTERS.
PHILOSOPHY.
  Logic—Formula, Induction, Deduction.
  Analyies—Examination, Solution, Proving.
  Synthesis—Classification, Arranging, Gathering.
LITERATURE.
  Bibliology—Authorship, Pantology, Editing.
  History—Records, Statistics, Museums.
  Music—Vocalics, Organics, Gesturics.
CULTURE.
  Education—Teaching, Studying, **Training**.
  Manners—Fashion, Habit, Custom.
  Morals—Sincerity, Purity, Probity.

ART.
ANGUAGE.
  Grammar—Etymology, Syntaxis, Orthography.
  Elocution—Oration, Conversation, Gesture.
  Printing—Publication, Typography, Binding-
ESTHETICS.
  Graphics—Drawing, Painting, Writing.
  Costumics—Fitting, Sewing, Upholstering.
  Sculptics—Engraving, Sculpture, Carving.
HAND-ART.
  Architecture—Machine, Carpentry, Ship-building.
  Earth-Culture—Textile cult. Fieldwork, Forestry.
  Manufactures—Instruments, Textiles, Wares.

1. Law of Relation. — The objects of the Universe are in Series or categories, and between these, in different series, exist definite relations of properties, existence, and motion, so that the truths of each category are repeated, within limited variations, in every other category. Universal laws express these relations, and the special laws of each series express the variations.

2. Law of Form.— Every object has the properties of form, space, and number ; and in every atom these inherent properties give rise to constant vibrations of a definite character. In objects more complex than single atoms, their forms are fixed expressions of the ratios with which the producing forces have acted.

3. Law of Trinity. — In every object and every action, are three parts or forces. The two side members of this trinity support the central member, and the general relation of the three is formal, static, and dynamic. The side members of a trinity are its chief instruments of differention.

4. Law of Structure-Units.—The unit of mineral structure is the Crystal, and that of organic structure is the Cell. The Plan of each organ is that of the leaf or Tree, that is, it contains tubes with branches and subdivisions terminating in cells.

5. Law of Differention.— In the evolution of an object, an individul, or a race, the parts and organs gradually become more complex and interdependent, the functions becoming distributed among a greater variety of unlike parts and organs, and any modifications of any one part being accompanied by a respondent change of the other parts.

6. Law of Rythm. — In all motions the central element is Time, and all motions are rythmical, or

have measurable forms and limits, and when these are reached, they tend to repeat themselves or return to equipoise. The smallest of these forms are the waves of the forces, and the largest are the paths of the cosmical bodies.

7. Law of Polarity. — All action is polar or displays the concert of opposite forces or tendencies, the attractive and repulsive, or positive and negative. Matter has bipolarity and tripolarity; and spirit has bipolarity, tripolarity, and circu-polarity. The atoms af matter arrange themselves in groups and forms according to their separate and composite polarities.

8. Law of Conservation. — The seven great forces are Gravity, Heat, Polism, Chemia, Cohesion, Light, and Nerve-force. All forces are convertible, transferable, or counteractive, in measured proportions, a definite quantity of one always producing or else counteracting, a definite quantity of another. The entire quantity of motion in the Universe remains always the same.

9. Law of Causation. — Every object has power to effect every other object, and each Effect is the Cause of another effect. In mechanics there is always a mutual action between the two bodies.

10. Law of Radiation. — The Forces all radiate from their points of emission in minute waves, the vibrations being transverse to the wave-course. Light, heat, electricity, magnetism, and nerve-force, may be transmitted along special conductors.

11. Law of Divergence. — The manifestation of force on a given surface decreases as the square of the distance from the point of emission. A single force, coming in contact with an object, is divided into a number of forces, differing in direction.

12. Law of Life.—The functions of living bodies are performed by organs, that is, by regular structures having definite and inter-related offices, and these organs maintain a constant adjustment of internal to external relations, and are capable of selfreparation and reproduction.

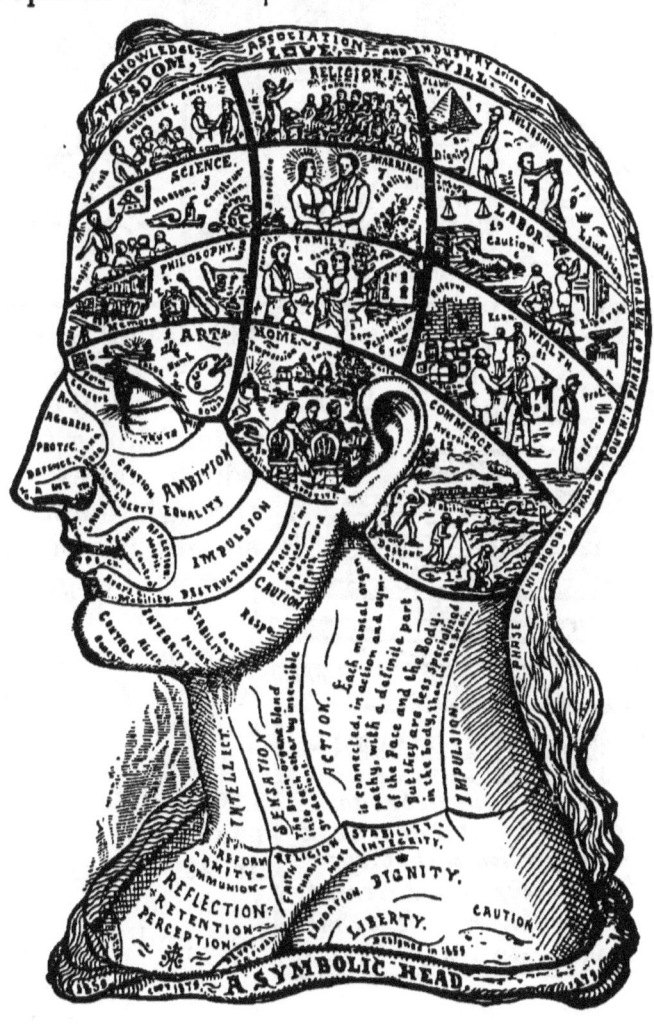

CHAPTER TWELFTH.
THE NEW EARTH.

Art is but that higher unfolding of nature which takes place through man. The stately temple or the powerful engine are as truly products of nature as the tree of the forest. Art is applied and embodied Science. Through these two great instruments man has made all of his great and permanent advancements in goodness and happiness in all ages of the world.

The parts of a building can have form, color, and arrangement. The geometric law teaches us how each form and curve affects the mind, and the mental laws of the trinity and of the nerve force show the same thing in regard to the arrangement and the colors of the parts of a building. On these three laws is based the system of unitary architecture. They unite the fragmentary parts of an ancient architecture into a system of surpassing beauty and enduring utility.

The engravings will illustrate this plan better than a word description

The unitary temple is constructed on the general plan of an ellipse, like the brain. Its great rooms are on the major and minor axes, and private rooms, for officers and members, fill the corner spaces.

The temple or dwelling is a medium of protection placed between man and the external world, and hence it should reflect the laws of both. In its structure we are obliged to use straight lines, such as characterize the mineral world. But we also use curves extensively, such as belong to the human form.

In the outside columns of the temple, the lower row has Egyptian, and the upper row has Corinthian, capitals. Both order of columns are used with modifications tn the interior.

The domes represent Intellect, Affection and Expression, or the Wisdomate, Socialate, and Laborate.

The Golden Portal, or front entrance, has three columns on each side, and three arches, symbolizing the three classes. The stones of these arches represent the twelve groups in order. The groups of the brain form a series of arches, whether we measure it from the front to the back or from side to side. And they support and balance each other, like the stones of an arch. For example, on comparing the map of the brain with that of the groups; we shall see that the groups of Science, Culture, Religion, Rulership, and Labor, form an arch. Religion is the key-stone. On its two sides, and equally supporting it, are Culture and Rulership. Farther down Science and Labor balance and support it. These principles were stated under the law of Polarity, but they are mechanical as well as vital laws.

In Free Masonry there was an instinctive sense that some truth existed here, but it was not guided by any real or exact knowledge, and their architectural symbolism was both crude and impractical.

The groups are represented by the flower, the sun, and the stones in the floor of the portal.

The great central court reaches from the first floor to the dome, from which it is lighted. It is surrounded by twenty-six columns. This is a place for social gatherings, as well as a passageway; and from the gallery around each story the members of the home can look down on what is taking place on its floor.

The Councilon is used as a counsel-room and also as a parlor. Above it a similar room, the Mimeta, forms the general parlor. The Auditum on the first floor is devoted to physical, and on the second floor to theoretic, instruction. Above the Appeton, or dining-room, is the children's play-room, or Formaton.

At the four corners of the great ellipse are the

GOLDEN PORTAL.

FRONT ELEVATION OF THE TEMPLE.

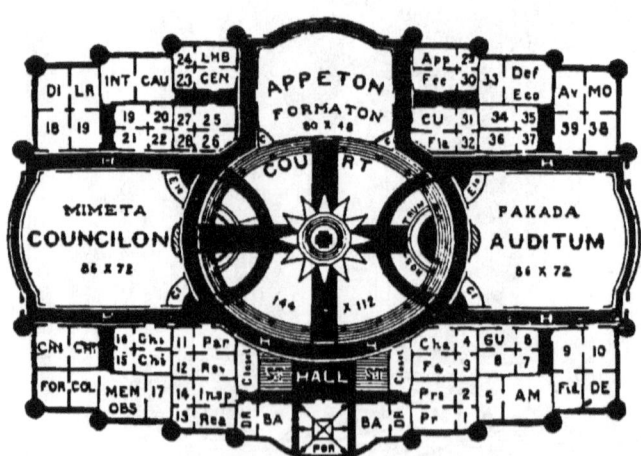

PLAN OF THE TEMPLE.

private rooms for officers and members. These rooms are arranged in series of twelve with bedrooms attached. The four stories include two hundred and eighty eight of these private rooms. Temples may vary in size from 260 to 360 feet in length. Or they may be still larger.

The colors of all rooms, private and common, are in harmony with the relations of the colors to the faculties. Thus, the rooms occupied by members of the Ambitious groupate are tinted with delicate crimson and purple, and trimmed with complementary colors. The rooms of members in the Parental groupate are tinted amber; and so of the rest. And thus the colors, the furnishings, and the arrangement of each room are in harmony with the character, tastes, and attractions with its occupant.

From the largest part to the minutest details, the temple illustrates the varied series of mental harmonies. In societies devoted wholly to instruction, where the temple is simply a school, its plan remains the same; for the school is a model of society itself, for which it is to prepare its members.

The plan of the Workshops is much the same as that of the temple. But the walls of the great rooms in these are usually straight instead of curved, and the corner rooms are less numerous.

The plan of the unitary Dwelling completly secures three great requisites. First, it gratifies the individual taste of each member. Second, it secures the utmost required privacy and seclusion to each member, along with the greatest facility in associating and working with those who are attractive and congenial. Third, it gives the greatest economy of material in its construction, and the greatest convenience in carrying on the various departments of domestic labor.

Costume. Our costume should secure three things:

1. Protection from the elements, from variations of cold, heat, and moisture. This will depend chiefly upon the material and the texture of our clothing, things which can be easily arranged from the abundant resources of our civilization. It also depends partly upon the form of the dress.

2. Our dress should secure freedom of muscular movement. To do this, the dress should not be too tight ; and when there are skirts, these should never reach below the knee. The costume of the two sexes certainly should not be any more different than their forms and characters.

3. The third requisite in costume is beauty of form and color. No dress can supersede the divine beauty of the human form by greater beauties of its own. The general form of the body and the limbs should not be concealed, nor should any long, straight, unyielding lines occur. Long skirts reaching to the ankles or the ground, obviously violate this law of beauty.

In proportion as dress follows or echoes the natural lines of division of the human body, will it be beautiful and useful. These lines are shown in the map and plan of the body, and the engraved " measure of man."

Dress is a social expression of character, it affects those with whom we associate. Hence there should be some unity of its forms. Slight variations of the dress, in different persons, would correspond to their different characters.

Colors of Costume. — In nature, Light is a far

more important and influential element than Sound; and when the harmonies of color are fully established in all the different departments of art, we have a right to expect that the effects will far surpass the noblest symphonies of sound.

A person should wear in his costume the colors which belong to his dominant organs ; or he may wear the polar complements of these colors in some one of the three degrees. A few examples will illustrate these applications clearly. A person with large Coactive organs should wear scarlet as the dominant color in his dress, and this might be trimmed with its complementary colors, green, salmon, or purple. A person with large Fraternal organs would wear green, or its complements, red amber or scarlet. Those with the Reasoning organs large would wear light blue ; those with Ambition large would wear crimson or purple. This law would not cause persons to wear colors which did not agree with their complexions. For difference of complexion indicates difference of character. The blonde and the brunette differ as much in their mental tints as in the tints of their faces.

The male and female of each pair differ by wearing darker and lighter shades of the same color. The centres wear brown and white, the masculine and feminine colors of unity.

The Banner. — The Banner and other official symbols of the kingdom are given at the head of this chapter.

The Banner has three upright bands, green, orange, and scarlet, representing the intellectual, social, and industrial departments of society. Its central sun indicates the twelve groupates. It is the Sun of Righteousness, for it shows the balance and righteous laws which rule these, and it truly symbolizes the perfect man. Its twelve rays have the same arrangement as the corresponding parts of the city.

The symbols of the officers and members are worn on their dresses. Their centers are circles in those worn by men, and ellipses in those worn by women. For the circle is masculine when compared with the ellipse.

Among the ancient Egyptian, Hindoo, and Semitic nations the Cross was used as a symbol of generation. It stands for the major and minor axes of the brain ellipse, and when crossed at the middle and formed of curved lines, it is the feminine symbol of marriage and of society. When crossed nearer the upper end, it is the masculine symbol of these.

Influence of Colors. — Every color is a definite kind of force.

The orange, yellow, and green rays of the sunbeam are the chief ones employed in constructing the delicate tissues of life. Now these are the very colors which the Author's observations and experiments have shown are radiated by the social groups of the brain—those of Affection. The Sensitive group radiates salmon ; the Parental, amber ; the Sexal, orange ; the Religious, yellow ; and the Fraternal, green. All of these faculties are related to the organs of nutrition in the body, those which organize its materials and build up its tissues. In the brain, these faculties attract human beings together, and produce all the complicated organizations of society. The colors of the intellect — different shades of blue tinged with green—are most closely related to the chemical force. The red of Expression is allied to heat. Hence we speak of a *cold* intellect, of *warm* affection, and of *hot* tempers.

In the sanitarium the different colors are important factors in toning up and restoring the diseased organs of the body. The Nervous system is toned and stimulated by colors in which blue predominates; the Nutritive system by those in which yellow leads; and the Muscular system by those in which red predominates. The details of these can be learned from the colored maps of the brain and body. By sifting the sunlight through differently colored glasses, we may select and use any one of these colors.

Correlation of the Senses. — We have dwelt largely upon color, althogh Vision through which it is perceived, is only one of the seven senses. The harmonies of one sense may give us a clue to those of the rest. The figures of speech in habitual use would seem to indicate an instinctive perception that there are fixed and close analogies between the different senses. Thus we say that we *smell* of a flower and *see* that it is sweet. Here we apply the word *see* to the sense of smelling although it really belongs to that of vision. So we speak of sweet faces, sweet flowers, and sweet sounds. We say that love, friendship, and social intercourse are *sweet*; and that hate is *bitter*; sarcasm is *pungent*, and tempers are sour. The basis of these correlations is believed to exist in the fact that light, heat, sound, odors, and flavors, all consist of waves, and that between these, in the different forces, are definite relations of length and form.

The organs of sense, the skin, the ear, the eyes the nose, and the tongue — are each adapted to a certain range of vibrations. The waves of sound are to long too set the rods and cones of the eye in vibration, and thus produce the sense of sight; and the waves of the nerve-force are not adapted to vibrate those rods and cones, except in unusual states of excitement and exaltation of sensitiveness. In this case, the rods are rendered more tense, and according to a well known law, they will then vibrate to the shorter waves of nerve-force. Then we see the nerve-force as light.

These explanations enable us to understand how one force can be converted into another. We have but to change the form and length of its vibrations, and the work of transformation is done.

We may perceive the vibrations of sound through the sense of touch, recognizing its pitch and its intensity. Yet in this case, as the Author's experiments have shown, the sensation is not precisely the same as it is when perceived through the ear. Probably no description of a sensation or an emotion could convey a perfect idea of it to a person who had never felt it in his own experience. Each mind must perceive them for itself. Yet the correspondences between the senses are so close, that the scale of harmonies for them all must be alike. The scale of musical accords and that for colors have already been worked out by science.

The senses are arranged in a series of octaves, and what appears as Sound to one of the senses, if transferred to the higher octaves would appear as Light or as mental Feelings.

The notes and strains of music have definite relations. Each has power to excite some one organ or group of organs. If the notes succeed each other, or are sounded together in the same order in which the faculties naturally follow or respond to each other in mental action, then the music will create a feeling of pleasure in the mind. It is harmonious; it awakens the faculties in their natural order. They respond in thirds, fifths, and octaves, as already explained in the chapter on Polarity.

Each odor and each flavor normally affects some special faculty or group. Hence we may have a scale of accords for eating, and arrange the articles of food so that their odors and flavors shall succeed each other in such an order as will excite the faculties harmoniously.

The following table presents some of these relations of the senses as at present understood. The base clef of sounds is below the parallel lines.

TABLE OF SENSE HARMONIES.

Culture	Green	Fa	Pears	Pinks
Science	Azure	Sol	Wheat-bread	Celery
Letters	Blue	La	Maize	Myrrh
Religion	Lemon	Mi	Rice	Jasmine
Marriage	Orange	Re	Oranges	Rose
Labor	Scarlet	Do	Lemon	Camphor
Rulership	Crimson	Si	Strawberry	Southernwood
Art	Gray	Sol	Oatmealbread	Vernal Grass
Family	Amber	Fa	Peaches	Pineapple
Home	Salmon	Mi	Grapes	Violet
Wealth	Red	Re	Melon	Musk
Commerce	Maroon	Do	Spices	Clove

Relations of Food. — Food can affect the body and the mind in three ways:

First. From the simple nutrition of its chemical elements. It must contain the carbon, oxygen, hydrogen, and other elements required in the body

Second. Food may modify character; may mold, develope, or depress the different faculties by the effect of its odors and flavors. For illustration, we would feed a person in whom the social organs were deficient upon food in which the sweet odors and flavors predominate. When we wished to develop the intellect we would feed the person upon wheaten bread or other food having alkaline odors and flavors. The flesh of animals, when used as food, stimulates the base of the brain. It chiefly excites the Impulsive, Defensive, Sensitive and Perceptive groups. It is not adapted to develop a noble, refined, and intellectual character. Its use as an article of diet belongs legitimately to savage life and the lower phases of society.

Third. Our food may affect us by calling the various faculties into exercise in cultivating and procuring its different varieties. The culture of grains and fruits tend to develop the social faculties and the intellect. When a people settle down to the pursuits of agriculture, it is at once an indication that the arts of peace are beginning to prevail over those of war. In savage life, hunting and fishing were common means for procuring food, and these required the exercise of perception, sensation, destruction, cunning, and mobility. In civilized life, the slaughter of animals for food called the same faculties into exercise. The structure of the teeth and other digestive organs in man proves that he is naturally adapted to live on grains and fruits when he arrives at man's full estate.

In a harmonized life, the cook must understand well the relations of food, and be as truly an artist as the musician or painter. In a far higher sense than in past times, the cook must cater to the appetite, but the appetite will be educated and trained to appreciate and seek the higher harmonies of food; and the pleasures conferred are increased to a corresponding degree.

The senses are the Portals of the Mental Temple. Through them all harmonies must enter to reach the halls of thought and feeling. These harmonies must be the effective instruments for reaching the most refined culture and the most exalted spirituality which a human being is capable of attaining. The education of the senses must therefore take a leading place in a true system of culture.

The color of the skin has an effect on the development of the senses. The most perfect complexion, in all respects, is that between the blond and the brunette. It belongs to the Caucasian race, distinguished alike for its high energy and sensibility, and its capacity for advancement.

Previous to the discoveries of this Book, the wisest of men knew a scale of harmonies of only one of the senses—that of hearing, as expressed by music. But we have shown above, that Heat, Color, Forms, Odors, Flavors, and Characters, have each their scale of accords. These make us masters of at least six times as many sources of pleasure as were known before. Until these were elaborated it was impossible to form a clear conception of how much is involve in a complete life of social harmony on earth, or in the supernal spheres; and it is equally impossible for us to take the steps essential to its practical realization.

The New Earth. — We have now cempleted the sketch of those basic laws of science which must guide the activities of the new life for humanity. The high promises of science confirm the voice of inspiration and both of these will justify the hand and inspire the hearts of those who work for the earthly redemption of man.

The immense transformation in the intellectual, the moral, and the physical life of man, will indeed make it appear like a new heavens and a new earth. In landscape art, the plan of the New Jerusalem will be taken as the model for all cities and towns. This plan is based upon the laws of form-beauty already explained in the first part of this volume. It combines in the highest degree the beauty of curved and straight lines with symmetry of its balancing parts. The streets are indicated by the dark lines. The great Temple in the center is occupied by the pivotal society or Band of Israel. Around this, on the four sides of the square, are grouped the twelve Bands, each having its buildings. There should be a natural limit to the size of a city, just as there is to the size of man. The city is a definite, organized structure, having a fixed relation of all its parts and activities. The capital city of the world need not contain more than 144,000 people as its fixed population.

The truths of science demonstrate that the long expected kingdom of righteousness must have a literal, material form, a definite and fixed constitution, and laws. The language of Bible prophecy on this point is clear and decisive. But its inner life is not less clearly marked. It is moved by the mightiest impulses of spiritual life, and these alone lift it into majestic power, and will maintain its triumphant course through the ages.

The past achievements of science and art lead us to exspect the most wonderful results in the future, from the modifications of the climate, the soil and the surface of the earth.

New chemical discoveries will unlock the icy zones of the earth, clothe them with verdure, and cool the hot breath of the tropics to the freshness of temperate climes.

With combined industry, the civil engineer will reclaim the deserts, and make them blossom as the rose. Vast industrial armies will be animated by a noble enthusiasm in making the earth a garden of beauty, the fit abode of a redeemed race.

Carried to its maturity, science here inspires the vital air of religion itself, and is moved by the same immortal impulses. Under their united light and power we shall mold all external conditions into enduring sources of pleasure, and make human life an eternal response to the spiritual symphony of the Universe

June 24, — אֱלִישׁוּעַ — 3468.

INDEX.

Food, its kind	11
Face and Indices	33, 38
Freedom Defined	123
Foundations	165
Fourth Seal	175
Fifth Seal	181
Fulfilled Prophecies	195
Future Measures	261
Food and Character	291
Gestures	85, 92
Grouping of Members	129, 130
Gathering of Tribes	166, O
Geologic Ages	3, 105
Greek Mental Life	104
Heredity	94, 137
Home Work	137
Household	138
Historic Numbers	254
Industry, Organized	128
Impeachment	125
Impressians	64, 66
Incense	168
Ishmael	253
Influence of Colors	287
Joining the Sticks	N.
Jerusalem	151, 176
Knowledge and Labor	4
Knowledge Classified	275
Laws of Nature	6
Lines of Evolution	101
Life in Israel	117
Lamb, Paschal	168
Length of Life	174
Logos, Meaning of	245
Lamb, Blood of	170
Motive System	13
Map of Organs	16
Minor Axis	40
Minor Currents	46
Measure of Man	48
Measure of Head	49
Mental Unity	75
Mental Chords	76, 77
Music	78
Analysis of Life	24
Adhesion of Impressions	59
Archetype	118
Authority	122
Atonement	171
Brain, described	18
Brain Centers	20
Brain and Body	31
Beauty, its laws	47
Bands of Israel	119
Battle with the Beast	184
Blessings of Jacob	X, L, M
Banner of Israel	286
Conception of Law	5
Criterion of Truth	7
Currents of Force	43
Conservation	56
Colors, Meaning of	63
Crown of Life	64
Caressing	67, 135
Civilization, Seven	106
Commerce	139
Character of Tribes	151
Cells	175
Covenants	D.
Character of Messiah	241
Course of Study	267
Costume	285
Corelation of Senses	288
Common Sense and Science	6
Control of the Will	57
Contraction of Muscles	13
Colors of Nerve Force	63
Caphalization	98
Chosen People	157
Design of this Book	4
Doctrines of Bible	149, 150
Duration of Life	A.
Destiny of Nations	252
Ellipse, law of	40
Embryonic Life	94
Elections	124
Employment	128
Exchanges, Social	163
Earthly and Heavenly	182
Education, Integral	265

INDEX

Mental Order, ... 79
Mental Act 30
Mimetic Law 85
Marriage 132
Mystery, mark of 184
Messenger. ....T.
Mosaic Polity 249
Messianic Prophecies. 104, 195
Measures of Time 261
Method of Study 270
Modified Currents 57

Nutrition 10
Nervous System 14
Nerve Cells 16, 17
Nerve Force 51
Nerve Currents 43
Numbers, Meaning 26, 30
Nerve Spheres 54
National Phases 100
New Jerusalem 151
New Birth 181
New Earth 279
New Covenant .... R

Order of Thought 79
Orders of Society 118
Ownership 126
Overcoming Evil 145
Obedience 172
Olah, incense 168

Proof in Science 7
Proportions 48
Polar Organs 71, 72, 78
Phases of Life 95, 100
Pairs of Sex 130
Purity 134
Penalties 173
Promised Land ...... E, F.
Plan of Salvation 237
Plan of School 266
Plan of Temple 281
Philosophy defined 8
Physiology Defined 10
Paschal Lamb 168

Responses 82
Rights Defined 125
Rights of Wealth 126
Representation 140
Religion 142, 145
Ressurection 181
Re-incarnation 181, 182
Reign of Peace 183
Rites of the Law 251
Radius Vector 45

Relations of Food 290
Science Defined 6, 8
Sensi-motors 15
Striatum and Thalamus.. 21
Sex in the Ellipse 43
Spiritual Atmosphere ... 67
Social Science 108
Social Structure ... 107, 110
Specialization 111
Spheres of Sex 130
Sexlove 133
Seventh Seal 150
Sealing in Tribes 160
Sticks 162
Second Seal 166
Sacrifices, Nature of ... 167
Sacrifices Restored 172
Spheres of Light and darkness 70
Symphony of Life 164
Second Coming 243
Solar Cycles 259
Seven Teachers 263
Seven Seals 193
Synthetic Laws 276

Test, Final 115
Transition Periods 259
Trinity in Mind 31
Trinity, Divine 250
Treasurer 146
Trustees 127
Transitions 145
Tribes in Jerusalem ...151- 152
Throne in Heaven 165
Tree of Life 176, 180
Theory of Mental Action. 81
True Messiah 235
The Turning 262
Temple, Plan of ... 279, 284

Universal Peace .... A.

Vital Trinities 12
Voice and Character ... 91
Vocal Inflections ... 91, 92
Veil of the Nations .... B

Waves of Thought 51
Waves in Dreaming ... 61
Worth of Life 174

Youth, Phase of 96

Zones, Mental 71

www.ingramcontent.com/pod-product-compliance
Lightning Source LLC
Chambersburg PA
CBHW032103230426
43672CB00009B/1621